Alexander Innes Shand

The Cookery of the Salmon

Alexander Innes Shand

The Cookery of the Salmon

ISBN/EAN: 9783744785051

Printed in Europe, USA, Canada, Australia, Japan

Cover: Foto ©Andreas Hilbeck / pixelio.de

More available books at **www.hansebooks.com**

THE SALMON

BY THE

HON. A. E. GATHORNE-HARDY

WITH CHAPTERS ON

THE LAW OF SALMON-FISHING

BY CLAUD DOUGLAS PENNANT

COOKERY

BY ALEXANDER INNES SHAND

ILLUSTRATED BY DOUGLAS ADAMS AND CHARLES WHYMPER

LONGMANS, GREEN, AND CO.

39 PATERNOSTER ROW, LONDON

NEW YORK AND BOMBAY

1898

PREFATORY NOTE

I wish to express my sincere thanks to the Marquis of Lansdowne, Lord Kilcoursie, the Bishop of Bristol, Sir Walter Phillimore, Sir John Fowler, Mr. Arthur Fowler, Mr. Henry Graham, Mr. A. M. Naylor, Mr. Craven, Mr. Henry Ffennell, and others, for information kindly supplied, and for permission to make use of their communications.

ALFRED E. GATHORNE-HARDY

CONTENTS

ILLUSTRATIONS

THE SALMON

CHAPTER I

NATURAL HISTORY

'THERE is a river in Macedon,' says Fluellen in
'Henry V.,' 'and there is, moreover, a river in Monmouth ; it is called Wye at Monmouth, but it is out
of my prains what is the name of the other river ; but
'tis all one, and there is salmons in both.' I had
intended to introduce this quotation as a proof that
Shakespeare, or rather Fluellen, did not know everything, but, curiously enough, the very first page of that
mine of information Day's 'Salmonidæ of Great
Britain and Ireland' mentions that Ælian, who
flourished about 180 A.D., alludes to a spotted fish in
Macedonia that in his days was captured by means
of an artificial fly, the mode of manufacturing which
he details Probably, however, this fish was a trout,

B

and although Day reports a stray salmon captured
off the coast of Malta, the normal distribution of the
species is confined to the Arctic and temperate
portions of the northern hemisphere, between latitudes
45° and 75°.

It is not my purpose to deal more than very
generally with the natural history of this king of
fishes. An exhaustive and scientific work would
require far more space than a single chapter of a
short treatise—and, I may add, far greater knowledge and research than I could bring to the subject.
My qualifications for the task I have undertaken, are
derived from a practical acquaintance with the
salmon in Norway, where I caught my first salmon in
1865 ; in Scotland, where I have spent most of my
autumns for thirty years ; and to a more limited
extent in England, Ireland, and Wales ; many of the
happiest hours of my life have been spent by salmon
rivers, *militavi non sine gloria*, and if I cannot
boast such a fishing library as the late Alfred
Denison, who collected 2,707 volumes on the subject,
it has also been a pleasure to me to read a good deal
of the literature of the disciples of Izaak Walton.
Next to catching a monster myself, there is nothing
that delights me more than to read of the success of
others, and an armchair and a cigar with Scrope or

Bromley Davenport is a delightful finish to a day's sport. If the supply of fishing books is large, so also is the demand ; and if I succeed in awaking pleasant recollections in the minds of experts, and exciting the tiro to higher ambitions, my aim will be accomplished.

British migratory salmonidæ may for all practical purposes be confined to three species :—the salmon, the bull-trout, and the sea-trout. These three vary greatly in different localities, in shape, appearance, and size, and other characteristics, and many naturalists subdivide the genus differently into from two to seven species. Day enumerates eighteen different authorities, ranging over two centuries, from Willoughby's 'Historia Piscium,' 1686, to Dr. Gunther's 'Catalogue of Fishes in the British Museum,' in 1866, no two of whom arrive at precisely identical conclusions ; however, it matters little to the fisherman whether peel and grilse, sewin and sea-trout, finnock and herling are local varieties, distinct species, or different names for the same fish. They are all at certain periods anadromous—that is to say, they run up rivers to breed and spawn in the late autumn in redds or beds in the gravel, their young, the parr, return later to the sea after acquiring the silvery appearance under which they bear the name of

smolts or samlets, and come back again enormously
increased in size to the same rivers which they left in
their infancy.

The able author of the Badminton volume on
fishing writes of the great progress of our knowledge
on the subject during the last two decades. No
doubt some problems have been solved by experiment and observation, but I incline to rather a
modest view of the advance made, and to dwell upon
the difficulties still unsolved, rather than upon the
additions made to our stock of positive information.
Let me take old Izaak Walton's 'Complete Angler,'
published in 1653, to see what was known at that
time by that not very accurate compiler and observer,
premising that most of his information was what
lawyers would call 'hearsay' only, and that it is not
certain that he ever saw a live salmon in his life. It
is true that he makes a casual allusion to having
caught them; but he gives no account of his
adventures with them; and they did not haunt his
usual hunting grounds.

'The salmon is accounted the king of freshwater
fish, and is ever bred in rivers relating to the sea.
He is said to breed or cast his spawn in most rivers
in the month of August, some say that then they dig a
hole or grave in a safe place in the gravel, and then

place their eggs or spawn *after the melter has done his
natural office,* and then hide it most cunningly and cover
it over with gravel and stones, and then leave it to
their Creator's protection, who by a gentle heat which
he infuses into that cold element makes it brood and
beget life in the spawn, and to become *samlets* early
in the spring next following.'

In this passage the inaccuracies and mistakes are
not very great. The salmon, of course, does not
spawn in the month of August, but from October to
January, or even later. The hen fish does not
deposit her spawn 'after the melter has done his
office,' but the two fish go to the spawning beds
together, where the redd is constructed, and the male
sheds his melt on the eggs and fecundates them after
they are deposited by the female. The process of
making the redd and spawning usually takes from
eight to twelve days ; but is more hurried when the
salmon have been prevented from ascending the river
until late by want of floods, or other causes. The
male fish fight for the possession of the female almost
as stags do for their hinds. It is still a debated question whether the redd or trough is made by the male
or female fish, but the better opinion seems to be
that it is mainly the work of the latter. It certainly
cannot be the case that the peculiar hook or beak

that grows upon the male salmon at this period is
used for making the redd.   Its position on the lower
jaw of the fish with its immovable neck would render
such a use impossible.   It is more probable that, as
has also been suggested, it is provided as an offensive
weapon for fighting like the horns of the stag.   The
eggs are 'hidden most cunningly and covered with
gravel' to some feet in depth—and the young fish is
born after a period varying from 80 to 114 days, or
even longer, according to the temperature of the
water.

The young fish of course in its early stage of existence is a parr, and not, as Walton says, a samlet or
smolt.   This was really settled decisively as long
ago, at any rate, as 1824 by the experiments detailed
by Scrope in his 'Days and Nights of Salmon Fishing.'
It is as well to be on sound ground for once, and I
hardly think this point can be contested by any
naturalist or sportsman of ordinary observation
and candour ; but even recently I have heard it
questioned or denied.   This, however, only proves
the vitality of error : there are still people who per-
sist in believing the Claimant to be Sir Roger Tich-
borne, in spite of overwhelming evidence to the contrary and his own confession, and I have known
keepers who would go to the stake for the faith that

is in them that cuckoos turn into sparrow-hawks in the winter, that the hairs of cows' tails are transformed into eels, and other and even stranger delusions.

Izaak Walton goes on : 'The salmon having spent their appointed time and done their natural duty in the fresh waters, they then haste to the sea *before winter*, both the melter and spawner ; but if they be stopped by floodgates and weirs, or *lost in the fresh waters*, then those left behind grow sick and lean and unseasonable, and kipper, that is to say, have bony gristles grow out of their lower chaps, not unlike a hawk's beak, which hinders their feeding ; and in time such fish so left behind pine away and die. 'Tis observed that he may live thus one year from the sea ; but he then grows insipid and tasteless, and loses both his blood and strength, and pines and dies the second year. And 'tis noted that those little salmon called *skeggers which abound in many rivers relating to the sea are bred by such sick salmons that might not go to the sea,* and that, though they abound, yet they never thrive to any considerable bigness.'

This paragraph is, of course, extremely inaccurate. Salmon certainly do not go back to the sea before the winter, merely leaving behind those unfortunate companions who are stopped on their return by

floodgates and weirs, or 'lost in the fresh waters'!
The bony gristle not unlike a hawk's beak is not a
mark of sickness common to both sexes, but the
ordinary and annual adornment of the male, and
does not 'hinder his feeding,' if indeed he feeds at
all to speak of in fresh water ; and 'skeggers'—if by
this word Walton means to designate samlets—are
young salmon in their silvery or smolt stage, and
not exclusively or at all the offspring of salmon
which do not go to the sea. I am inclined to
think from the context that the author means to
include sea-trout with smolts under the general
designation of skeggers, as he makes no allusion to
them as a separate species. In the only other reference to skegger in his work, he is, however, undoubtedly referring to smolts : ' In divers rivers, especially that relate to or be near the sea, as Winchester or the Thames about Windsor, there is a little
trout called a samlet or skegger trout, in both which
places I have caught twenty or forty at a standing,
that will bite as fast and freely as minnows ; these be
by some taken to be young salmons, but in those
waters they never grow to be bigger than a herring.'

The bony hook which grows on the salmon's lower
jaw is still a puzzle to the student. Walton says that
' if the old salmon gets to the sea, then that gristle

which shows him to be kipper, wears away, or is cast off *as the eagle is said to cast his bill*, and he recovers his strength and comes next summer to the same river.' This is, after all, a fairly accurate statement, and although the hook, which is formed of connective tissue, is absorbed and cannot be shed, much later observers than the father of angling make mistakes upon this point. A writer in the ' Field ' in 1884, quoted by Day in a note, states, that ' when the fish has reached a certain stage in the kelt state, the hook gradually loosens at what seems, on examination, to be a kind of joint just where the point of the nose should be in the fish ; a slight tap when it has arrived at this stage, or slight pressure on the gravel will dislodge it.' Although this excrescence is usually distinctive of the male, small knobs frequently, and large ones occasionally, are found even in gravid females. It is still a moot point whether salmon breed annually, or every second or third year—opinions differ—and no definite conclusion can safely be arrived at.

To revert to our author, he next quaintly observes that the salmon, having recovered his strength, comes next summer to the same river, if it be possible, to enjoy the former pleasures that there possessed him : ' for, as one has wittily observed, he has—like some persons of honour and riches, which have both their

winter and summer houses—the fresh rivers for
summer and the salt water for winter, to spend his life
in ; which is not, as Sir Francis Bacon hath observed
in his "History of Life and Death," above ten years.
And it is to be observed that though salmon do
grow big in the sea, "*yet he does not grow fat but in fresh
rivers, and it is to be observed that the farther they get
from the sea they be both the fatter and better.*" ' This
last statement is indeed a staggerer, and the exact
reverse of the truth. Salmon come up fat from the
salt water, and subsist mainly in the rivers upon the
fat they have accumulated in the sea, where food was
abundant. It has been frequently contended that
they do not feed at all in fresh water, and a recent
author states dogmatically that it is impossible that
they could feed in the rivers, as if they did they
would destroy everything in them. This seems to
me to be an extravagant proposition. It is possible
to feed without making it the main business of life ;
and it would seem that grilse and salmon, during
their fresh-water stage of existence, 'take the goods
that God provides them,' without going out of their
way to search for nourishment. Their digestive
organs dwindle and shrink ; but food is frequently
found in their lower intestines. Setting aside, for the
moment, the well-authenticated instances of food

being discovered in the stomachs of salmon taken in
fresh water, I should have thought that the experience
of the angler was conclusive on this subject ; granting
that some other cause than the gratification of the
appetite may be assigned for *Salmo salar's* predilection
for a ' Jock Scott ' or a ' Blue Doctor,' as to which I
have something to say later on, surely the fact that he is
often caught with worms, minnows, dace, prawns and
such natural baits, is proof positive that he is not averse
to an occasional relish when in his fresh-water
habitation. Some go so far as to advocate the
destruction of kelts on the ground of the mischief
their ravenous appetites do to the young fry, and
although I have no desire to keep or eat anything so
nasty, I doubt if much advantage results from rod
fishers being compelled to put them back.

Walton next states quite correctly that ' though
they make very hard shift to get out of fresh water
into the sea, yet they make harder shifts to get out of
the salt into the fresh waters to spawn or possess the
pleasures that they have formerly found in them.'
He describes how they force themselves over floodgates, weirs, or stops in the water, to a height above
common belief, and quotes Gunn as speaking of such
places as ' being above eight feet high above water.'
This estimate of eight feet as the extreme height of a

salmon's direct leap is not, I think, far from the mark. Scrope, whose opportunities of observation were very great, combats Yarrell's account of their power of leaping ten or twelve feet perpendicularly, saying that he has never seen a salmon spring out of the water more than five feet perpendicularly. He mentions having measured the fall of the Leader into the Tweed, which salmon could never surmount, and determined it to vary from five and a half to six feet, according to the level of the flood. He adds that large fish can leap higher than small ones, and that deep water gives them a better opportunity than shallow. 'They rise rapidly, from the very bottom to the surface of the water, by means of rowing and sculling, as it were, with their fins and tail; and this powerful impetus bears them upwards in the air, on the same principle that a few tugs of the oar make a boat shoot onwards after one has ceased to row.' This is a better method of accounting for the height of a salmon leap than old Izaak quotes from Michael Drayton's 'Polyolbion':—

'and stems the watery tract
Where Tivy falling down makes a high cataract
Forc'd by the rising floods that there her course oppose,
As tho' within her bounds they meant her to inclose;
Here when the labouring fish does at the foot arrive,
And finds that by his strength he does but vainly strive,
His tail takes in his mouth, and bending like a bow

That's to full compass drawn, aloft himself does throw,
Then springing to his height as doth a little wand
That, bended end to end, and started from man's hand,
Far off itself doth cast ; so doth the salmon vault.'

Mr. Day, in his book already quoted, gives a clear
jump of six feet as probably as much as a salmon
under ordinary conditions could accomplish, but
quotes, in a note, Swift's 'Travels in Iceland,' who
declared, that from personal observation he knew that
they were able to dart themselves nearly fourteen feet
perpendicularly out of the water, and Professor
Landmark, who in 'Nature,' August 16, 1885, stated
that he had witnessed their jumping sixteen feet perpendicularly. I have certainly myself never seen a
salmon jump more than six feet direct, if as much.
There are two curious snapshot photographs of
salmon leaping at a fifteen-foot fall, reproduced in
'Scribner's Magazine' for September 1897, but it is
obvious these leaps are at the head of a rapid, and
not directly perpendicular.

'His growth is very sudden : it is said that after
he is got into the sea, he becomes, from a samlet not
so big as a gudgeon, to be a salmon in as short a time
as a gosling becomes to be a goose. Much of this
has been observed, by tying some riband or some
known tape or thread, on the tail of some young

salmon which have been taken in weirs as they have
swarmed towards the salt water, and then, by taking
a part of them with the known mark, at the same
place, at their return from the sea, which is usually
about six months after—which has inclined many to
think that every salmon usually returns to the same
river in which it was bred.'

Here we have an account which could hardly be
improved upon now. The rapid growth of the fish,
the experiment of marking—although I should hardly
think a 'riband or tape' put on to a samlet's tail would
be likely to be found on a grilse on his return —the six
months' average stay in salt water, and the homing
instinct of the fish which brings him back to the same
river, are all correctly described.   The marking of
salmon with disks, rings, branding or cuts on the fins
or tails, is the foundation of most of our knowledge
of their growth and migration.   We still wonder at
the marvellous instinct which brings them back to
their native river, like the swallow to its chimney or
the pigeon to its dove-cote, although tacksmen will
tell you that they recognise occasional wanderers
in the wrong river, asserting that they recognise them
as strangers by their shape and appearance ; and
although stray fish are sometimes captured in the
tideways of rivers like the Thames, which cannot have

bred there, as salmon have long since disappeared entirely from their main streams.

Walton next tells us that the he-salmon is 'usually bigger than the spawner; that he is more kipper and less able to endure a winter in the fresh water than she is, yet she is, at that time of looking less kipper and better, as watery and as bad meat.' All who have caught autumn fish will confirm this account. The kipper, with his ungainly shape, his dark red marking, and his great beak, is ugly enough to frighten his captor when lifted out of the water, but although he is a bit soft to eat, he does not make bad cutlets when fried; while the hen fish, with her deceptive appearance of being in good condition, for all her silvery sides and ordinary shape, is far more watery, tasteless, and insipid.

Walton concludes his observations on salmon by noticing the variations of seasons in different rivers, by telling you to observe that he does not stay long in one place, 'but covets still to go nearer the spring-head,' that he does not as the trout and many other fish, lie near the water-side, or bank, or roots of trees, but swims in the deep or broad parts of the water, and usually in the middle or near the ground. And he then proceeds to tell you how to catch him. Sometimes or seldom he will bite at a minnow, *not usually at a fly,* but more usually at a worm, and then more usually at a lob or garden worm, which 'should be scoured,' and notes that 'many used to fish for salmon with a ring of iron on the top of their rod, through which the line may run to as great a length as is needful when he is hooked. And to that end some use a wheel about the middle of their rod or near the hand.' He then imparts the secret of old Oliver Hanley, 'a noted fisher, now with God,' who used to put his worms into a box with oil of ivy-berries, 'and make his worms so irresistibly attractive that he could catch more fish than I, or anybody who has ever gone a-fishing with him, could do, especially salmon.' On the authority of Sir Francis Bacon he believes that fish can hear, and probably smell, in the water, and concludes by telling you trout and salmon in season have their bodies adorned with red or black spots, 'which gives them such addition of natural beauty as I think was never given to any woman by the artificial paint or patches in which they so much pride themselves in this age.'

For the duration of life of the salmon, which Walton, on Sir Francis Bacon's authority, fixes at ten years, I do not think we have, or can have, any data to go upon, and it must be mainly guess-work. What with all the enemies that dog his career from the cradle

to the fish-kettle : the birds, insects, and fish that feed
upon the spawn, and harry his young fry ; the otters
in the stream and the porpoises and seals in the bay
that hunt him in his maturer days ; and last, not least,
the numerous engines, nets, traps, poisons, prawns,
flies, and minnows devised for his destruction by
mankind, few indeed must be the fish that succumb
to senile decay.

> Fate cropped him short, for be it understood,
> He would have lived much longer if he could.

Day tells us that it has long been known that fish
possess the sense of smell. Blind salmon are often
captured in good condition, which must have obtained food by the use of this sense. The organs of
smell are situated as in other animals, but do not
communicate with the mouth, and are not related to
the function of breathing, as it would injure their
delicate lining membrane to be in incessant contact
with currents of water. The nostrils are depressions
or cavities, with two external openings situated on
either side of the middle of the snout. He also tells
us that 'hearing is developed in fish, and it is
remarkable how any diversity of opinion can exist as
to their possessing this sense.' He quotes Lacépède
for fish which had been kept in the basin of the
Tuileries for upwards of a century, coming when called

C

by their names, and carp, tench, and trout in Germany
summoned to their food by the ringing of a bell.   I
should be better prepared to credit this latter testimony if Mr. Day had seen it himself, or if I could
cross-examine the witness he cites.   If any food was
thrown on the water, or the surface was disturbed, it
would be more likely to account for the assembly
than the calling of the names or the ringing of the
bell, and I am a little sceptical as to whether this
may not have been the case.   If fish do hear what
passes on the bank they certainly do not heed it, and,
timid as they are, I have never known them take the
slightest notice of shouting, whistling, or any other
noise ; nor would I hesitate to allow a school-feast, an
Eisteddfod, or a monster concert to take place within
earshot of the pool I was fishing, if I could be certain
that none of the assembled crowds would approach
near enough to cast a shadow on the surface of the
stream, or risk the danger to himself and the incon-
venience to me, of my hook, while I was casting,
lodging itself in some portion of his person or garments.

> But if a man who stands upon the brink
> But lift a shining hand against the sun,
> There is not left the twinkle of a fin.

With this corroboration of his views on the sense

of smell and hearing in fish, I take leave of Izaak Walton, protesting that Mr. Andrew Lang, in his preface to the edition of 1896, does scant justice to his author when he writes 'that as to salmon Walton scarcely speaks a true word about their habits, except by accident.' His comments are probably not the result of original observation, but I should think they fairly epitomised the contemporary gossip on the subject. I would rather urge that few treatises on natural history of so early a date contain so much that is confirmed by later and more scientific observation.

Much of the life history of the salmon still remains obscure, notwithstanding our boasted advance in knowledge. We know that the smolt goes down to the sea a few inches long, and returns a grilse weighing many pounds, but cannot ascertain how far they go from the estuary or how they contrive to attain such large dimensions so rapidly. They are voracious feeders, and consume large quantities of herrings, pilchards, and other fish and crustacea when mature ; but it is not known where or how far they go in the salt water, nor are they ever captured in the intermediate stage of their existence, between their start as smolts and their return to the estuaries as grilse. Their path on their return journey is unfor-

C 2

tunately too well known, and consequently beset with
dangers. We have seen that it is still uncertain how
often they breed, or how long they live; and, as
their growth is in the sea, it is curious that some
rivers are never visited by fish of very large size, and
that, even with long and large rivers like the Tay and
Tweed, monsters are far more often met with in the
former than in the latter. Another puzzle is to
account for the reason for their jumping. I do not
mean at a fall, but when in the pools and heads of
streams. It is not at flies or insects, as in the case of
trout, and they might easily get sufficient exercise in
their native element. Again, why do salmon take
flies? Some have quaintly suggested that they do so
from irritation; but if so, how is it that they are 'put
down' instead of 'up' when a 'Captain' or 'Blue
Doctor' has passed over their heads a great number
of times? I am more anxious to murder an organ-
grinder after two tunes than one, and my wrath
increases in geometrical proportion to the pertinacity
with which he grinds his instrument of torture. I
can well imagine *Salmo salar* being bored at seeing a
small object opening and shutting and jumping backwards and forwards, as he is vainly endeavouring to
get forty winks at the bottom of the pool, and even
his making up his mind that if it went on any longer

he would 'go for it'; but then the secret of success
in salmon-fishing would be a dogged persistency, and
instead of resting a rising fish, it would be advisable
to keep at him until he could bear it no longer. Of
course I do not believe in any such fanciful reason,
and have no doubt that flies are taken for food of
some description. Although they are not like any
inhabitant of the rivers, their appearance and motion
greatly resemble that of the crustacea, which, like our
trade prosperity in years unhappily passed, advance
by leaps and bounds, and anyone who has seen a
shrimp or prawn shifting his ground in a salt-water
vivarium, and then watches the 'play' of a salmon-fly
in the stream, cannot fail to be struck by the resem-
blance between the two. The motion of the feathers,
now closing when pulled against the stream, now
opening as the pressure ceases to be felt, is just like
that of the numerous legs and appendages with which
its prototypes in the sea are so bountifully provided.
Salmon doubtless do not feed greedily or regularly in
fresh water, but I feel sure that the reason food is so
seldom found in their stomachs is that they always,
when practicable, eject it as soon as hooked. Mr.
Naylor, in a letter to the 'Field' newspaper dated July
1897, records the capture of a salmon of twenty-eight
pounds killed on a spoon in Norway. It was hooked

in such a manner that its mouth was completely closed,
the triangles being fixed in the upper and lower jaws.
On cutting out the hooks a partially digested parr fell
from the fish's mouth. It was, no doubt, the peculiar
way it was hooked which prevented it from suppress-
ing the evidence of this meal taken in fresh water.
Mr. Marsham also, in September 1897, killed a 20 lb.
male fish fresh from the sea in the Teith, inside which
he found a black and white slug $1\frac{1}{2}$ inches long.

I do not believe that salmon or any other fish
feel very acutely, a reassuring theory for the tender-
hearted fisherman. I once caught a sea trout about
a pound and a half in weight which had been
recently completely transfixed by a heron's bill. The
wound was perfectly fresh, and could not, in my
judgment, have been made more than half an hour,
and yet the fish was already feeding and taking the
fly. So, too, the desperate struggle of the fish to get
free confirms the same view. Not all the instinct of
self-preservation would induce a man to put a strain
of even a pound on a fishing-rod if the hook was
attached to some tender part of his flesh.

Scrope, in an amusing passage, quotes Sir
Humphry Davy, ' the eminent author of " Salmonia,"
and Dr. Gillespie, as authorities for the statement
that " fish seldom feel any pain from the hook." '

The bit of special pleading which follows is so good that I am tempted to quote it.

' I take a little wool and feather, and, tying it in a particular manner upon a hook, make an imitation of a fly; then I throw it across the river and let it sweep round the stream with a lively motion. Up starts a monster fish with his murderous jaws, and makes a dash at my little Andromeda. Then he is the aggressor, not I ; his intention is evidently to commit murder. He is caught in the act of putting that intention into execution. Having wantonly intruded himself upon my hook, which I contend he had no right to do, he darts about in various directions, evidently surprised to find that the fly which he had hoped to make an easy conquest of, is much stronger than himself—I naturally attempt to regain this fly unjustly withheld from me. The fish gets tired and weak in his lawless efforts to deprive me of it. I take advantage of his weakness, I own, and drag him somewhat loth to the shore, where one rap on the back of the head ends him in an instant.'

Let us hope that these eminent authorities are right. At any rate we may comfort ourselves with the reflection that salmon have to be caught some-how, and that a long and fruitless struggle in a net must be at least as disagreeable as the nobler fate of a contest in which the fish is matched against the angler with a fair chance for life and liberty. We may reverse Macaulay's famous saying about the Puritans' objection to bear-baiting, and submit with confidence that we love fishing not because it gives pain to the salmon, but because it gives pleasure, health, recreation and excitement to its votaries.

So prolific are the salmon that were it not for the waste caused by the innumerable enemies of the eggs, the fry, and the mature fish, the offspring of a single baggit hen would suffice to stock a good-sized river.

It is very easy to breed these fish artificially ; and even to produce hybrids, which are occasionally fertile, between the various species of salmonidæ ; even the non-migratory *Salmo fario* interbreeding with the anadromous *Salmo salar* and *Salmo trutta*, a fact alluded to by Kingsley in his delightful 'Water-babies,' where the student of fish-lore may find much keen and shrewd information upon the subject conveyed in a humorous form. Various attempts have been made to introduce them into the Antipodes by sending over the fecundated ova, but hitherto without success, although the introduction of the common trout into those regions is a most successful instance of acclimatisation. All the salmon requires in order to increase and multiply to any reasonable extent is to be left with healthy surroundings and a longer respite from persecution. No reasonable man desires that they should be allowed to multiply to such numbers as swarm in some rivers in Newfoundland—too great really either for sport or food—where the water is thick with fish, and anyone can get as many as he wishes with gaff or spear ; while the banks are fœtid with decaying corpses, and bears and other animals are sated with the spoil. But the number of salmon in British and Irish rivers have diminished, are diminishing, and ought to be increased. My own experience and communications from numerous reliable sources assure me of this fact. It puts me out of patience to see the wasteful and wanton destruction of a source of national wealth and enjoyment which could so easily be preserved by more reasonable treatment. Here is a creature which does absolutely no damage to man—by consuming his food or destroying his crops—which grows from ounces to pounds in a few months, and provides wholesome food, wealth, or recreation to thousands. All it asks is fair and sensible treatment. If it resents the unmeasured and unrestrained pollution of our rivers, the interest of the tenants of the banks are in this respect absolutely identical with those of

the inhabitants of the water.   It cannot be said that
a fish which manages to survive the passage through
the mouth of the Tyne at Newcastle is unreasonably
exacting in its requirements.   Yet one sees from
time to time such paragraphs in the newspapers as
I quote with shame from the *Scotsman* of August 22,
1897.

    There was a wholesale destruction of salmon in
the river Ribble last week.   Large numbers of fish
were seen floating down the stream dead, and eighteen were taken out dead from one pool.   These fish
had all been poisoned by foul refuse. which had been
flushed into the river by the heavy rain.'   This is not
an isolated instance, but the record of an occurrence
only too frequent.   Rivers like the Teviot and some
of the Wicklow streams pursue their rocky course
absolutely void of their former denizens, some of
them so poisoned that no living fish can exist in their
polluted waters.   The legislature has done something
to check this wanton waste ; perhaps it might do
more, but there is a danger in restrictions in advance
of local opinion, and what is certainly more required
than new Acts of Parliament is the intelligent and
vigilant enforcement of existing laws by the local
authorities.   Large powers have been recently conferred upon various areas.   County, district, and

parish councils are now elected by a democratic popular vote. It rests with those representative bodies to justify their existence by a prompt and resolute interference with the selfishness of such individuals and corporations as carelessly pursue their trades and occupations with injury and destruction to the health and wealth of their neighbours. In some cases the mischief has already been done beyond repair, but it is the plain duty of every Englishman to see that this wanton destruction goes no further. But it is not enough to provide the salmon with a suitable environment. The breeding stock must be protected from excessive and indiscriminate destruction. Poaching on the spawning beds, and the massacre of immature fish, do some mischief, but I have no hesitation in stigmatising the greed of the net fisher, and the defective laws under which he plies his trade, as the greatest causes of the diminution of salmon in British waters. Our ancestors no doubt used the prototypes of the same engines, with little care for times and seasons, and also indulged in cruives, traps and weirs of a very destructive character; but side by side with the rise in the value of salmon as a saleable commodity, and the greatly increased facilities for its transport by rail and steam, and its preservation by ice and canning, the human enemies

of the salmon have multiplied twenty-fold, their nets
and engines have developed and improved in efficiency ;
and they have learned to manage them with greater skill
and knowledge of the habits of the fish, and its course
from the sea along the estuary and to the spawning
beds. The old Scandinavian legend ascribes the
invention of salmon-nets to the principle of evil, and
relates that by a just retribution, like Perillus and
other scoundrels, the inventor perished by his own
wicked contrivance —

Infelix imbuit auctor opus.

Loki, the god alluded to, had carried on his
various tricks with impunity for a long time, but at
last his mischievous pranks culminated in the death
of the innocent and beautiful Baldur, whose virtues
and good qualities made him as obnoxious to his
destroyer as Aristides was to the Athenians. Everything on earth and sea had been sworn to do him no
harm ; but the ingenious Loki fashioned an arrow
out of mistletoe, which, owing to its peculiar habit of
growth, had been omitted from the solemn league
and covenant, and putting it into the hand of the
blind god Hodur, urged him to shoot, which he did,
with fatal effect. This was too much for the forbearance of even the most easy-going gods, and they

went for the murderer in a body. He fled from his pursuers, invented salmon nets, and subsisted on the proceeds of his fishing. Tracked at last to his place of refuge, he burnt his nets to avoid the possibility of their being used against him, and, turning himself into a salmon, plunged into the river. His precautions were of no avail ; for the fresh ashes of the twine remained in the shape he had given them, and the gods easily reconstructed the destroyed nets from the pattern. The first time they dragged for him, Loki, who had acquired the instincts with the form of the fish, put his head under a stone, and the net passed harmlessly over his back. Before making their second venture, they added weight in the shape of a lot of spare shields and bucklers ; but this time he escaped them by jumping over the middle of the primæval seine. But 'there is luck in odd numbers,' and the third time, Thor wading behind the net, probably even deeper than the point represented by Scrope's limit of the fifth button of the waistcoat, an adornment with which he dispensed, caught him by the tail as he attempted to repeat his previous method of escape, and put an end to his mischievous career.[1]

Of course I do not seriously object to nets or net-

[1] See *Forest Scenes in Norway and Sweden*, Rev. Henry Newland.—G. Routledge, 1855.

fishing, without which it would be impossible to
catch a tithe of the salmon which the consumer
requires, and which the most greedy rod fisher can
well spare. My real contention is that in this
respect the interests of all classes of fishermen
are identical, and that, if the experiment was fairly
tried, it would soon be discovered that 'the half was
greater than the whole.' We hear some philanthropists
and more politicians advocating a compulsory eight
hours movement, and one argument used by them in
its favour is the increased productiveness which
would result from the better quality of the labour
done during a shorter period than the present
customary working day. I do not desire unnecessarily to enter upon a controversial topic which does
not directly bear upon my subject, but I believe that
there can be little doubt, if any, that shorter hours of
labour in the particular trade of which I am writing
would in the long run benefit the salesman, the
consumer, and the humble rod-fisher as well, by
greatly increasing the supply of fish in the river.
The key to the situation, in my deliberate opinion, is
the lengthening of the weekly close time, and the
rigid enforcement of the amended law which I
suggest. Few indeed are the fish which during the
net-fishing season succeed in running the gauntlet

through all the engines prepared for their destruction
between the estuary and the breeding grounds high
up the river, and the proprietors of the upper reaches
take little trouble to preserve and protect the
spawning fish, as they complain with some justice
that they never get a chance at a salmon in a clean
condition. Legislation is, of course, essential for any
practical improvement in this direction ; even if one
could meet with a tacksman so far-sighted and
provident as to refrain from killing the 'goose with
the golden eggs,' his self-denial would be unavailing if
his more selfish neighbours were permitted to capture
the fish he had spared. If the present period of
sanctuary was doubled, I believe that in a year or
two at most the nets would be catching far more fish
than they now do in the longer period, and that the
most discontented would acquiesce in restrictions the
wisdom of which would have been demonstrated
beyond cavil. Some such measure is imperative, and
the reward of the intelligent gratitude of all well
wishers to the national prosperity awaits the states-
man who has the firmness and courage to initiate
and carry through the necessary amendment of the
law. However, knowing by experience the great
difficulty of forcing any measure through the Houses
of Parliament which is not of a political nature, I am

glad to hear that Mr. Malloch of Perth is endeavouring to form a syndicate to take all the net fishing on
the Tay and introduce the change I suggest voluntarily. Needless to say, I wish all success to the
experiment.

CHAPTER II

EGGS FOR GRANDMOTHERS

' MY first salmon !' What fisherman is there 'so dead in memory—so old in heart' that he does not recall to mind that eventful landmark in his career? The girl's first ball, the blissful day when the Etonian is told he may get his colours for the eight or the eleven, the election to a scholarship, or the first class or fellowship, the barrister's first brief—even if it be 'soup' at sessions—the maiden speech : all these are great days in a career ; but about some of them at least there is a fearful joy ; and they may be damped by the recollections of failure. But the fisherman who has worked his way through minnows, dace, roach, perch, and gudgeon to pike and trout, from paste and gentles and worm, to the delight of fly-fishing, must, if he has the root of the matter in him, have been fired with a higher ambition and longed for the day when he should measure his skill with the king of fishes, whose acquaintance he has hitherto made 'beautiful in death'

on the slabs of the fishmonger's shop, or on the table,
only. There is such an appearance of ' power ' in the
small head, broad shoulders and wedge-like shape—
such a glamour in the bright silvery sides—such grada-
tions in the shading—altogether such a fascination
about the glittering prize, that no minor triumph will
satisfy the inward longing ; and the wanderer is driven
forth, like Io by her gadfly, to go, if needs be, to the
uttermost parts of the earth to satisfy his ambition.
And the salmon really sometimes seems to enter into
the spirit of the thing. His prowess is so well known,
his strength so great, his cunning so matchless, that
he can well afford to yield for once to the awkward
blandishments of the tiro. Has he not been known
to tire the arms and defeat the skill of a Lovat, a
Denison or a Bromley Davenport. His moderation
cannot be mistaken for weakness ; if for once he yields
to a Briggs or a——, he

> Strikes down the lusty and approved knight,
> And lets the younger and unskilled go by,
> To win his honour and to make his name.

The eventful day has come and the neophyte is at
last, breathless with excitement, duly equipped with
waders and a long rod, standing by the side of a real
salmon river, in charge of a trustworthy nurse who
selects the right fly for the day and tells him to ' cast

there.' The rushing water boils and bubbles over rock
and boulder, dark ; but clearing after the night's flood,
for in this case the predestined captor has found the
river in order—an event which is not always or even
often the case. Perhaps the beginner has served a
long apprenticeship to trout. If so, he has not so
much to learn, although there is a great deal of difference between the neat turn of the wrist which sends
the fine line and gossamer cast with dry fly attached
to fall just over the rising trout, and the sweep of the
arms which urges the ' Jock Scott ' and treble gut across
the torrent ; but it may be that he has never handled
a fly rod before in his life. Even then he need not
despair. The gillie may be stifling or uttering male-
dictions in a strange tongue, if he is an Irishman, or
bearing his trial more stolidly if he be an elder of the
kirk. The rod may describe strange curves in the air,
the line may be serpentine in its convolutions, the fly
may bump into the water only a few yards from the
end of the rod with a splash like a Solan goose coming
down upon a herring ; but it is a long line which
knows no straightening, and the kindly stream hangs
the fly at the right angle, and on a taut line for a
portion—although probably only a short portion—of
every cast which has not hitched it in a tree or the
performer's clothes. A few yards down the stream

and there is a boil and a momentary glimpse of a
broad back. Well had it been for the novice had
there been more slack line at the time, or had his eye
been less vigilant, for at the first motion of the water
he strikes with a suddenness which takes the lure
away from the jaws just opening to seize it, and
attaches it firmly to the branch of a birch tree twenty
yards above him. It is a work of time and labour to
dislodge the fly, and there is no need for once to give
the fish a rest. Personally conducted a little distance
above the rise, the novice is suitably admonished not
to be in such a hurry : he had far better not strike at
all in such water, and quivering in every nerve he sees
his fly once more working at or near the same
spot. Again there is a boil—a glint of silver—and
this time an electric shock as the connection is complete, and the first fish is on. A whirr of the reel, and
a singing of the line as the salmon dashes madly down
the stream ; but, alas ! the point of the rod is
instinctively lowered, which is just what it ought not
to be, and the line is going out with fearful rapidity.
' Up with the point of your rod, mon : up with it—
keep a good strain upon him.' No time now for
courtesy or respect ! be he baron, duke or royalty
itself, the words will out without the preface. Fifty
yards of line out—and is that the fish jumping opposite

to him ? and yet there is a strain upon the rod which makes his arms ache. Yes, the fish has got the advantage of all that slack, and is heading upwards with all the weight of the water bellying the line. 'He has drowned it.'

Thrice lucky the sportsman if he has not got it round a sunken rock, loosened the hold, or broken off. But Providence is kind, and the tackle strong, and, under the guidance of his mentor, Mr. Briggs has managed to reel in a good deal of the slack, and got his rod in the orthodox curve, and breathes again. There is an interval of rest—more welcome to the inexperienced fisherman than to his attendant, who knows the difficulty and delay caused by the tactics of a sulky fish ; but it is not for long, for after two or three shakes of the head, the salmon dashes down the stream, pursued by the excited sportsman, and Pat or Donald shouting 'Canny noo,' or 'Be aisy,' as the case may be. Sometimes the rod point is dangerously lowered ; but its general tendency is in the right direction ; now all depends on the humour of the fish. He is within half-a-dozen yards of the bottom of the pool, and if he takes a fancy to face the broken water that dashes and eddies through the boulders to the next cast it is a guinea to a gooseberry that he cuts the line, but he turns just at the

nick of time—and soon his runs become shorter and
shorter—there is an occasional slow wave of a broad
tail on the surface, and ' Mentor ' takes his stand on
a large flat rock, where there is a still deep back-
water, and takes the cork off the gaff. A few moments
later the fish turns on his side, apparently almost life-
less, and is slowly towed towards the gaff. The victory seems won, and the proud and happy sportsman
is already mentally calculating the weight of his
prize at something varying from a half to a third
more than the steelyard will record later—yet if he
knew ! the next few minutes are the most perilous
of the whole contest. There is 'life in the old dog
yet,' the hold is dangerously worn with the long and
not very scientific fight, and that log-like form is good
for at least one more wriggle, dash and jump, if he
catches sight of the gaff and its wielder. But I
cannot find it in my heart to rob my imaginary
sportsman of his success. I like to bring down the
curtain with united hands and ' Bless you, my children.' There is a quick stroke of the gaff and the
fish is gasping on the stones. What matter if
he be a trifle red, and only turn the scale at eight
pounds. He is a 'fish,' and the proud and happy
victor is mentally vowing that his first salmon shall
not be his last, while ' Mentor ' shall not lack the re-

freshing dram, if he 'tastes,' or at all events the half-sovereign or more which he has so richly earned.

Who shall say that my picture, if an imaginary one, does not describe a scene which, with slight variations of incident, has occurred again and again ? I shall not, I hope, be accused of depreciating a sport to which I am devoted, if I express my conviction that skill counts for much more in trout fishing, especially with the dry fly, than in salmon fishing. Take a good day and equal conditions on the Anton or the Test, the Mimram or the Lea, and match an unfortunate beginner, with the best professional advice, against such masters of the art as Lord Granby, Mr. Croft, or the late Mr. John Day. Not only are the odds a thousand to one that the expert beats the tiro, but the latter may consider himself fortunate indeed if his basket contains a single fish at the end of the day. As he pursues his course up-stream the river is furrowed by departing fish, and if he succeeds in keeping out of sight long enough to try for a rising trout, the flop of his fly upon the water, if it ever gets there, is the signal for its departure. The slightest splash, the least drag, is fatal, and the fly refuses to float, while he finds it much easier to hit the weeds and cressets which occupy the greater part of the stream than the narrow belt of water where the gnat or dun disappeared at his approach. So, too, he is obliged to cast from his knee, and as he flicks the line behind him in desperate efforts to dry his fly, it disappears with an ominous crack, and it is necessary to go into dock for repairs. The difference between the two sports is almost like that between chess and whist. In the one case the professor has the indifferent performer absolutely at his mercy—in the other, while he is secure of considerable winnings in the long run, it is possible that luck may from time to time give the victory to his less skilful adversary.

I hope that no one will infer from these remarks that it is an easy thing to become a good salmon fisher. It is beautiful to see a real master at work, and I would almost as soon watch such a one as catch fish myself. First, there is the cast. Salmon do not always obligingly put themselves just where the stream will bring the fly over them wherever it may have fallen. Often the place where they lie by some submerged boulder is a long way off, and can only be reached by the highest combined strength and skill. The wind is gusty and squally, there are trees or high rocks behind, and there is but a narrow and treacherous ledge to support the feet, and that is often deep under water in a strong stream. It is no child's play—a false step might be fatal—yet see, the fisher-

man has lifted the point of his rod, keeping all his
line still in front of him, and then with a strong,
resolute swish has brought the part nearest to the top
in contact with the water, and the line, as if by magic,
unrolls itself straight towards the place where the fish
usually rises, the fly alighting last of all, just in such a
position that without loss of time or trouble it will
hang at the right moment in the right position, to
present a temptation to the fish, which ought to be,
and often is, irresistible. This is the 'Spey cast,' and
when executed by an expert it almost deceives you
into believing it to be easy. If you think so, try it
yourself, and you will soon be undeceived. Only long
practice and great natural aptitude has rendered possible that brilliant feat. As a rule, the work done
behind you is more important than what you see in
front ; which is in a great measure its result. As in
golf, the swing forward is the reflection of the back
ward movement, and if the line has been corkscrewed
or curved behind your shoulder it will not be straight
when it is brought forward. When the fly has come
round to a point near the bank you are standing on or
under, lift your rod till the fly and gut cast are loose
at the top of the water, then with a strong sweep of
the arm send the line flying straight back over your
shoulder and make a similar movement forward the

moment the fly has reached its furthest limit behind, neither delaying nor hurrying the motion. But if there are rocks or overhanging boughs behind you, and you have not acquired the 'Spey cast,' another method of overcoming the difficulty is to stand facing directly down-stream, throw the line straight back over the shoulder nearest the water, looking round as you do so to see that your fly keeps over the stream and does not go back as far as the threatening boughs or rock, and then with a direct and strong sweep toward the opposite side you may succeed in throwing a fairly long and straight line across the stream and a little down it. This used to be called on the Tay the 'cradle' cast, from a pool not far from Stanley, which could only be properly fished from the bank by this method. There was a long, deep, submerged shelf of rock some twenty or twenty-five yards from the side, and the overhanging trees made it impossible to bring your line behind you. I remember a day—I am afraid to say how many years ago—when I got three fish out of that hundred yards of water, each weighing between eighteen and nineteen pounds. What especially fixes the incident in my memory is that I hooked the first fish almost immediately—that he was a singularly sulky customer, dived deep and hugged the rock, never at any time running more than ten or

a dozen yards, and that it took me three-quarters of
an hour to bring him to the gaff. I hesitated whether
I should have my lunch before or after recommencing
operations, but thought I would 'just try one or two
more casts.' The very first offer was accepted by a
fish, the exact counterpart of the last, only of a more
accommodating disposition, as he ran freely and well,
but speedily exhausted himself by his efforts to escape,
and he was on the bank beside his companion in
less than six minutes. I do not usually time myself,
but I had looked at my watch to see whether it was
lunch-time. I mention this occurrence to illustrate
the great difference in the time which may suffice to
tire two fishes similar in size and condition.

I hope I have made myself fairly clear, but if it is
difficult to cast a good line with obstacles behind you,
it is hardly less so to describe the operation in such a
manner as to be intelligible to the reader. The best
description is but a very poor substitute for a
practical demonstration by the river-side, and I have
but one hint to add before I leave the subject of
casting. Whether you be an old hand or a beginner,
examine the point of your hook from time to time.
A sharp rap against the stones behind you may occur
without your being in the least aware of it, and will
often break the best-tempered hook that was ever

made. The feathers and general aspect of the fly remain the same, and give you a false feeling of security. Then, when one or more good fish have risen, and you have just felt them without their taking hold, and at last you make the examination you ought not to have delayed so long, all Walton's advice to anglers, ' to be patient and forbear swearing, lest they be heard and catch no fish,' is apt to be thrown away upon you.

After the cast comes the working the fly. As to this it is difficult to lay down any definite rules, so much depends upon the nature of the water, whether still, rough, or rapid, and on the conditions as to wind and depth. As a rule, it is a mistake to cast a long line when the fish are lying near the side from which you are fishing, but if the stream is very rapid it is necessary to have a fair length out, or your fly will dance about too near the surface of the water. A series of slight lifts of the point of the rod should, of course, impart to the ' fly ' that lifelike appearance caused by the opening and shutting of the feathers as it dances up and falls down the stream ; but the action should be varied, as a skilled bowler alters his pace to overcome the resistance of an obstinate bat. Generally speaking, the line should be jerked up and down more in still water than in rapid ; and you

should fish deeper for autumn fish that have been in
the river some time than for salmon fresh from the
sea.   But there is no rule without an exception, and
if a fish declines your lure or rises short when it is
presented to him in one way, try another method.
Do not, however, go on too long at a time at short
rising fish ; mark the exact place either physically,
mentally, or both, and when you return after fishing
the rest of the pool, your patience will often be
rewarded by a taking rise and a tight line.   Next
comes the most debated point on which to give
advice, namely, 'the strike.'

' To strike or not to strike, that is the question.'
Here again it is impossible to lay down a hard and
fast rule.   In a strong stream it is better certainly not
to strike at all, unless for some reason a whole succession of fish have been 'rising short,' in which case
a sharp and decided stroke may hook one foul, when
'look out for squalls,' especially if the fly fixes itself
in the middle of the fish.   A foul-hooked fish always
makes a desperate fight, as you have no control over
his movements, and the water does not get into his
gills to exhaust him ; and if he happen to be hooked
in the side he catches the whole weight of the water
even after he is fairly killed, and it is most difficult to
bring him to the gaff.   I once remember severely

straining a strong salmon-rod in landing a little grilse
of eight pounds on the heavy stream known as the
Cat Holes, in the Tay. A fish hooked through the
tail gives you a better chance : as, although he has
the advantage of you at first, and fights like a tiger,
you become master of the situation, and may tow him
safely to harbour if you once succeed in lifting his tail
out of water. His strength is gone, and he is as
powerless as Antæus when Hercules prevented him
from touching his mother earth. But how often the
hurried strike of a converted trout fisher snatches the
fly from the jaws of a rising fish. Heaven defend
me from the gillie who shouts or whispers ' There it
is.' It is difficult enough to keep cool and check the
instinctive action of the wrists even without such a
temptation, and poor human nature succumbs when
encouraged in vice by another. If the flesh is too
weak it is not a bad plan to try Tom Purdie's dodge
as reported by Scrope. He had risen the same fish
four times, and began to suspect that he had given
him too little law, ' or jerked the heuck away before
he had closed his mouth upon it. . . . I keepit my
een hard closed when the heuck was coming owre
the *place*. Peace be here ! I fand as gif I had catched
the branch o' an aik tree swinging an sabbin in a
storm of wind.'

What I recommend, and try to practise myself in strong water, is a steady pull at the fish, not when the rise is seen, but when it is first felt. There is a good chance that the point of the hook will be thus driven in well over the barb, and if the hold is so slight that the fly comes away you are saving time by hastening a catastrophe which would certainly have occurred later on. But in a lake or the still part of a sluggish river it is necessary to strike fairly quick, although hand and eye should not act together as rapidly as if you were fishing for trout. Dig it into him just as he turns, and if he has meant business you are nearly sure to have him fast. Of course, even in still water, when the fish are taking low down, you often feel them before seeing the rise at all, but then the question settles itself, and there is no need for advice.

Next comes the important operation of playing the fish, and here there is at one time little or no difficulty, but at another all the highest qualities of the sportsman may be brought into play. Knowledge, presence of mind, courage, strength, endurance, activity, readiness of resource and invention may all be required to meet the cunning and wiles by which the 'foeman worthy of your steel' endeavours to overcome you, and too often succeeds. A spring fish in a rocky pool is indeed no contemptible adversary, and a tussle with such a one may be an experience to last a lifetime. Well for you if you know the bottom of the water, for, depend upon it, the fish does, and will be ready to take advantage of any submerged stump or boulder if you give him the chance. Nothing, of course, can check his wild impetuous rushes when the reel screams and the line hisses through the water, but it is astonishing how he may be led and directed if you know how to do it. But such knowledge cannot be communicated in writing, and comes only by instinct and practice. A few general rules of universal application are all that I can offer. Keep a good strain on your fish from the first moment you hook him, and keep as much line on the reel as you can. It is better to follow the fish, if possible, than to let him run out much of the line, for the weight of the water on a great length is apt to bring the strain upon the hold in the wrong angle; and if the salmon tries the common manœuvre of a rapid turn and a dash up-stream, it is not always easy to reel up so fast as to prevent him from making the line slack for a moment or two; when, of course, he has a good chance of ridding himself of the fly. Now he leaps high into the air, and the point of the rod must be momentarily lowered, but recovered as rapidly as it was lowered. Now he rests, and you may be glad of the temporary relief, but you should not, if it can be avoided, allow the rest to degenerate into a sulk. Perhaps, however, the minutes wear on and he declines to move, the only sign of life being a 'jigging' at the line as he turns his head from side to side, either trying to shake the fly loose or rubbing it against some rock at the bottom, and something must be done to make him move. Throw a stone or two in above him, but beware lest you hit the line. Some desperate individuals have been known to put their bunch of keys round the line and let it down on his nose; but they are of the class who 'burn their boats and destroy their bridges.' If the fish is lost after all, the despatch box and cigar cabinet must visit the locksmith before the contents are available, or the portmanteaus and bags must make their next journey open. Personally, I have shrunk from such a risky proceeding, but if the fish has remained stolid in spite of my trying him at different angles, and from down-stream below him, I have often found it effective to let a few inches of the line out of the reel below the hand and suddenly let it go, thus giving a little momentary slack as it runs through the rings and a jerk as the rod tightens it again. Another dodge is a smart rap

K

on the butt of the rod. If all resources fail, there is
nothing for it but patience ; and I have known the
fish to yield to the strain at last, and come quite
gradually and steadily to the top of the water, just
when I was becoming convinced that the line was
fixed round a rock or stump, or one of those terrible
bits of wire-fencing which are always falling into
some rivers that I know, as the crumbling and overhanging banks give way after a spate ; and reluctantly
making up my mind to break and have done with it.

But how if a fish seems quite determined to run
out of the pool into broken water, or straight to some
dangerous obstacle, perhaps under the archway of
some bridge, where you cannot follow him ? Well, if
he must, he must, and every fisherman's experience
will tell of salmon lost in spite of all that skill and
patience could do. But usually there is a moment
of hesitation before the desperate passage, as no
salmon likes to leave his pool. At such times do
not reel up line, but, keeping the strain as steady as
possible, walk backwards up the stream. I have
often known a fish under such circumstances to allow
himself to be led for a considerable distance from
the point of danger, when a turn of the handle of the
reel would probably have been the signal for an
onward rush and a broken cast

Lastly comes the process of landing the fish, and it is at this supreme moment that a mistake is most apt to be fatal. When the line is quite short and the salmon is gasping at the top of the water, floundering and flapping his broad tail, a well-directed stroke of that natural weapon may break the cast or release the fly, and you must keep a vigilant eye and a cool head. You have steered him clear of the dangerous rock, coaxed or guided him from the very verge of the perilous rapids, pursued him over slippery boulders, perhaps over your middle in the strong stream—your arms ache with the strain of the long struggle. A little patience, and he is yours. Do not, I entreat, spoil all by too impetuous handling. I grant that the sight of the spent giant makes you long to have him on the bank, but beware of reeling up the line too short ; perhaps you may get the knot which attaches the casting-line through the top ring of the rod—at all events, you will get a heavy strain in the wrong place, and there will be danger if he nerves himself for a final rush. Above all, keep your gillie cool, if you have one with you, and impress upon him, if he be inexperienced, that it is not his business to catch the fish, but to land him, and that a gaff should not be handled as if it was a hatchet, or a spear, or a fleshhook dashed into a pan or kettle, or cauldron or pot, to impale and bring up some portion of the contents. I write feelingly, as I have more than once had my line gaffed by men who ought to have known better, and I have even seen a salmon literally knocked off the line by a blow of the cleek from above. Perhaps it is owing to this disagreeable experience that I prefer when it is feasible to land or gaff my own fish ; but of course this is not everywhere practicable. A deep, still place should be selected to gaff a salmon, and if you prefer to beach him you should keep some little distance from the water and rather take advantage of the fish's own movements than drag him *nolens volens* on the shore. A steady, direct pull, and then, when he is gasping high and nearly dry, down with your rod and run in behind him and throw him up upon the shore. A smart rap above the snout with a stone or stick will put an end to his floundering, and whatever may be your fortune for the rest of the day, at least you will not return empty-handed.

CHAPTER III

TACKLE AND EQUIPMENT

THESE subjects have been so fully and ably treated
in the Badminton volume on fishing and other works
that it is not my purpose to deal with them except in
the most general terms. A few hints derived from
my own experience may not, however, be out of place,
and the experienced sportsman can skip them if he
will.

Gentle reader ! whatever may be your particular
taste or fancy, let me at least entreat you to spare no
reasonable expense to provide yourself with the best
and most reliable tackle of all sorts that can possibly
be procured. An expensive article is not necessarily
a dear one. Deal with men who have a reputation
to maintain, and rely upon it that the very dearest
bargain you can possibly acquire is the cheap rod
which snaps at the ferrule like a carrot when you are five
miles from home, and the water in order : the reel which
catches at a critical moment, or the gut which breaks

at the knot as you strike hurriedly at a rising fish, or
wears and gives in the long struggle, just losing you
the prize at the moment he seems to be your own.
Salmon fishing at the best of times must be an
expensive amusement, and you are lucky if in tips,
rent, and travelling expenses, your fish cost you less
than five pounds apiece. It is indeed 'spoiling the
ship for a halfpennyworth of tar' to grudge the
necessary cost of thoroughly reliable workmanship
and materials.

The angler must of course be prepared to face all
weathers; often the most disagreeable day, with a
strong wind and heavy showers, proves the most
productive. Flannel next the skin and a good homespun suit will turn a lot of water, or prevent much
risk of chill if you happen to get a ducking, but you
or your attendant, if you have one, should carry also
a good stout mackintosh. Don't have it made too
short; shopkeepers are very apt, if you do not take
care, to sell you what they call a fishing mackintosh,
which just reaches down to your hips. Remember
the heel of Achilles; or, if you are a mechanical
engineer, unversed in the classics, that no chain is
stronger than its weakest link. If you have to face
an Argyleshire shower with a practicable breach
between your wading stockings and your coat, or if you

have to sit in a dogcart with the rain pouring off you
and deluging your seat, you might almost as well have
spared'yourself the burden of any protective covering
at all. Of course, if you have wading trousers instead
of stockings my remarks do not apply—but I do not
recommend them except for very deep wading in very
still water. My own conviction is that when you are
going into a rapid stream deep enough to feel the
water trickle into your stockings, you have gone deep
enough.⎺· Few ͺanglers have waded much without
going through some disagreeable if not dangerous
adventures ; and once at least I can remember being
in serious peril. I had waded down the North Esk
trying a minnow in a very heavy flood, in what was
ordinarily a shallow. Step by step I advanced, but
keeping within a few yards of the left bank, I
imagined myself secure, and went deeper than I would
otherwise have ventured to do. When I found that I
only stood with difficulty, I thought it time to beat a
retreat ; but when I tried to move I found the water
deepening into a hole, and that escape in that
direction was impossible. A heavy and dangerous
fall was just below, ending in a torrent rushing among
great rocks and boulders, and, good swimmer as I
am, I doubt if I should have ever regained the shore
had I once been swept off my feet. There was

nothing for it but to make for the further bank at a long distance across the raging flood. Leaning the butt of my rod, reel and all, into the gravel at the bottom, and supporting myself upon it as best I could, I crossed sideways with short and laborious steps. Well for me that I carried weight, and was young and strong. More than once I thought that I could stand no longer.

> Yet through good heart, and Our Ladye's grace.
> At length he reached the landing place.

I was fairly exhausted when I emerged, dripping but safe, on the friendly shore.

Stockings, or wading trousers if preferred, are always better than any kind of boot. The inside gets damp with perspiration, but dries easily when turned outside after the day's work. Boots are very difficult to dry. Of course, the foot should be protected by a knitted stocking over the india-rubber, and the brogue over the whole should be well studded with stout nails to give a good foothold and prevent slips. Any mackintosh covering is hot and uncomfortable to walk in ; but unless I am obliged to go a long distance on Shanks's mare I always prefer to wear waders. Even in small rivers, where the casts can be easily fished from the banks, it is a great convenience to be able to cross at any ford or shallow—or if boat fishing to

be able to step out in a foot of water or thereabouts, to land a fish and follow him. Some hardy individuals take to the water in ordinary costume ; but they are rather beacons to warn than examples to follow. Such habitual rashness usually ends in rheumatism or worse evils : and Scrope's advice, I should imagine, was partly satirical. He considers Mackintosh's invention wholly ' uncalled for,' ' accounting it an unpardonable intrusion to place a solution of india-rubber between the human body and the refreshing element. It is like taking a shower bath under the shelter of an umbrella.' In another passage he advises you ' never to go into the water deeper than *the fifth button of your waistcoat* : even this does not always agree with tender constitutions in frosty weather. As you are not likely to take a just estimate of the cold in the excitement of the sport, should you be of a delicate temperament, and be wading in the month of February, when it may chance to freeze very hard, pull down your stockings and examine your legs. Should they be black, or even purple, it might, perhaps, be as well to get on dry land ; but if they are only rubicund, you may continue to enjoy the water if it so pleases you.'

There were giants in those days ! For my own part, I have never found it necessary to examine the colour of my limbs, but when wading in the Tweed or Deveron in the early spring, have sometimes found it advisable to come out of the water and dance about the bank to warm myself, in spite of my having taken advantage of Mackintosh's obnoxious invention and being clad in the warmest wool and homespun. But I leave my readers to choose between the advice of my honest friend and his effeminate disciple.

A good form of hat is a cork-lined helmet, similar to those worn in tropical climates. The shoot at the back throws off the rain, and it is very handy to stick flies inside. I tried one of these hats accidentally on my return from Egypt, and have used one of the same pattern ever since, except in a strong wind. A good sized bag with canvas for fish on one side, and an india-rubber pocket for the reel and boxes on the other, and a net with a telescope handle with a knuckle joint at the end, and a clip to hang it by the bag, is convenient if you are alone and carry your own things. The gaff can be taken in the pocket and screwed into the net handle when required, while the net saves you many a sea trout too small to gaff, as these tender-mouthed fish often get off if you have to lift or drag them to land. The gaff, *crede experto*, can always be screwed on without difficulty at some period during the playing of the fish.

With regard to the rod, of course much depends upon the water for which you are bound—much also upon your individual preference and physique. Some prefer greenheart, some split cane, others a spliced and whippy Castle Connell. One man selects a long heavy rod which will do a good deal of his work for him, another likes one as light as is consistent with the possibility of covering the cast. Personally, I generally use a three-joint fifteen-foot split cane, with patent fastenings and a cork grip, which is both pleasant to the hand and comfortable if it happens to be wet. I like a light weapon, and such a rod, well balanced and well made, will throw a long line and kill a heavy fish ; but I am far from saying that for big rivers, where long casting is required, or for very rocky ones, where great power of guiding the fish is wanted, and it is useful to be able to get well above him, a stouter and longer rod is not preferable. Lord Lovat used to fish with one twenty foot in length ; but a grilse or even a salmon had but a short shrift with him, and not every one has his giant strength. One advantage of having a light rod is that a sea trout gives some fun upon it, whereas he affords little sport upon a heavy one. It is astonishing how light a rod will kill salmon with patient handling and a steady strain. I have taken many—the largest over twenty

pounds—with an ordinary single-handed trout rod ;
but most of them in a river where the water was
exceptionally still, and the banks so clear that it was
everywhere easy to follow your fish.

Probably it has fallen to the lot of most fishermen
of any wide experience to capture salmon with trout
tackle on more than one occasion.   Kelts, of course,
in the spring are a regular nuisance to the trout fisher,
as they take the ordinary March brown or dun
greedily, and generally select the moment when there is
a fine rise of fly upon the water.   Probably the wisest
course when one is hooked is to break : but I hate to
do this on purpose, and have wasted many a half hour
pulling the ugly heavy brutes out of the water.

The best of rods will break sometimes, if the fish
rise at a wrong angle, just as the line is coming out
of the water, or if the fly catches in something behind
you without your knowing it : and it is a most pro-
voking thing to find yourself by the side of a river
some miles from home, with fish rising well, and a
rod snapped off short at the ferrule with no sufficient
ends to splice.   I now always have my rods made
with a spare second joint as well as three tops.   It is
not a great additional expense, and gives a feeling of
security ; besides, even if you are spared the crowning
calamity of an accident by the water side, it is always

a good thing to be able to send away a joint for
repair or inspection without putting a favourite rod
hors de combat. Of course, necessity is the mother
of invention, and one can generally engineer a rough
splice, even in the case of the most awkward frac-
tures. I have killed fish with a rod with the two
upper joints awkwardly cobbled together round the
ferrule with a piece of luncheon-paper string. My
brother-in-law, Colonel Malcolm, sends me the following account of a similar experience of his own in
Canada.

'Once in Canada an unnoticed rootlet caught my
foot on the bank of the St. Anne du Nord, and
brought me down, making four smashes in my top
and second joint, three of which were mended up
with string, roughly but efficiently, and the fourth
somehow did not show till I had hooked a salmon,
and then the way the thing gaped was a caution.
This could only be met by turning the rod round,
and the tenderest care. Thus deprived of strength
the fish led me down the river, and behold ! a small
islet on the wrong side of which he was determined
to pass, but gentleness coupled with firmness brought
him into the right path, and down to a lovely back-
water, where he was more easily managed ; then I discovered that a young Irish officer had left the gaff

behind in the inn where we had put up our trap, so
of course we had to keep the fish on much longer than
would have been otherwise necessary ; but the culprit,
having taken off shoes and stockings, got behind him
as I turned him into a sandy dock, and all was well.'

The reel should be an ordinary check winch,
not too large for the balance of the rod. There
should, of course, be plenty of line, but if the reel be
too small to hold enough taper salmon, a quantity of
thin strong line not taking much room can always
be spliced to the heavier and more expensive portion
used for casting. There are many inventions of
different kinds for 'improving' reels, but although
their merits may be great, personally I dislike any
sort of complication. The line should be made to
suit the rod, and should not only be always carefully
dried on returning home, but also periodically tested
whenever it has been used. When a fisherman returns with a glum face, and a story that his 'beast
of a line' broke, and lost him the fish of the
season, you are usually safe in conjecturing that it
is his own fault, but you would not be wise to
tell him so.

Your casting lines should be of the best selected
gut, and a short length of twisted gut next to the
reel line is a good thing, even when you are fishing

with a fine cast, as it tapers the line for casting. Strong twisted treble gut is desirable for a very rocky stream, as all is not then lost even if one strand is cut, but good single gut will bear as great a strain as twisted. In clear bright water it is wonderful what can be done with a fine cast, but for such fishing the rod should be as light as is consistent with the possibility of killing your fish, as it is very difficult to acquire the lightness of hand requisite to avoid breaking fine tackle with a heavy rod. Gut should be always carefully soaked in cold water before you attempt to tie any knot in it, as it is extremely brittle when dry, and every strand and knot should be invariably tested before use, and not merely periodically like the line. A kink, a knot, a tangle, or bend, may crack a cast or tippet of the best material, and it is better to find out all weak places before and not after you have risen and hooked your fish. It is a good plan to soak, prepare, make up, and test at least one cast before starting in the morning. Such work is more deliberately and better done at home than at the river side, where, in spite of all counsels of perfection, it is hardly in human nature not to hurry if the water looks grand, and the fish are moving. I must myself confess in sackcloth and ashes that I have been broken more than once, owing to

the neglect of the obvious precautions I am suggesting
to others, tempted beyond my powers, and sinning
against knowledge.

Coming lastly to the fly, I know that I am on
more delicate and disputable ground. I am inclined
to think that colour matters very little indeed, but
am conscious that, nevertheless, I nearly always take
advice and use the fly that is most in vogue on the
water that I happen to be fishing at the time being.
I have the assurance at any rate that the particular
fly recommended to me has caught fish lately, and
therefore that it will in all probability do so again
under like conditions; and although I may feel
pretty certain that a different one would meet with
the same success, I am not disposed to try experiments on a strange water. As regards colour alone,
I must express a conviction that as a rule the reason a
particular fly kills most fish on a certain stretch of water
is that it is more used than any other, and faith is
a great element of success. On certain days a salmon
will take almost anything that is offered to him, on
others nothing will stir him. To quote Scrope
again, 'sometimes they will tak' the thoom o' yere
mitten, if you would throw it in, and at ithers they
wadna look at the Lady o' Makerstown and a' her
braws.' I was struck only the other day when fish-

ing in Tweed by my attendant telling me a 'Jock Scott' used to be a good fly, but that the fish did not take it much just now. He was a first-rate fisherman of great experience, and I hardly dared to tell him that I thought old 'Jock' would turn out as useful as ever if it was given the chance; but the sequel proved that I was right, for a few days afterwards I killed two fish on that fly in that very water. My belief is that a few patterns, each of different sizes, are a sufficient equipment. A 'Blue Doctor' is my favourite fly, and with that and a 'Silver Doctor,' a 'Butcher,' a 'Black Dog'—a fly with a black body with silver twist, a red head and a rather sober wing— and 'Jock Scott,' I am inclined to think that one can catch fish anywhere. I like my flies tied upon double hooks. Apart from the greater likelihood of securing fish, I think they hang and work better in the water. In places where the river is clear of obstacles and weeds I am guilty of the heresy of using a dropper, a small sea-trout fly, and have often caught salmon as well as trout upon it. I think there is something particularly attractive about the play of the dropper, as on some occasions nearly every fish of the day has risen to it. In illustration of the theory that numerous changes are not very necessary, I have often changed the tail fly two or three times to

F

humour the supposed caprice of a fish I have risen but not hooked, and have caught him after all on the dropper which had remained the same all the time. But while I have no great faith in colour, I attach much importance to the size of flies, and believe that, as a rule, sportsmen are apt to use them too large. As I have said, I do not like experimenting in strange water where I am a guest, but in the little river which I fished for many years, I gradually and consistently reduced the size of my flies with uniform success. In clear low water it is hardly possible to have them too small, and I believe that with small flies and fine tackle one need never despair of success. On one occasion I killed twelve salmon in a day in a single small pool after a long drought, all upon small sea-trout flies, and in the middle of the day I tried for a short time the experiment of substituting a little salmon fly, some two sizes larger; but although the fish rose at it every time, not one of them took it into his mouth, although with the smaller flies both before and afterwards nearly every rising fish was hooked.

For minnow, prawn, and worm fishing, I must refer my readers to other and more exhaustive treatises. Whatever merit there may be in these brief hints is derived from the fact that they are the

result of my own experience, and although I have
caught salmon with minnow and worm, and have seen
them caught with a prawn, I hardly ever use anything
but the fly, and have no claim whatever to be considered an expert with other lures.

I cannot leave this subject without confessing the
magnetic attraction a tackle maker's window has for
me as I walk the streets of London. We are apt to
jeer at the fair sex when we find it difficult to get them
past a splendid array of new bonnets or the newest
fashionable millinery, but they might justly retaliate if
they saw us with our noses flattened against certain
windows in Pall Mall, the Strand or Temple Bar.
The long array of rods, the display of bronzed winches,
the tempting flies, the appetising prawns in their grave
of glycerine, move one's wonder that any fish can have
self-denial enough to resist such attractions, and turn
our thoughts to Melrose, Abbotsford, and the Tay, and
the memories of long past conflicts.

CHAPTER IV

BOAT FISHING

THE most satisfactory method of fishing for salmon
is, no doubt, casting, either from the bank or wading,
as described in the previous chapters—but there are
rivers—and some of the best and most sought after—
where this is often impracticable, owing to the width
of the stream, the nature of the banks, and the posi-
tions of the pools in which the fish rest and take the
fly.   I will briefly describe some examples of various
methods of boat fishing, mainly derived from my own
personal recollections.

The first scene is a certain wide stretch of the Tay
not far from Dunkeld ; the time, I am sorry to say,
a good many years ago.   A little above us on the hill,
among beautiful woods and grand Scotch firs, stands
an immense modern mansion, which, on close inspection, turns out to be a shell only, a still existing
example of the folly of beginning to build without
counting the cost ; and close beside it the picturesque

old Scotch castle which it was intended to supplant, well known to the art connoisseur as the subject of Sir John Millais' fine picture of 'Christmas Eve,' so well etched by Macbeth. No wonder that the great artist did justice to his subject, for at the time of which I write he was a near neighbour, and a frequent guest within those hospitable walls, and in later years rented the fishing of the adjoining beat of the Tay, and the shooting of the surrounding woods, chase and bog. We are not far from the scenes depicted in 'Chill October,' 'Murthly Moss,' and 'The Fringe of the Moor.'

There are two of us sitting in the boat facing the rectangular stern, and Miller and his man have selected two good-sized flies, one a 'Butcher,' the other something like a Popham, and attached them to the treble gut casting lines of a pair of stout eighteen-foot rods, which point outwards from the corners of the stern. A third rod hangs straight between them, on which is a medium-sized phantom minnow. Fortune has so far favoured me this morning, for I have won the toss, and therefore the first chance with the minnow. We have just finished such a breakfast as Queen Elizabeth might have envied, and start from the bank in high spirits, for the river is in first-rate order ; it is about a week since a heavy spate substituted the 'Pleasures of Hope' for the possibility of sport for a day or two, and before we can get into the boat the sight of some magnificent fish splashing about in the pool in front of us brings our hearts into our mouths ; for my companion has never before seen a salmon alive, and I have seldom had a chance of an encounter with the giants of the Tay. Perhaps it was not altogether a good sign for the fish to be taking quite so much air and exercise, but it was something to be assured that the pool was not empty, and of that there was ample ocular demonstration. We let out line as directed, until a bit of silk whipped round it discloses that the orthodox twenty yards has passed through the rings, a rather smaller allowance being considered sufficient for the minnow ; and after giving each one turn round a fair-sized stone at the bottom of the boat, plant the butts of our rods against notches in the plank behind our feet, light our pipes, and begin to pursue 'the contemplative man's recreation.' But not for long—for the steady strokes of the two oarsmen have not propelled the boat to the opposite side before one of the three stones gives a jump in the air, and my companion has hardly time to seize his rod before the line is screaming through the rings —and seventy yards are out before his rather awkward movements have brought his rod into position,

'HARLING' ON THE TAY

although the two boatmen have backed water rapidly
as the great fish pursued his headlong course down the
stream. In the meanwhile I have rapidly reeled up
the other lines to prevent the entanglement which occasionally at this kind of sport necessitates two men
playing the same fish, both sometimes ignorant till
near the conclusion of the fight to which it really
belongs. Miller has now guided the boat to a convenient landing-place, and the excited sportsman is
assisted on to the bank, with many injunctions to be
especially careful as he steps to land. And now the
conditions become the same that I have previously
described, and there is no incident of a particularly
exciting character, till a fine twenty-one pounder is
duly gaffed and weighed, for although the point of the
rod is occasionally dropped too low, and there are
moments of a slack line and awkward strain, the
fish has been firmly hooked, and could only have been
lost by criminal awkwardness or great ill-fortune.
Then we recommence operations—highly elated with
the good beginning—and proceed through the day,
one of us being occasionally landed to cast in any
of the very few places which lend themselves to such
an operation—and if the performance is one which
does not call for any great physical or intellectual
effort, I can affirm that two very elated individuals

walked up to the Castle in the evening followed by
the bearer of seven salmon—two of these grilse of
eleven or twelve pounds—the others ranging from
seventeen pounds to twenty-three.

It must not be supposed that our host was under
the delusion that this was the highest form of sport
that the river could afford. When it was possible to
give a beat to a single rod, and he was a fisherman of
experience, he was allowed to cast from the boat
instead of occupying the position of a sort of auto-
matic trimmer. But all who remember that delightful
time, those elastic walls, and genial hospitality, will
bear me out in testifying that it was no easy task to
provide sport for the numbers who were welcomed
there ; and that occasionally it could only be secured
by putting the proverbial 'three men in a boat.'
Somehow or other, however, it was contrived that
every guest should go out expectant in the morning
and come back radiant in the evening, for the place
was like the conjurer's magic bottle, and every taste
was provided for.

Sometimes the fish were obstinate, and there was
ample leisure for the passengers in the boat to think
of other things as well as the care of their rods and
lines. Many were the good stories told, and the
songs and parodies composed on such occasions for

the evening's consumption, when music and merriment were the order of the day ; and not a few
surprises and jokes, good, bad, and indifferent, were
devised and executed. On my first visit I had come
straight from grouse-shooting with Lord Cairns at his
pleasant autumn quarters in Forfarshire ; and his
servant had presented me with an unexpected gift in
the shape of a gigantic wooden bootjack which he
had placed in my portmanteau on my departure. I
received in the evening a serio-comic letter from my
late hostess reproaching me for repaying her hospitality by annexing her property ; and the sight of some
of the days' catch going off as presents with their tails
protruding from a neat covering of reeds suggested to
me a suitable reprisal. I begged the tail of a fine
twenty-pound fish, and sent off the stolen property
suitably directed, disguised as the counterfeit present-
ment of a large salmon. Lady Cairns was equal
to the occasion ; for when she wrote thanking me for
the fine fish, she mentioned that she was unable to
enjoy it herself, as she was leaving on a visit, but that
she had sent it on direct to her neighbour, Lord
Dalhousie, at Invermark, a little higher up the glen.
Of course this was an invention, but I could not help
wishing that it had been true, and that I could have
seen the face of the old laird when he opened his

parcel and imagined that he was being made a fool of by the Lord Chancellor.

The honours of the day in harling rest with the boatmen, who are responsible for bringing the flies properly over the fish, and I have officiated in that capacity as well as with the rod. There was a stretch of water about a mile and a half below the house where there was one very good cast—Burn bend— where early birds used often to secure a fish before breakfast, but where most of the water was considered useless, and never harled, as the bottom was smooth, and salmon did not lie there as a rule. Once, however, when there was an extra large party in the house, three of us went over there, borrowed a boat, and tried the water by ourselves. Sir Frederick Milner will doubtless remember the twenty-two pound fish he got on that occasion ; and I can answer for it that one at least of his amateur fishermen was as proud of his success as the captor himself. I have also with a friend harled in the mouth of the Rauma in Norway, the two of us managing both the boat and the rods, and getting fair success with grilse and sea-trout ; and I do not think the operation at all a difficult one for anyone with the ordinary proficiency with the oar acquired at least by every wet bob at Eton.

Whatever may be thought of harling from a
sportsman's point of view, there can be no doubt that
it is a most deadly method of killing fish. There are
casts which even the most skilful fisherman cannot
negotiate properly, and wind and current sometimes
sweep the fly round tail foremost and loose instead of
with the lifelike motion which attracts the fish and the
taut line which hooks him. But in harling, as the
boat goes from side to side, the oarsman keeping his
eye on a mark on the opposite bank and regulating
his pace by the speed of the current, the line is always
straight, and the flies and minnows visit in turn, and
in correct position, every nook and corner of the
stream. The fish under such circumstances are very
easily caught, and I can remember at least one fisherman—my own father—who made his *début* as a
salmon fisher at Murthly, and came back from his
first day's apprenticeship the proud captor of no less
than ten salmon.

I have not disguised my opinion that this method
of fishing is a very inferior class of sport to the more
legitimate casting from the bank or wading, but I
agree with Mr. Fraser Sandeman, in whose book—
'Angling Travels in Norway'—a number of valuable
hints on this subject will be found, that it is the only
practical method by which certain pools or even

some entire rivers can be fished ; still, I think that he
somewhat exaggerates the difficulty of the operation
and the skill necessary for its performance. To go
slow from side to side, to 'keep at it,' and to drop
four to five feet at each transit, does not seem to me
hard to do except in very rough water ; but it is
certain that there are degrees of proficiency in this, as
in all sports, and that it is a great handicap to have a
fool for a boatman.

It is usually the oarsman's business to land the fish
either with net or gaff, and a bungler who knows little
of the sport and cannot manage a boat properly may
involve you in difficulties and dangers more serious
than the mismanagement of a pool or even the loss
of a good salmon. There are occasions when you
are offered the alternative of a break, or of following
your fish into unknown rapids, or even into similar
perils consciously encountered ; and your life may
depend upon the activity, readiness, and presence of
mind of your boatman, and his proficiency in his
craft, if, as is usually the case, you face the risk in the
excitement of the moment.

To hold a boat properly with the oars for the
fisherman to cast a likely spot in mid-stream or at
some distance from the shore requires far greater
skill than mere harling. Every current and every

rock should be known to the oarsman, who should not merely be able to tell you exactly where you may expect the fish to rise, but also should avoid unnecessarily disturbing a likely place with his strokes or the boat. So, too, the wielder of the rod may have quite as long and difficult a cast to make as if he was on the bank, except that he has not got to avoid overhanging branches or a precipitous bank behind him. He has also the supreme satisfaction of knowing either from his own past experience, or from information received at the time, the precise spots where he should exercise the greatest caution and deliberation, and feel the strongest expectation and hope. Mere 'chuck and chance it' work is never very satisfactory, and a long monotonous pool or stream, though it may be very productive, loses half its charm if each successive cast is or ought to be a complete replica of the one before it, and as likely to be followed by a break in the surface and a tight line.

A different method of boat-fishing is pursued on Tweed. There also you have a wide stream, a strong current, and great depth in many places, and wading and bank fishing is in most spots quite impossible. The precipitous sandstone banks and overhanging trees which give such a charm to the landscape at

Dryburgh, Melrose and St. Boswell's make the use
of the boat imperative, but I have never seen harling
attempted on that classic ground.

I need not make any serious call upon my
memory to describe a day upon Tweed, for it was
only yesterday (September 13, 1897) that by the
kindness of my friend, Mr. Walter Farquhar, I
enjoyed a pleasant day's sport in the Mertoun
water—a typical stretch of the river, and the scene
of many an episode in Scrope's work. I had been
trouting at Dryburgh just a week before, after a
succession of heavy floods, when the water was
still out of condition for salmon-fishing—so had a
good opportunity of measuring the exact effect of a
week's dry weather upon the stream. My letter of
invitation, written on the 9th, told me that the river
was then in fine order, and was running down slowly,
and that my friend had got five fish and a sea-trout
the day before—an excellent bag considering that the
nets were still on. I arrived at the stables at Mertoun at about twelve o'clock, after a drive of nearly
ten miles and a railway journey of half an hour, and it
was not long before I had commenced operations
at the House stream. Goodfellow, the presiding
genius of the beat, was away for the day on business,
but he had left a worthy substitute in the person of

his second in command—one of the numberless
Elliotts who still frequent the Border counties. I
cannot say that he was sanguine—no fish had been
got on Friday or Saturday, although one had been
lost on the afternoon of the latter day—and the river
had got very low and clear, too much so to be really
in order. Tweed unfortunately does not rise in a
lake, and the days of her perfection are few and far
between, as she is generally too thick immediately
after a flood, and then subsides very rapidly. Still
there was something in my favour. The fish had
enjoyed their Sabbath rest ; there were certainly some
in the pools, and they were settled down and not
knocked about by perpetual floods, and the sky was
slightly overcast instead of the brilliant sunshine
which all, except fishermen, had so much enjoyed
the week before, after a long spell of cloud and storm.
A little wind would have been an advantage, as the
deep, still places were glassy, but we agreed that
there was a chance, although not a first-rate one.

The House stream, as its name implies, is a rapid,
not very deep run just below Mertoun House. Here
the coble was duly launched, and I tried the cast over
with two flies ; first a " Blue Doctor " mounted on a
No. 8 hook, and then a " Jock Scott " on a No. 5. The
boat was here managed by a simple process : Elliott

waded down the stream holding on to the side of
the bows, and let her down about a yard at a time—
in fact I was to all intents and purposes fishing from
a moving platform a few yards from the side instead
of going into the water, which at its then height could
easily have been fished by a wader, had it been
necessary. No fish moved here or in the willow
bush pool a little lower down, nor indeed did we
linger very long over the latter, as the best part of it
was very still and clear, and did not look at all likely
in its present condition.

Elliott now rowed us across—my Eton boy was
with me fishing for trout—and told us that if we
would go up to the bridge he would wade across the
stream a little above it and join us, and, as we had
our lunch, we watched him attempting to do so, but
the rapid was a little too deep to be negotiated in
ordinary wading stockings, and he had to come round
by the suspension bridge after all. Before he reached
us I met one of the house party who had been fishing
in the beat below mine, and he somewhat revived my
flagging hopes by telling me that a fish had been
risen there that morning. He added that one of the
pools above had been very much disturbed by a
horse which had fallen over the cliff and been
drowned. I imparted the news, not of the horse, but

of the fish to Elliott when he came up, and began to unlock the next boat, but he did not seem much impressed by the good augury, merely replying 'that would be early in the morning.' However, he rowed me across, and I began to fish the Bridge pool, commencing about 200 yards higher up.

Here the river is deep under the Mertoun side, where a long submerged shelf of rock extends along the bank, ending four or five yards out in a straight descent into deep water, forming just such a resting-place as salmon love to frequent. It was obviously unnecessary to throw a very long line, as it was a place where fish would be sure to lie close to the boat. Here again the fisherman waded along the shelf of rock holding the boat, and although the trees above would be rather awkward it would have been perfectly feasible to fish it from the bank. Half-way down my patience was rewarded by my first rise, a fair-sized fish came at the 'Jock Scott,' but did not touch. We stopped, moved the boat a little higher, and exchanged the fly for one a trifle smaller, but to no purpose, as our friend refused to repeat his attempt, and after finishing the pool we judged it prudent to leave him for the present and make our way up to the Craigs pool, which we were agreed was our best chance for the day.

G

The Craigs pool, where another boat awaited us, is one designated by Scrope as Craigover, and is the scene of one of those terrible poaching proceedings— sunning the salmon—which he describes with such astounding candour ; but for which he ought to have done at least a month on the treadmill. It is the very ideal of a salmon pool, and I was not surprised when my attendant remarked that it always held some fish at any period of the season. There is a gravel bank on the Mertoun side, but the Craigs, a precipitous sandstone rock, rises opposite at an angle of the stream, which just above descends in a rapid almost amounting to a small fall. At the bottom of the rock numerous boulders, the 'tumbled fragments of the hills,' tell of similar débris beneath the waters, forming the subaqueous caverns and buttresses which salmon love to haunt. Two small natural cairns protrude into the water, one at the lowest corner of the rock, and the second twenty or thirty yards lower down ; there is sufficient stream to hang the fly properly, but the black surface denotes great depth, and altogether it looked an ideal spot at any height of the river, but especially promising when she was low and bright. Here a rather long cast is required, as the deep water extends a long distance from the rocks, and the boatman cannot wade in far. Here he cannot follow the boat, but has to let her gradually down by a rope, leaving the outer oar reversed on the thole pin to steer automatically. Hopefully and carefully I cast my fly right under the rock, working it right round until it was opposite the boat, as even there the water was plenty deep enough for a fish to rise, and before very long a sudden check of the line told me that I was into the first fish of the season, although not even a boil broke the surface of the water.

I cannot, I regret to say, truthfully record any very exciting incident in the playing of this particular fish. He behaved in a most gentlemanly manner. He did not sulk, but his runs were short and demure, and long before he was the least tired I had guided him down the stream into the deep still backwater, where he spent most of the few remaining minutes of his existence. He did not jump, and my companion suggested that he was only a small one, but I drew a different augury from the strain on the rod and the fact that he never showed himself, and felt sure that he was at least a moderate sized fish ; and soon his runs became shorter and shorter, and as he broke the surface we could see that I was right. And now Elliott put his large circular landing net into the water; but as I guided the fish into it, he made his first really disagreeable plunge, and shot out into the pool, taking

with him some thirty yards of line ; but it was his last
effort, for in another minute he was scooped up and
deposited on the gravel, a nice clean male fish just under
fourteen pounds.   Both the barbs of the double hook
were deeply embedded in his jaw, and it was evident
that nothing short of a break could have given him his
liberty.

While he was still on, I had seen another fish
break the water a little lower down, close into the
second cairn, and without wasting any time we
resumed the offensive, and I recommended casting
just below the place where I had hooked the fish.
The pool had been very little disturbed, and even
if it had been more so, I should not have thought it
necessary to wait, as I have risen fish immediately
after a hooked companion has been jumping and
swaggering about the pool in a manner calculated
to frighten them into fits.   They seldom, it seems,
take warning from the misfortunes of others.   The
casting now became a little more difficult ; not only
was it necessary to throw a fairly long line, but as the
fly came round below the point of the rod it was
sucked into a sort of eddy or backwater which
drowned the cast and made it very difficult to get the
line clean out of the water for the backward movement.   Once at least I succeeded in tying my cast

into one of those complications of knots which would
be impossible if voluntarily attempted, but a little
patience soon got rid of the tangle, and with an
excitement which years of experience have not wholly
abated, I found myself nearing the spot where I had
marked the rise, and at the very first cast over the
place found my fly taken ; again under water. This
time I had no reason to complain of want of excitement, for just a second after feeling the hook, a heavy
fish dashed down the stream, taking out line at a pace
which made me hesitate to leave the boat, as I had
rather a small reel and a short allowance of line for
so wide and strong a river as the Tweed is near St.
Boswell's.

However, he turned as rapidly as he had
started, heading up-stream at a pace which made
it impossible to reel up quite sufficiently fast, and
just opposite to me, a really beautiful fish turned
a complete somersault in the air. ' It is another fish,'
said my boatman, but I shook my head, although I
could easily see what had deceived him, for the place
where the fish jumped was a good deal above that
where the line touched the water. Speedily as I
reeled up, there was a moment of slack when I was
uncertain whether I had not lost him, but only a
moment, for almost as soon as I felt him again the

line fairly whizzed through the water as he dashed to
the opposite side. It was a sharp and exciting
contest, but too sharp to last long, and before many
minutes he was visibly tiring, and his runs became
shorter and slower, and he yielded to pressure. As
he came near the top the fisherman and I both noted
with some surprise that there was a mark on his side ;
and when he also was duly netted, and had received
the *coup de grâce* with a stone, the cause was apparent
in a large still bleeding scar on both sides immediately
above the belly. At first I thought that some
poacher had endeavoured to sniggle him with a triangle
and that he had broken away ; but on investigation it
was plain that the wound was not due to human
agency, as the marks of teeth were clearly visible.
He had indeed had a narrow escape for his life, as
the seal had gripped him right across the middle, but
he had escaped his voracious foe to fall a victim to a
human enemy before many hours had passed. He
was indeed a magnificent specimen, in perfect condition, and I herewith give his portrait, roughly but
accurately drawn to scale, showing the marks of the
seal bite as a further example of the insensibility to
pain before referred to. The scars on the right side
extended four and a half inches in width along the body,
and to a height of two and three-quarter inches from

the belly. On the left side was a corresponding half-
moon-shaped gash seven inches long by four high,
with outlying tooth-marks. Though practically

healed and filled up, these marks were nearly half-an-
inch deep in some places. I should think the seal
must have dived under him and gripped him from
below. We fished the pool again, and tried two flies
over the one that had risen above the bridge, before
we left to catch our train. Goodfellow met us at the
stables, and was much elated by my success. He
constrained us to take our fish with us ; and as we
had no bag or baskets, they created some sensation
among the tourists at St. Boswell's station. I weighed
the biggest at the parcel office, as my little steelyard
only worked up to eighteen pounds, and found him a
few ounces over twenty pounds. Both fish were
much admired by my travelling companion in the
carriage to Hawick—a commercial from Bradford,
who said I had earned a good day's wage—and

'supposed I was going to sell them.' It must not be thought that what I have described above represents an extraordinary day's sport on Tweed. I have purposely selected a moderate one. On November 9, 1885, and the four following days Mr. Farquhar and Lord Brougham, fishing on alternate days, killed 18, 17, 11, 12, and 10 fish on the same beat, the two rods in the week securing 95 fish.

Of harling in a loch I have no knowledge, and from what I have heard I do not feel any great ambition to tackle the big fish in Loch Tay. The fishing there is best in the spring, and it must be desperately cold work trailing the big phantom minnows after your boat in a north-east wind, or sometimes in a snowstorm or in frosty air. But I have had some good days in a certain 'damp climate contiguous to a melancholy ocean,' and although my experience is not very recent, bear my testimony to the excellence of the free fishing at Waterville in the late 'sixties.'

It was in the height of the Fenian agitation that I visited that beautiful coast with an Oxford friend ; a large and weighty box of books testified to our inten- tion of reading, but served no other purpose beyond that of trying the temper of the cardrivers and the strength and pluck of their game little horses. My

relationship to the then Home Secretary drew upon
me some attention from the Royal Irish Constabulary,
although I certainly found no necessity for their protection.   Paddy has his faults, but I do not think
he has any inclination to visit the sins of the fathers
upon the children.   We secured the services of two
experienced fishermen and their boat for the period of
our stay, and beyond the fact that they loved whisky
' not wisely but too well,' and were quarrelsome in their
cups, we had little fault to find with them.   Their
boat was more like a substantial gig than a Tay or
Tweed coble, but a flat-bottomed craft would not have
held the water enough for a drift, and would certainly
not have been safe in the violent squalls and heavy
storms which we occasionally had to encounter.   The
favourite fly was a moderate sized sea-trout fly, with a
rough body of fiery brown pig's wool and a plain
wing of native manufacture, and I had not then
sufficient confidence and self-assertion to experiment
with the smarter specimens of the tackle-maker's art
which we had brought with us from the metropolis.
The method of fishing was like that for ordinary loch
trout, rowing up-wind and drifting sideways along the
likely bays and headlands, casting before you with
the wind with a fourteen-foot rod and a moderate
length of line.   The sea-trout, which were numerous

and plucky, but not very large, rose almost anywhere. The salmon had favourite haunts and lurking places where submerged rocks rose nearly to the surface in the deeper water. There was of course some competition to secure the first turn at the favourite places, and all were eager to come in in the evening with the best baskets landed. Many a bright sea-trout and shapely peel of four or five pounds, and occasionally a brown salmon of from ten to fourteen pounds, roused the envy of less successful competitors. Luncheon on one of the islands with a freshly caught fish broiled in the embers as a *pièce de résistance* was a delightful meal. Our boatmen were full of stories : there was of course a ' worm ' in the lake, perhaps twin-brother to the mysterious monster whose attempted capture was described in the ' Badminton Magazine ' for July, 1897.[1] Then there was also a horseman, who, at certain periods, rode over the surface of the lake on a charger shod with silver

---

[1] This creature answers the description of what Newland (*Forest Scenes in Norway and Sweden.* Routledge, 1855) calls ' the fictitious mal, a great-headed wide-mouthed monster with long beard, of the same colour as an eel, slimy and without perceptible scales. It is said to grow to the length of 12 or 14 feet, and to carry on its back fin a strong sharp lance which it can elevate or depress at pleasure. It is supposed to lie, seeking whom or what it may devour, in the deepest and muddiest holes of rivers and lakes.'

shoes ; and a disused chapel and burial-ground on one of the islands contained a stone which no one could carry away safely. Several had tried it, but always some misfortune had happened to them to prevent their success. The last rash accepter of the challenge had fallen down and broken his leg ! I particularly remember this legend because an Oxford undergraduate a year or two after was dared into undertaking the quest; and, although no physical misfortune happened to him, was very properly fined by the magistrates and compelled to take back the desecrated stone.

The best day we ever had there was one of some risk. A regular gale was blowing, and none of the boats started in the morning at the usual hour. The wiser old stagers never made a start at all, but we were young and rash, and pressed our boatmen to brave the elements, being all the more eager from the certainty that we should have the best places all to ourselves. Mickie and his colleague shook their heads, and protested that it was not safe ; but at last we bribed or cajoled them into consenting to launch forth and drift down the sheltered side of the loch— the wind was blowing from the hotel end—on condition that we took a spare pair of oars with us and agreed to lend a hand on the return journey.

For a time all went well : the fish rose freely and greedily, as they often do on a loch in the most disagreeable weather, and before we had finished the drift we had secured over two dozen sea-trout, a big brown fish, and four peel, and were congratulating ourselves on our pluck and foresight, and thinking what a laugh we should have at the less venturesome sportsmen who were cultivating the fireside while we were enjoying such excellent sport. But the end was not yet, and the laugh turned out to be not altogether so entirely on our side as we supposed. In the first place we had to fulfil our pledge of rowing home in the teeth of the wind ; but when my companion, a stalwart and practised oarsman, bent himself to the job with a vigorous pull, the crazy oar snapped short in the middle, and the boat swung round, nearly capsizing, and shipping a quantity of water. For a time we tried the three oars, but the balance was so bad and trimmed the boat so awkwardly, that the attempt was soon abandoned as hopeless, and we continued the voyage in our waterlogged craft with two rowers and two passengers. Our progress was terribly slow, the wind had increased in violence, and although our boatmen stuck gallantly to their work, we could perceive from their faces and their muttered appeals to the Virgin and the saints that they did not feel at

A GALE ON THE LOCH—THE CRAZY OAR SNAPPED

all confident of ever reaching the shore. Soon the
boat was nearly half full, and we were sitting almost
up to our knees in water, and it was plain that she
would never keep afloat till the end of the journey.
Things looked black indeed, but fortunately the low
shore of one of the islands loomed through the scud
and rain, and we just managed to drag her ashore
and empty her. Thankful for our escape, we held a
council of war, and determined that it was impossible
to make the regular landing-place ; so relieving the
boatmen at the oars and guided by their local knowledge, we rowed laboriously to shore at the nearest
available spot, dragged the boat to land, and walked
home, dripping and uncomfortable, not quite so sure
that we had done such a very wise thing after all.

Another description of boat fishing for salmon is
practised in Wales and its borders, where the coracle—
the lineal descendant of the prehistoric British boat—
is employed both for rod and net fishing. These
clumsy-looking contrivances consist of a framework
of laths or basket-work covered with tarpaulin, straight
at one end and spade-shaped at the other, with a
board in the centre to sit upon, supported upon another
set edgeways below it. They are about five feet by
three, and are worked with a single paddle somewhat
of the shape of an elongated cricket-bat, which the

occupant, who is seated facing the broad end with a
foot in each corner, works by making figures of eight
either in front or at the side.. Of course it is impossible to propel these crafts against the wind or
stream, but they draw little water, and are very easily
carried on the back, a strap running through the seat
being placed round the neck. A gentleman living in
the neighbourhood of Usk used to do great execution
in the Association waters, fishing before him from a
coracle with a short rod made on purpose : as he was
able to avail himself of certain long pools with bushes
on each side which were too deep for wading and
could not be approached from the banks. I
remember being greatly impressed by his success
during a visit to that river, when I was very lucky
myself for the first three days after a flood, after which
the fishermen came down in too great numbers, and
nearly every pool was occupied by an early hour
in the morning. I took one of the coracles home
with me to Kent, and used it for pike fishing in a pond,
finding it by no means so difficult to manage or easy
to capsize as I should have supposed from its
appearance. I sometimes wonder that they are not
used for small reedy hill lochs in Scotland, as they can
be bought for a few shillings, copied by any carpenter
of ordinary intelligence, carried with great ease, and

mended without difficulty with patches and a fresh coat of tar if they spring a leak. Of course they would not be safe for large lochs or in rough and squally weather ; but they will float in a few inches of water, and can be guided on to a convenient shallow and left there when a large fish is hooked.

CHAPTER V

SMALL HIGHLAND STREAMS

I HAVE in a previous passage alluded to the price
which the angler must expect to pay for his sport; and
it may be taken as an established fact that the rents
of really good stretches of water go on steadily increasing, and that in the rare instances where there is a
fall of price, it is only because for some reason the fish-
ng has greatly deteriorated, and the fact has become
public property. Rivers which used to let for 200*l.* or
300*l.* a year are now subdivided into numerous beats,
each commanding a similar rent, and well-known
fishings fetch a fancy price, and, like the choicest
grouse moors, seldom get into the agents' hands, but
are eagerly competed for on the death or departure of
an old tenant. It is highly advisable before renting
a salmon river to obtain information from some one
who has previously and recently fished the water.
An experienced sportsman may form a trustworthy
opinion of the merits of a grouse moor by walking on

the ground, and noting its capabilities as to heather, water supply, and the like, and the indications of the presence of birds ; but I defy anyone to tell by the appearance of a river in June or July what sort of sport it is likely to afford in August and September. I have seen streams that looked absolute perfection, apparently alive with salmon, where it was really hardly any use to fish during the autumn months ; and there is nothing so disheartening as going on flogging such water day after day without any real hope of success. I dispute the proposition that a blank day is sheer waste of time ; but I cannot say that it is amusing to go on fishing pools when once you are convinced that under no conditions can salmon be caught in them at the time of year. I become filled with hatred of the fish which jump over my line in derision, or fling summersaults all round my fly, but never take it ; and under such circumstances some misguided men are driven to desperate courses, which cannot be justified, but are in some measure palliated by the temptation.

It sounds trite and commonplace to say that those who rely upon accounts of previous bags should ascertain the time and method of their capture ; but I have so often known people to take an autumn river in spring or a spring river in autumn, that a

H

word of warning against such an error is not altogether
out of place. Spring fishing is really the cheapest in
proportion to its merit ; the competition which sends up
rents to famine prices is not so severe then as later.
Comparatively few can get away in the early part of the
year, and even of those who are free to select the period
of their holiday, most for various reasons prefer the
autumn. The greatest drawbacks to early fishing are
kelts, frost, and east wind ; but there can be little
doubt that a real spring salmon gives better sport,
and is altogether a more desirable acquisition, than
two or three fish caught in the late autumn. On the
other hand, the advantage of an autumn river is that
it works in with other sports, and that if a long spell
of dry weather spoils your chance of a salmon, it is
favourable for grouse shooting or stalking. I have
fished in a good many such rivers in August, September and October, and a short account of the sort of
sport to be obtained in some of them may be of
interest.

The little river that I know best, having fished it
regularly for the best part of a quarter of a century, is
the Add, which rises in the hills near Loch Fyne and,
after a short but rapid course through gorges and over
rocks, descends into the plain, and for the last few
miles of its career meanders slowly through the

partially reclaimed peat moss which fills the valley opposite Crinan Bay, into which it ultimately discharges its waters close to the western outlet of the Crinan Canal. The lower part of the river winds round and round through the soft soil, the curves being so sharp that a straight line of about a quarter of a mile in length would cross the river three times. The stream has cut itself a deep channel through the peat, and the banks are high above the water, protecting it from the wind, which, as the current is naturally sluggish, is very necessary for successful fishing, except immediately after a heavy flood. The river, like all small West Highland streams, rises and falls with extreme rapidity, and the upper part of the water is only really in order for one day after a flood, and the lower for two—the first day being usually the best. By this I do not mean to imply that fishing is useless except for these short periods. The lower pools are deep, and there is always a prospect of getting a fair basket of ·sea-trout, and an off-chance of a salmon or two as well if there is a fairly strong breeze. The run of fish does not begin until nearly the end of July, and the rod fishing continues until the end of October. Except in one or two places where there are small fir plantations on one side of the river, there is hardly a yard where the banks are not perfectly clear, and the casting can be managed with a light rod. Waders are not absolutely necessary, but as there is usually a shallow on one side or the other of a pool, they are a convenience, especially as they enable one to cross and recross the numerous fords and take advantage of the wind, which, when right for one cast, is wrong for another.

The principal difficulty of fishing is caused by the wind, which makes the best curl on the water when it is against the stream, and it is often both strong and squally. I once succeeded in sending the point of my hook right through the palm of my hand, hooking myself so firmly that after vainly endeavouring to break off the barb, I had to cut the feathers off the fly and pass it through the other way. Notwithstanding the deep channel and the high banks, I have seen waves almost breaking on the pools, and, if only the wind is fairly steady, it is hardly possible to have it too rough. Usually a perfectly calm day is fatal to all prospect of sport, but occasionally a sort of temporary insanity seems to come over fish, and they take the fly in a manner and under circumstances wholly unaccountable and incomprehensible. I remember especially one day when, at dead low water and with a glassy calm, I stood by a still pool, and after watching for some time a shoal of small salmon and grilse swimming round and round, threw my fly over them, more in idleness and from curiosity than with any other motive. To my great surprise one fish after another followed the fly, and more than one took it under water, and I caught three and hooked and lost one or two others, although I myself, my rod, and my cast must have been quite as visible to the fish as they were to me. It is very seldom indeed that there is not some curl on the lowest horseshoes, and it very rarely happens that one cannot at least secure one or two sea-trout ; but these game little fish have certainly decreased in numbers during my fishing career. It is useless to fish for either salmon or sea-trout long after the flood tide has begun to make. For a few minutes at 'first of flood' the fish rise furiously, but generally short ; but when the sand and gravel off the shallows begin to float, and the stream to turn, you may as well put up your rod and walk home.

The part of the river of which I am speaking is perfectly fresh water long after it has been touched by the tide ; but there is a stretch lower down, near the old Crinan ferry, where great sport can sometimes be had in what is practically part of the estuary at 'first of flood' at spring tides. I never myself did very much there, as it was rather far to go for a very short bit of sport, but the old laird told me that he once

caught ninety-nine sea-trout there at a single tide,
and I have no doubt that his account and memory
may be strictly relied upon, although I run the risk of
having a well-known 'chestnut' quoted against myself
and him.   Probably it was the fact of the day's catch
being just one short of the 'century' which fixed the
number in his recollection.   I have no doubt that at
that time sea-trout were far more numerous than they
are now ; but over-netting has told greatly upon their
numbers.   I fear the countless yachts which frequent
the west coast are not altogether guiltless of this form
of poaching.   Some owners regard neither the law of
the land nor the rights of property when anchored in
waters at all out of the way, and make havoc with
scringing and splash nets.   The committees of the
various northern yacht clubs are doing something to
discourage the poaching propensities of certain of
their members ; but I am afraid that not unfrequently
out of sight is still out of mind.

The fish in the Add run small, the average weight
working out at about $7\frac{1}{2}$ lb.   The largest I ever
caught there weighed just over twenty pounds, and I
never heard of anything much heavier being taken with
a rod and line.   The largest number I ever caught
in a season was forty-nine salmon and 167 sea-trout.
My best day, eliminating the altogether exceptional

experience of 1892 before referred to, was seven salmon, and I have several times caught six.

Some unique features are presented by the fishing at Cambusmore, on the east coast of Scotland—one of the few places where salmon take the fly actually in the sea—and Mr. Henry Graham, who leased it from the Duke of Sutherland for several years, has, at my request, supplied me with the following interesting account of its peculiarities :—

' The foundation of the fishing was a little stream absurdly misnamed the " Fleet," which meandered—or for the most part stood still—over a short course of seven or eight miles, until it was artificially discharged into a sea loch of the same name.   Most of its passage was through marshy land which had been, early in the century, reclaimed from the sea by a high embankment called the " Mound," over which the main road ran, and in which flood gates, opened twice in the twenty-four hours, allowed the accumulated fresh waters to run into the loch.   Above the Mound was a lake of brackish water, in which, as well as on the sea side, it was possible for a wader to obtain with a fair breeze a good basket of sea trout.   But the salmon fishing proper of the so-called river was concentrated in two long pools higher up, which, except under some exceptional spate, or for the short time during which the opening of the sluices below set the upper waters moving, presented the appearance of a sluggish canal, and would only yield their treasures under very lively breezes. They did, however, get filled in autumn with small fish of from 3 lb. to 17 lb. in weight, and on their banks we would sit for hours, hoping for winds from the right airt which might bring good sport to our twelve-foot rods with light tackle and small salmon and sea-trout flies. In the lower of these pools, called " Torboll " from the neighbouring farm, two of us during a day of equinoctial gale killed eleven fish on a bank of about forty yards' length ; but this experience was never quite repeated. Into this pool a little tributary stream called the " Carnach " ran down from the moors, upon which a mile further up a most elaborate and beautiful salmon-ladder was constructed many years ago in a picturesque spot, and although the sport above it could not be said to justify the cost of this structure, yet we did catch a certain number of fish there—never more than a dozen a year—with trout flies, among the heather and grouse. By opening a siuice in a ioch ten miles up this stream we could create an artificial spate to bring fish up the ladder ; but I think they generally knew it was not the real article. Below the Mound we had another chance of fish, for they would lie and splash outside

the great doors, waiting for water to get through them ;
and when these were opened and a lively stream
running, they would often take our flies, or at least
get foul hooked in jumping over them, and then run
down the loch and force us to follow in a boat or be
broken. The duration of this fishing depended upon
the amount of water which had to run away, and
sometimes the guardian of the gates would let in
some of the rising tide so as to increase the outflow.
When the gates were finally shut, a shoal of fish
would often lie close under them, and there were
methods—when all others failed—adopted by the less
respectable members of the family for securing one
for dinner, which I only refer to in order to abhor and
condemn.

'But perhaps the most interesting and peculiar
feature of our fishing—for I am not aware of anything
similar elsewhere—was at a place called the " Ferry,"
two miles off, where the two shores of Loch Fleet
(which must be five miles in circumference) converged
into a narrow channel, of eighty or ninety yards in
width, between the Cambusmore side and a series of
sandbanks stretching to the opposite shore. There,
between their frequent pilgrimages to the sluice gates,
the fish would lie, and when for two hours before low
tide. the returning salt water was forced with the

current of a rapid river through these straits, they
would rise to bigger flies and give an eighteen-foot rod
as much exercise as on any fresh waters that I know of.
Unluckily our sport was limited by the shortness of
the time before the loch had emptied itself and the
current became slack.   I may add that the fresh water
of the Fleet was a mere driblet in this torrent of
ebbing salt.   Some years the fish did not frequent
this channel at all, but fixed themselves further up the
bay, where, with the exception of one short place
behind a rock called the "Stone," there was no current
in which a fly could work.'

The more ordinary type of small Highland river is
very interesting to fish, and of course far more beautiful in its surroundings than the sluggish streams above
described ; but an account of fishing in such waters
would present few exceptional features. The sportsman
should 'gang warily,' as there are often dangerous
places and slippery rocks from which the pools and
casts can alone be reached, and an attendant may be
very useful, not only to supply the necessary local
knowledge, which is more constant than in streams
with a soft and shifting bottom, or to land the fish in
difficult places, bu' sometimes to rescue the fisherman
himself from an awkward predicament.   Many of
these rivers unfortunately afford examples of anglers

having gone out alone and never returned alive. The
rise and fall of the stream is often extraordinarily
rapid, and the force of the rushing water very great ;
but the hills are now so thoroughly drained that few
rivers, except those which have a large lake near their
source, remain in fishing order for more than a very
short time. It is curious how seldom salmon take a
fly when such a river is only at its ordinary or normal
height, and there has been no recent flood. The
pools may be full of fish, and the stream may in many
places look just the right depth and strength, but
experience teaches one that there is hardly any chance
of a taking rise. It would seem that the psychological
moment is either when a fish has just shifted his
ground and taken up new quarters, or when he is just
about to do so. When actually running, salmon never
take, and when quite settled in a pool, they become
dour and sulky. It is for this reason that I like to
have some pools occasionally touched by the tide.
The fish in such places are kept moving, and there is
always a chance.

It would be foreign to my subject to describe the
great floods which have from time to time devastated
the Highland straths, although probably the most
singular capture of a fish recorded in all salmon lore
is that narrated by Sir Thomas Dick Lauder in his

account of the historical flood of the Findhorn in 1829,
when his gardener caught and killed a fine salmon
with his umbrella, at an elevation of fifty feet above the
ordinary level of the river.

An interesting account of the four devastating
Highland deluges of 1829, 1849, 1868, and 1892 was
published by Mr. Nairne at Inverness in 1895, but
from a salmon fisher's point of view the most noteworthy feature of such destructive natural phenomena
is the way in which they alter pools even in the
most rocky channels, and render futile the most
elaborate attempts made to construct artificial salmon
casts.   I remember admiring two beautifully constructed artificial pools between the Lynn and
the junction in the Broom at Braemore.   Sir John
Fowler had applied his great engineering skill to
the improvement of the river which runs through
his beautiful Highland home ; and by means of
concrete dams and breakwaters consisting of larch
piles in a double row filled up between with stones
and gravel, had turned a long stretch formerly useless
for fishing purposes into excellent and productive
salmon casts.   Alas ! the great flood of 1892 washed
these attempts to ' bridle the stream with a curb of
stone ' completely away, and the only traces of the
improvements which remain to tell of what had been

done, are fragments of the concrete blocks deposited here and there at the will of the torrent.

Some salmon rivers run through deep and picturesque gorges, and it is not always easy to negotiate the pools. A sportsman not long ago had, after a long and arduous descent, just begun to wet his line when a big boulder splashed into the water at his feet. When a second followed, he and his gillie abandoned their now useless attempt to fish, and sheltered as well as they could under the rocks at the side until the danger was over. When the torrent of missiles came to an end, an investigation into the cause of the phenomenon disclosed the fact that the angler's own manservant had been amusing himself and a companion by rolling stones down the brae, to see them splash into the water, in ignorance of the fact that he was endangering the life and spoiling the sport of a justly incensed master.

CHAPTER VI

SOME FISHING RECORDS

PROBABLY the most remarkable fishing, as far as mere number is concerned, that ever took place in the United Kingdom, was that enjoyed by Mr. Naylor in the Grimersta river in the Island of Lewis, in the year 1888. The numbers caught and the manner of their capture were so extraordinary that an account of the circumstances cannot fail to be of interest to all who care for salmon lore. Mr. Naylor has, at my request, most kindly furnished me with a narrative of the details, mainly taken from his Diary. The fishing consists of a small river which runs out of Loch Langabhat, a lake ten miles long by one mile wide, not far from the boundary between Harris and Lewis, and, after running a distance of nine miles and con-necting four lakes, discharges into a sea loch. The Diary runs as follows :—

Arrived at Grimersta on July 30, 1888. The river hardly running, and only a couple of inches deep where it runs into the sea. A few salmon in the pools, and thousands leaping in the sea. We got several to take the fly in salt water, but generally caught what we required for the table by letting the fly sink in the middle of a shoal and foul-hooking one. In the salt-water bay at the mouth of the river the air seemed full of salmon, hundreds leaping out of the water at the same time, while shoals of 50 to 2,000 or more kept on swimming slowly round and round past the mouth of the river close to the surface, with their dorsal fin appearing above the water. Towards the middle of August the fish commenced to die from a disease which attacked them on the head and gills, and great numbers were found dead at each low tide. The only chance of saving the fish was to make an artificial spate, and so let them up the river. Collecting all the available men about the place (about fifteen in all) we set to work, and after about four hours' hard work succeeded in deepening the outlet from Loch Langabhat about a foot. We then went down to the lower end of the first loch, and constructed a strong dam of turfs and rocks across the river at its exit from the lake. In five days from that time the water in the first loch had risen a foot, and on August 21 the dam was knocked away, and a good spate came down the river.

A small shoal of about thirty salmon was the first

to come across the fresh water, which was now running freely into the sea, and they immediately turned and rushed up the river. Presently a larger shoal came tearing up, and in a few minutes the fish were crowding into the narrow mouth of the river in such quantities that many were pushed out on to the shore among the stones. There were so many fish that numbers had to get up the river in quite shallow water, and it was astonishing to see how they would rush up a steep run where the water was only three inches deep. They appeared to hold on to the rocks by their pectoral fins, and force themselves up by a vigorous motion of the tail, which, being more than half out of water, sent up showers of spray. We spent several hours in watching the fish going up ; and the water accumulated in the first loch was sufficient to keep the river in spate for forty-eight hours, in which time all the fish went up the river ; but many of them remained in the pools between the sea and the first loch (a distance of little more than a mile) ; and on looking down into these pools from the rocks above, the bed of the river seemed paved with fish, nearly all of which had a white fungus spot on their head. For some reason most of the fish remained for several weeks in the first loch, instead of running further up as they usually do.

BIG DAY ON THE GRIDIRON

Two days after we let down the water I got 31 in the first loch, but for the next few days the weather was bright and calm, and not many fish were got by any of us; but on August 27, the rod which fished the first loch got 36. Next day I got 54. The rod on that beat the following day got 46, and the next day I had it I got 45. The total take of the three rods for the six last days of August was 333 salmon, and 71 sea-trout. All the fish were fairly caught with fly. We might have killed many more if we had all fished in the first loch each day, but we did not care to break through the rules as to the division of the beats (under which the whole of the first loch formed part of number 1 beat), consequently only one of the three rods was among the fish each day, the other two not getting many.

The average weight of the fish caught in each of these exceptional large takes was 6 lb.

The numbers and weights for the six days were as follows :—

	Salmon	Weight	Sea-Trout	Weight
Naylor	143	856	31	23
Hansard	106	680	26	19
Probyn	84	490	14	10
	333	2,026	71	52

I

Mr. Naylor's individual take for nineteen days' fishing was 214 salmon weighing 1,307 lb., and 304 sea-trout weighing 161 lb. On his great day, August 28, he fished for nine hours, from 9.30 A.M. to 6.30 P.M. The largest number caught in an hour was ten, and the smallest two. When he left off there was still an hour and a half of daylight, and his gillies implored him to continue fishing. To use his own expression, he 'was tired of the slaughter,' and did not care to go on, although he has no doubt that he might have caught eight or ten more fish.

This is indeed a most remarkable record, and I imagine that while there are few anglers who would not dearly like to have one or more such experiences, such extraordinary success would pall if often repeated. Mr. Naylor assured me that no skill was required to hook or land the salmon, that three or four rushed at his fly every time it was cast into the water, and that although he began with two flies, as was the usual practice in these waters, he very soon left it off, as it interfered with landing the fish sufficiently rapidly to catch so large a number in the time. I have never myself caught two salmon at one time, although I have often caught a salmon and a sea-trout, and have had two salmon on together for an appreciable period on several occasions during my fishing career. The

critical period is of course when the fish are being
landed, as it is next thing to impossible to prevent a
dead strain upon the second fish when the first is
gaffed and lifted ashore, of which he usually takes
advantage. One of my relations once accomplished
the feat through the quickness of his gillie, who cut
off the dropper, upon which the first salmon was
hooked, at the moment he gaffed him, thus preventing
any pull at the one upon the tail fly. Mr. Naylor tells
me that he has several times succeeded in landing
two salmon together, by the ingenious contrivance of
putting on his dropper by a ring instead of a knot, so
that it can shift freely along the casting line. I do
not, however, think that anything but great good
fortune could enable two fish to be landed together
when the second takes the fly after the first has been
played some time and is nearly tired out. The
difference of pace and movement almost always causes
a break either of the tackle or the hold.

For number of fish taken I have little doubt that
Mr. Naylor's record is and will remain unique. It is
said that the late Lord Lovat once got thirty-six
fish in a day, averaging 14 lb. each, which, of
course, would make a much larger aggregate weight,
but I have also heard that he had three gillies and
their rods with him, and that although he rose and

1 2

hooked all his fish himself, he then immediately
changed rods and left his attendants to land the salmon.
Some such plan must, I think, necessarily have been
adopted in order to get the number in the time, as
although Lord Lovat was notoriously very hard on his
fish, it would have been hardly possible to have
landed such a quantity of good-sized fish in such a
stream in the time.

The marvellous readiness with which the salmon
took the fly as soon as a way was engineered for them
into the river and lakes after their long involuntary
detention at the mouth, seems to throw some additional
light upon the question, before referred to, of their
feeding in fresh water. They are very seldom
captured with any kind of lure in the salt water when
gathered together and waiting for a flood to take them
up the stream, but it would seem that they take the
fly very greedily when from prolonged drought they
have been compulsorily detained in salt water for
an abnormal period. I cannot boast of any such
extraordinary results as I have quoted from Mr.
Naylor's Diary ; but the largest number of salmon I
ever killed with rod and line, in a given time, was also
after a prolonged drought, when, in October 1894,[1] I

[1] See 'Nil Desperandum,' *Badminton Magazine*, October
1896.

caught in two or three pools of the Add, to which fish had access at every high tide, thirty-five salmon of from $17\frac{1}{2}$ to $4\frac{1}{2}$ lb. in five days. There had been no rain since early in August, and the water was extraordinarily low, bright, and clear; nevertheless the fish, which were swarming in the pools, beyond which they could not get, rose very readily at a small fly on fine gut, and I easily beat any record I had previously made with the water in perfect order, getting ten one day and twelve another. I cannot suggest any satisfactory explanation of their conduct, except that they were remarkably hungry after a long involuntary fast.

The great success attained by Mr. Naylor's artificial spate invites imitation, and is not an isolated instance of the regulation of the height of a salmon river by engineering works. It is obvious, however that such experiments can only be successfully under-taken in a limited number of places and under exceptionally favourable conditions. It is a ticklish thing to meddle with the free flow of a West Coast burn, thereby incurring the responsibility for the destruction caused by floods, which would be almost sure, rightly or wrongly, to be attributed to the man who had dammed the stream. A chain of lochs, as at Grimersta, is almost essential for the conduct of such engineering works, as otherwise one or more artificial reservoirs would have to be constructed. A very large supply of water would be needed to materially affect the volume of a typical Highland stream, and I should not recommend any one, without considerable engineering skill, to risk attempting to dam, divert, or lower the lakes and burns furnishing the water supply of any cultivated or inhabited district, however slight may be its claims to such a description, without first squaring every possible dissentient.

For another curious record I am indebted to Mr. Henry Graham, who has kindly supplied me with the detailed account of a remarkable day's hauling enjoyed by himself and Lord Muncaster in the Cargill water of the Tay on October 10 (the last day of the season) in 1872. The river was just in splendid order after a spate, and no fish had been caught for about a week before. The two rods were fishing from the same boat, and one or other of them put down the hour and minute at which each fish was caught or lost during the day. I am grateful to them for the opportunity of laying the time table before my readers, as I think they will find it in many respects interesting and suggestive.

Fishing commenced at 10 A.M.

A.M.

10.5 . Salmon, weight 11 lb. . Muncaster
10.20 . „ lost . „

A.M.

10.30		Salmon,	weight	22	lb.	Muncaster
11.0		,,	,,	20	lb.	. Graham
11.15	.	Grilse,	,,	9½	lb.	. Muncaster
11.25	.	,,	,,	5½	lb.	. ,,
11.30	.	Salmon,	,,	16½	lb.	Graham
11.45		,,	,,	14½	lb.	Muncaster
11.55	.	,,	,,	18	lb.	. ,,

P.M.

12.10	.	Grilse,		lost		,,
12.25	.	Salmon,	,,	26	lb.	. Graham
12.30	.	,,		lost	.	,,
12.40	.	,,		,,	.	,,
12.55	.	,,		,,		Muncaster
1.5		,,	,,	17½	lb.	. ,,
1.15		,,		lost	.	Graham
1.25	.	,,		,,	.	,,
1.45	.	,,		,,		Muncaster
2.0	.	,,	,,	23	lb.	. Graham
2.10		,,	,,	14½	lb.	Muncaster ⌉ Both
2.10		Grilse,	,,	7½	lb.	Graham ⌊ landed together
2.20		Salmon,	,,	18	lb.	Muncaster
2.30	.	,,	,,	27	lb.	Graham
2.55	.	,,	,,	11½	lb.	. Muncaster
3.10	.	,,	,,	12	lb.	. Graham

An interval of forty minutes was then taken for luncheon, and fishing recommenced at 4.10 P.M.

P.M.

4.45	.	Salmon,	weight	18	lb.	. Muncaster
5.0	.	,,		lost	.	Graham
5.30	.	Grilse,	,,	5	lb.	. ,,
5.40	.		,,	8	lb.	. ,,

Left off at 5.50.

Result of seven hours' fishing { Salmon 15
{ Grilse 5
—
20

Weight 304½ lb., or an average of a little over 15 lb.

From this it will be seen that in rather heavy water it took on an average 13¼ minutes to hook, play, and land fish, three-quarters of which averaged nearly 20 lb. in weight. How many rose without taking hold is not stated, and probably could not be ascertained, as in harling many of the fish come at the fly deep under water, and are felt and not seen. But the most instructive part of the record is the manner in which, for a little more than an hour, from 12.30 to 1.45 fish after fish was hooked and lost.

During the first hour and fifty minutes eight fish were brought to the net out of nine hooked ; in the next period of the same duration seven out of nine were lost, notwithstanding the fact that the fly was to all appearances presented to the fish under precisely the same conditions, there being no such disturbing element as might possibly be presented by casting or striking. To an outsider it would hardly seem possible that such a difference should be caused by the way in which similar fish took a barbed hook into their mouths ; but every fisherman must have had some very similar experiences, although it is not often that they are so plainly recorded and contrasted.

Usually there is a time in the day when fish will not rise at all, and there is another when almost every fish hooked manages to effect his escape. The same curious discrepancy occurs in the detailed account of Mr. Naylor's ten hours' fishing in the Grimersta, when the number caught in an hour varied from ten to two. There was no record kept of the fish lost on that occasion, but I am told that there was the same example of a series of fish escaping at one particular period of time. It will be observed that if one sportsman had had the boat to himself, he would in all probability have got nearly the same number of fish.

Tay salmon are fine fellows, but there are always a few grilse caught in that river to reduce the average weight. I know of no river where the general run of the fish caught is larger than in the Cascapedia River in Canada, part of which is fished by the Governor-General. I am indebted to the Marquis of Lansdowne for access to his fishing register for the four years ending 1887, which records a total calculated to stir up feelings of envy in the breasts of less fortunate fishermen.

In 1884, between June 14 and August 5 inclusive,

Lord Lansdowne caught ninety-one fish averaging
23¼ lb., fourteen of them weighed 30 lb. and over, the
largest of which was 43 lb.   The rest of his party
made up the total to 262 fish ; weight, 6,003¼ lb. ; 30 lb.
and over, thirty-six.

In 1885, the fishing season was from June 13 to
July 30.   Lord Lansdowne caught eighty-two fish,
weighing 1,973½ lb. ; average weight, 24 lb. ; over
30 lb., nine ; largest, 39½ lb.   Total number caught,
392 ; weight, 9,920¼ lb. ; average, 23½ lb. ; over
30 lb., fifty-four ; largest, 45 lb.

1886, June 12 to July 24.   Lord Lansdowne,
101 ; weight, 2,500 lb. ; average, 24¾ lb. ; over 30 lb.,
twenty-four ; largest, 39 lb.

Total for the season, 271 ; weight, 6,687½ lb. ;
average, 24⅓ lb. ; over 30 lb., sixty-five ; largest, 41 lb.

1887, June 25 to August 19.   Lord Lansdowne,
ninety-four ; weight, 2,232 lb. ; average, 23¾ lb. ; over
30 lb., seventeen ; largest, 38½ lb.   Total for the
season, 320 ; weight, 7,277½ lb. ; average, 22¾ lb. ;
over 30 lb., fifty-five ; largest, 41 lb.

Grand total for the four years : 1,245 salmon,
weighing 29,188 lb. ; average weight, 23½ lb. ; over
30 lb., 210 ; largest fish, 45 lb.

This record, large as it is, pales before that made
by Mr. Charles Ellis, Mr. Iveson, and Captain Percy

in the same river in 1879, when in fifty-three days from June 9 to August 15, 640 fish were caught.

Mr. Ellis got 269, weighing 6,714 lb. ; over 30 lb., fifty-three.

Mr. Iveson got 216, weighing 5,483 lb. ; over 30 lb., forty-eight.

Captain Percy got 137, weighing 3,451 lb. ; over 30 lb., twenty-seven.

The best day was June 18, when Mr. Ellis caught seventeen fish, weighing 465 lb., of which the individual weights were as follows : 38 lb., 36 lb., 36 lb., 32 lb., 32 lb., 32 lb., 32 lb., 31 lb., 30 lb., 24 lb., 24 lb., 22 lb., 22 lb., 21 lb., 21 lb., 20 lb., 20 lb., and on July 11 he caught seventeen, weighing 415 lb.

Lord Kilcoursie, who was on the staff of Lord Stanley of Preston (now Lord Derby), when Governor-General in 1891 and 1892, has very kindly supplied me with the following graphic account of the scenery and method of fishing.

'From the mouth of the Cascapedia, in the Bay of Chaleurs, for a distance of about twelve miles, the fishing has been for many years in the hands of an American syndicate, and it is only from that point upwards, for about thirty-five to forty miles, that the Governor-General has the fishing rights. The scenery is simply magnificent, for, although on the

lower or tidal reaches the banks are low, and the
country "cleared," from a point about six miles
from the mouth to the upper waters runs one un-
broken forest, dense and deserted, except for the
"lumberers," whose timber slides for shooting logs
down into the stream appear at two places. So thick
is the forest growth that the river itself is the sole
route, and the method of climbing up its rapid and
beautiful course is always the same, viz. by canoe,
with a man in bow and stern "poling," as it is called,
up stream, keeping as near either bank as possible to
avoid the stream, and putting the poles in with a
rhythm and a musical twang on the pebbles which, in
the great silence, is weird to a degree, and can be
heard for miles. If out fishing, the fisherman sits in
mid-canoe, and is thus poled up to his beat by two
half-breed Indians. The beats in the last years of
Lord Stanley of Preston's term were as follows :—

' At the twelfth mile from the mouth at a sharp turn
stands " New Dereen," built by Lord Lansdowne, a
rough wooden shanty which will hold four rods
comfortably. From this lodge the fishing during the
first fortnight or three weeks is chiefly carried on, the
rods dividing some ten or more miles of fishing,
all above the lodge itself. As the fish move up so do
some of the party—usually two—who are "poled" up

to what is known as " Middle Camp " : two log huts
of the roughest description, swarming with mosquitoes
and undermined by "ground hogs," a sort of cross
between a guinea pig and a hedgehog. From this
camp the two rods work some twelve or fifteen pools
between them ; and then, again, comes one more
move upwards to "Lazy Bogan," the best of the
three divisions because the highest, the most deserted,
and the fullest of glorious pools and big fish. To get
to " Lazy Bogan " 28 miles above Middle Camp, and so
two days' "pole"—to go out and get five or six fish
between 5 P.M. and 8 P.M., of which the lightest
perhaps is 28 lb., and then to come back to the camp
for tinned soup, trout, and some beef brought up
from below, and to smoke one's pipe in the glow of
the Northern Lights, which simply electrify the sky—is
a joy too great to be put on paper.

'The method of fishing is the same throughout the
river. On the way up are passes, a few large, dry
beaches which form the bed of the river when in
spate in the spring after the melting of the snows.
Here you halt, and an Indian gets out and selects a
large stone, called on the Cascapedia a " killick."
This acts as an anchor. A knot, also peculiar to the
river, is tied round the stone, and about three fathoms
of rope are sufficient. You then pole or paddle to the

head of your pool ; down goes the " killick," and also
the Indians, glad enough of rest and a smoke. You
then stand up, take the rod, a spliced greenheart
supplied from St. Johns, New Brunswick, which has
been lying along the canoe all ready, and begin to cast.
The moment a fish is hooked, you sit down ; the
bow Indian lifts up the " killick," and both take the
paddles and work the canoe up and down according
to the run of the fish. As many of the pools are at
the head of a strong rapid, it is furiously exciting
if the fish makes a bolt down stream, as the least
mistake will not only probably lose you your fish, but
possibly your life. Finally, comes the most marvellous
piece of work of all, namely, the gaffing. It is all but
true to say an Indian *never* misses. I have had a
fish gaffed absolutely in the centre of a rapid, if we
managed to get up alongside him in the canoe, and
while fish and canoe were being literally hurled down
stream, only steered by the one Indian with a
paddle !

' The best flies are the Jock Scott, Durham Ranger,
Silver and Blue Doctors, and Black Fairy. The
average weight of one hundred and forty-four fish
killed in 1891 was 25·05 lb., and of one hundred and
thirty-three fish killed in 1892 was 26·82 lb.'

I may refer those who wish to supplement this

description of Canadian fishing to an account of sport
in the neighbouring Metapedia river by Sir Henry
Stafford Northcote in 'Blackwood's Magazine' for
1877, and reprinted in the first volume of their series
entitled 'Travel, Adventure, and Sport.' From this
it will be seen that fifteen years have not materially
altered the method of fishing, and that the most
serious drawback to the sport then, as now, consisted
of the various flies and mosquitoes which take a
fiendish delight in penetrating an unacclimatised
skin.

Mr. Arthur Fowler, who has fished in Canada as
in most other parts of the world, assures me that
Lord Kilcoursie has not in the least exaggerated the
marvellous dexterity displayed by the Indians in the
use of the gaff. It would appear that this is an
attribute of semi-civilised races, for he adds that the
only attendants whom he has known to compare
favourably with the Indians in this respect were the
Lapps on the Tana River, which he visited in 1896.
A greater contrast than this river presents to the
beautiful stream just described, rushing between
virgin forests, can hardly be imagined. There is no
scenery ; the river is from three hundred yards to half
a mile wide, and scrub birch is the only tree. For
thirty miles the land is sand and mud, not a stone in

the river bed. There are very few birds : the cuckoo
is common. Hours there are not regular, but it
does not matter, as night and day are the same ; in
fact, a bright midnight is lighter than a cloudy midday. Two Lapps navigate each canoe. They are
splendid boatmen, going one hundred and ten miles
in thirty-six hours against a three-mile-an-hour stream.
They never seem to tire ; all they want is half an
hour's rest, and coffee and food every three or four
hours. They are just like jolly boys, always laughing
and chatting. They vary much in appearance.
Their features are not Tartar. Some are like
American Indians. One would be very like a
Soudanese if he were black. Some you would take
for Scotchmen, or rather Lewis men. They are
cleanly. To give an idea of the size of the river :
seventy miles from the mouth at dead low water the
breadth is two hundred and thirty yards, the average
depth four feet. The current runs about two miles
an hour, which gives 390,000 cubic feet per minute.

It will be readily understood that, in a river of
this description, harling is the only method of fishing
which affords a fair chance of success. It would be
very tedious to cast in such wide and monotonous
water. A pine-built, flat-bottomed canoe is used,
managed by two Lapps, who are splendid boatmen,

but very small in stature. Two rods are usually
used, one with a fly on the cast, the other with a
spoon, and it is necessary to balance them in the
fork of a birch twig, as there is not a high enough
freeboard for harling in the ordinary way. The
fisherman sits in the centre leaning against a back-
board ; the man in the bow uses a short paddle, the
one in the stern a pole. They do not pole down the
rapids as the Indians do in Canada, but shoot them
paddling, a difficult and dangerous feat. They land
to gaff the fish. They themselves fish with a short
line fastened to a larch pole, with home-made tackle,
and a spoon beaten out of an old brass kettle or
biscuit tin. When a fish runs to the end of their line
they heave the impromptu rod overboard, and pick
it up again when it floats.

The walls of the hut at Levyck on the Tana,
usually occupied by sportsmen for the fishing, are
marked with the records of the bags caught by
various parties from time to time. In 1873, between
June 23 and July 26, three rods got one hundred and
fifty-six fish, weighing 2,676 lb. On July 6 fifteen fish
were caught, weighing 278 lb. On July 7 seventeen
fish, weighing 340 lb. The accounts are irregular
and imperfect, but the best year recorded during
ten following was 1874, when three rods caught two

K

hundred and seventy-four fish, weighing 4,746 lb., in a
month's fishing, from July 9 to August 10. On July 16
twenty-four fish were caught, of an aggregate weight of
401 lb. Two rods in 1880 caught one hundred and
three fish ; in 1881, seventy-five ; in 1890, one hundred and twenty-nine ; 1893, seventy-nine. The
average weight of the fish caught is about 18 lb.
The heaviest fish recorded 45 lb., but in several years
only the number and aggregate weight are mentioned.

It will be observed that, notwithstanding the large
average size of the fish in these rivers, no capture of
a fish of 50 lb. and upwards is recorded in any of these
years in either the Cascapedia or the Tana. I shall
give one instance of a large fish caught in the former
river in the next chapter, where the subject of monsters
will be dealt with. Some of the best fishing in the
United Kingdom is in the Duke of Richmond's
water near Gordon Castle. Some remarkable records
of sport there may be found in Vol. CLXIII. of the
'Quarterly Review' : two hundred and ten salmon
were taken in the first nine days of one October,
and the salmon run large, and are usually in fine
condition.

CHAPTER VII

THREE FISHERS, AND SOME BIG FISH

I CANNOT better illustrate the charm of salmon-
fishing, and the hold which it keeps upon its votaries,
than by taking as examples three noted fishermen of
different professions and characters, who shared a
common passion for the sport upon which I am writing,
Mr. John Malcolm of Poltalloch, the Hon. and
Rev. Robert Liddell, and Mr. Alfred Denison.
All these three were famous upon many rivers, but
it was on the classic banks of Tweed that they found
their happiest hunting ground. I will first say a
word or two of Mr. Liddell : the other two may be
taken together, as for years they shared a sitting-
room at the Cross Keys, Kelso, from which town they
used to fish adjoining beats of the Tweed.

Robert Liddell was best known to fame as the
earnest and hard-working incumbent of St. Paul's,
Knightsbridge, and the hero of a famous ecclesiastical
suit, but it is only as a devoted follower of the

K 2

Apostolical recreation that I venture to allude to him
here. A keener hand on Tay, Spey, and Tweed
never existed, and although he had no river of his
own, he was a deservedly popular guest on many of
the best stretches of water in Scotland, notably at
Gordon Castle and at the celebrated Pavilion beat
near Melrose. He not merely cast a beautiful line,
but knew every trick of the trade, and was an adept
at making his own flies, an accomplishment which is
gradually becoming rarer with the improvement of professional work, and the development of the modern
tendency to specialise. He also used to write inter-
minable cantos in the metre of Sir Walter Scott's
narrative poems, describing minutely his day's sport
and recording in verse every change of fly, rise, and
incident of the play till each fish was gaffed or lost.
Some of these verses were privately printed and
given to friends, and I have read them at different
places where I have been a visitor with him, but
cannot remember more than their general nature,
metre, and subject. As might be supposed, they were
more interesting as literary curiosities than as lyrical
effusions ; for I doubt whether Tennyson, or Shelley
himself, could have found much inspiration in such a
subject. His generous disposal of his spoils was
once the cause of great expense to his parish. A

horrible stench pervaded the house which had been
built for the assistant clergy in Wilton Place, close to
his church. Engineers, plumbers, and workmen were
called in. The drains were of course discovered to be
defective, and were relaid at a heavy cost. It was
not till some time after that the real *corpus delicti* was
discovered in the shape of an 18-lb. fish which the
rector had despatched, carefully packed, as a present
to his senior curate, which in the absence of the
recipient had been left in his room to await his
return. Mr. Liddell died in 1888 in his 80th year,
having preserved to the last his keenness for the
sport, which doubtless did much to keep him in
health to such an advanced age, in the intervals of
very hard work cheerfully and conscientiously
performed. On September 28, 1885, three years
before his death, he caught with his own rod no less
than twenty fish at Taymount on the Tay.

Mr. Malcolm, of Poltalloch, although in the last
two or three years of his life he was unable to use his
legs enough to enjoy his favourite pastime, did not
altogether give up the rod and line until nearly eighty
years of age, and continued to lease the celebrated
Makerstoun waters on the Tweed some time after he
had passed his seventieth year. I can well remember
with what delight he used to cast off the cares of his

large establishment to go to his October quarters at
Kelso, and take 'his ease at his inn' with his old
friend and companion.   No school-boy escaping from
Dotheboys Hall could have taken greater pleasure in
the prospect of a holiday, or enjoyed it more when it
came.   He was an excellent performer on many
streams—the Lochy, the Spean brawling through its
rocky course, the slow Add meandering across Crinan
Moss, were all thoroughly familiar to him ; but in his
eyes no water could compare with Makerstoun, with
the Troughs, the Red Stone, and other famous casts.
There he would fish with his attendant, George Wright ;
and when 'she' was in order, no start was too early
and no day too long for him ; but he never prolonged
his holiday quite to the close of the Tweed season, as
he had an invincible prejudice against catching salmon
which had been any time in the water, and scorned
the red kippers or teeming baggits which were good
enough for less particular sportsmen.   I wish I could
have a shorthand note of some of the conversations
between him and Alfred Denison during those *noctes
Ambrosianæ*, for I am sure many wrinkles worth
recording might have been collected from their experiences as they fought their battles over again.   It is
curious that Mr. Denison's best day should have been
upon his companion's water, the Lower Makerstoun

beat, where, on October 13, 1873, he caught sixteen
salmon, weighing 22 lb., 18 lb., 9 lb., 20 lb., 27 lb.,
23 lb., 17 lb., 6 lb., 9 lb., 16 lb., 22½ lb., 21½ lb., 25 lb.,
7 lb., 18 lb., 20 lb., losing four, and having also eleven
' rises ' and ' pulls.' On the three previous fishing days
Mr. Malcolm had caught twelve, fourteen, and fifteen
large salmon, and I think he always a little grudged
the chance that he happened to have given away the
fourth, although he was by no means given to the
failing of jealousy over his sport.   I have often heard
him tell the story of the great week, and I think he
would have been just as well pleased if the sixteen
had fallen to his share, and one of the other three good
days to that of his guest upon that occasion.   Long
after he was unable to fish himself, he still took a deep
interest in the sport of others, and often made his
way round to the gun room at Poltalloch to look at
the fish that I, Egremont Lascelles, or some other of
his connections or guests, had brought back in the
evening.[1]   Alfred Denison was an even more constant
and devoted disciple of Izaak Walton ; for as a
bachelor he had more time at his disposal, and in the
autumn of life was able to devote nearly all his

[1] Much of my information as to Mr. Alfred Denison was
kindly supplied by his nephew, Sir Walter Phillimore, some of
it having been previously published in a letter to the *Field*
newspaper at the time of his death.

well-earned leisure either to the active enjoyment of the
sport or to the kindred hobby of collecting the literature of the subject—his fishing library, which is now
an heirloom at Ossington, being the most perfect private
collection in existence. Among his treasures are the
‘ Book of Angling,’ printed in 1606, of which there are
said to be only three copies known ; a Flemish treatise
by Van der Goes, printed as early as 1492 ; and the
Book of St. Albans, ascribed to Dame Juliana Berners,
containing the quaint ‘ Treatyse of Fyshynge with an
Angle.’ He was the eighth son of John Denison,
Esq., of Ossington, Notts, born on August 23, 1816,
and was a commoner of Christ Church, Oxford.
After taking his degree, he went out with his brother
Henry to seek his fortune in New South Wales. When
his brother, Sir William Denison, became Governor-
General of Australia, he served as his private secretary.
After many and pressing difficulties, with which he had
to contend single-handed, his sheep-farming proved a
success, and in the year 1857 he was able to return to
his native country with a modest competence. His
elder brother, the Right Hon. John Evelyn Denison,
afterwards Viscount Ossington, was chosen that year
Speaker of the House of Commons ; and during the
whole period of his tenure of the office which he so
adorned, from 1857 to 1872 inclusive, Alfred was his

private secretary, and was most popular in the House, giving diligent and unwearied attention to his official duties. It was in that capacity that I first met him ; when he most courteously found me a seat in a very crowded house, to hear my father speak in the Irish Church debate. From his return to England until his death he was a regular visitor to the Scotch salmon rivers ; the Ness first, and afterwards the Tweed also.

An entry in his Diary for 1883 records that since 1860 he had caught with his own rod, in the two rivers, 3,795 fish. In the subsequent years, up to the date of his death, he records further sport to the amount of 806 fish, making the astonishing total of 4,601. As to the weight of those fish, it may suffice to give as an example the year 1883, when the fish killed were 235, and their weight was 2,708 lb. As a poetical friend wrote of him, 'he weighed his fish by the ton.' His best day on the Tweed I have already mentioned. His best on the Ness was August 7, 1876, when he records as follows : 'Began fishing at ten minutes to nine. Killed 15 lb., 10 lb., 8½ lb., 7 lb., 7 lb., 10 lb. 9 lb., 11 lb., 9 lb., 6 lb., 11 lb., 9 lb., 9 lb., 10 lb., 9 lb., 8 lb., lost two, and had ten rises. The first six fish I killed in an hour and ten minutes. Water rather falling—dark. High S.W. wind.' In 1885, which he calls 'the good season,' he killed in the Ness 120 fish, weighing 972½ lb., and in the Tweed 180 fish, weighing 2,651 lb.   Besides his salmon-fishing he was well known as a trout-fisher, and a member of the Stock-bridge club.   He continued to enjoy his favourite sport until the last.   He came down as usual to Ness House on August 1, 1887, although he had suffered severely from an illness at Stockbridge in the spring and early summer.   Arriving by midday, he fished that afternoon and caught two fish.   During the dry season that followed there was little opportunity for fishing but on Friday, Sept. 2, and Saturday, Sept. 3, he caught nine fish, six of these on Saturday.   It was remarked of him that he never threw a better or straighter line than on that Saturday ; but the over-exertion and a chill proved too much for him.   On Sunday morning, Sept. 4, he was taken ill, and died in twenty-four hours.   His body lies in Ossington churchyard, by the side of his brother Henry.

I have often heard from his old friend the story of his celebrated encounter with the salmon which eventually defeated him after ten hours' hard work. At six in the evening, on a Friday, in the Holm pool in the Ness he hooked a salmon which he knew to be of immense size.   After one long and violent rush, during which angler and gillie had the greatest diffi-

culty in keeping up with him, the fish pursued the
usual and more fatal course of sulking. Three
successive attempts were made to gaff him in deep
water, but in vain, as each time he moved on a little,
but could not be persuaded to run. The contest
continued till darkness set in; reinforcements then
arrived in the shape of refreshments and a brother
angler, but all efforts to bring the fish to the gaff
were frustrated by his weight and strength. Through
the long night Mr. Denison persevered, keeping a
steady strain on the monster and meeting every new
manœuvre with the patience and skill of a prince
among anglers. At last, about 4 o'clock in the
morning, its matchless strength was nearly exhausted,
and after several short runs the big tail gradually began
to stir the top of the water, and the stubborn resistance
seemed at an end. Slowly the giant bulk was towed
towards the shore, the gaff was stretched out to
secure it, and the prize seemed gained, when the fish
made a last expiring rush—and alas ! the line caught
on the angler's watch-chain. There was a dead pull :
the line snapped, and the fish floated away, after a
contest of no less than ten hours. A few days before,
Mr. Denison had got the fish of the season in the same
pool, a remarkably handsome fresh-run salmon of
33½ lb., but, like Mr. Bromley Davenport's fish in

'Sport,' it only looked like a small bit of the monster that escaped.

Mr. Bromley Davenport's work is too well known for anything more than a passing allusion to his fishing adventure. If any of my readers have not yet read 'Sport,' they have a treat before them, with which I should be loth to interfere, and I refer them to its brilliant pages for particulars of the loss of 'the biggest fish that ever was seen.'

Another most vivid and picturesque account of 'a night with a salmon' may be found in a volume of essays by the Bishop of Bristol, published by Smith, Elder & Co., 1895, under the title of 'Off the Mill.' It attracted much attention when first printed in the 'Cornhill Magazine' for 1869, and I have the authority of its author for stating that all the details are exact in every particular. It is most instructive, not merely from the dramatic incidents of the struggle, but also as a record of salmon taking a bait in salt water, and may be taken as another typical instance of failure in spite of every possible exercise of pluck, patience, skill, and resource.

The scene of the adventure is that part of the Tay where the Earn joins its waters with the larger stream, and the estuary proper commences. The rise and fall of the tide amounts to twelve to fourteen feet, and as the stretch of the water is three-quarters of a mile across at high tide, harling is the usual and only reasonable method of fishing adopted. The fly was practically abandoned, not rising more than one to six as compared with the minnow, and that one never more than a sea-trout.

The 'Night with a Salmon' was the last night but one of the rod season of 1868, and the fish was hooked at about half-past twelve in the morning, high tide having been about ten. The monster took the minnow on the lightest of the three lines, a mere makeshift, composed of two trout lines seventy and fifty yards long, the splice of which had not been tried. He first went nearly out to sea, playing the boat rather than the boat playing him, and having the full advantage of both tide and current. Many dangers had to be surmounted : first the sperling nets with their high poles and ropes, and then the channel of the South Deep, where Mugdrum Island divides the Tay into two streams and the bottom is 'gey foul,' and the tide runs like a mill race. At half-past three the boat approached Newburgh, with its wild expanse of estuary beyond, and for the first and last time touched the shore for a second, but not long enough for either passenger to land. The writer gives a vivid account of the sorrows of the unfortunate third man, not an enthusiastic angler, wet, cold, and hungry, and longing to get ashore —at one time even threatening to jump overboard and swim. The change of the tide made the fish frantic, but he decided on going up with it, and did so at a great pace, and shortly afterwards showed himself at last, springing two feet out of the water—a monster as large as a well-grown boy—and proving that he was not foul hooked, as had been surmised from his behaviour, for the line led fair from his snout. Soon afterwards a strand of the line parted within twenty yards of the end, through the constant friction of the wet line running through the rings for so many hours; and the problem became complicated by the necessity of keeping the flaw as far as feasible on the reel. The necessity of keeping close on the fish led the boatman such a life as he will never forget. At last night came on in earnest; it was half-past six and all but dark before the pier was reached from which the boat had started seven hours before.

Here, after one churlish refusal, a boat was induced to come alongside, and the unfortunate passenger was transhipped at about eight o'clock with injunctions to send off food and a light. It was an hour before the boat returned with an excellent lantern, a candle and a half, a bottle of whisky, and cakes and cheese

A NIGHT WITH A SALMON

enough for a week. Dr. Browne now put in force
what, in a letter to me, he states that he 'regards as
the most brilliant idea that ever came into his mind.'
A spare rod, short and stiff, was laid across the seats
of the boat, with the reel all clear and a good
salmon line on, with five or six yards drawn through
the rings. They waited until the fish was quiet a
minute or two under the boat, and gently taking hold
of the line he was on, passed a loop of it through that
at the end of the salmon line. After two or three
failures the loop was got through, a good knot tied,
and the old line snapped above the knot. The danger
surmounted might then be properly estimated from the
fact that the flaw when examined turned out to be seven
inches long, and half of one of the remaining strands
was frayed through. The only thing now to be avoided
was coming into close contact with the fish, as the
loop, of course, would not run through the rings.
This was rendered more difficult, as the manœuvre
of transferring the fish from one rod to another was
facilitated, by his being attracted by the light and
keeping close to the boat. For a few moments it
was proposed to hang the light over the stern and
gaff him when he came up to it, but this method was
rejected as unworthy of so noble a foe. I quote the
conclusion of the article.

'Time passes away as we drift slowly up the river towards Elcho. Ten o'clock strikes, and we determine to wait till dawn, and then land and try conclusions with the monster that has had us fast for ten hours. The tide begins to turn, and Jimmy utters gloomy forebodings of our voyage down to the sea in the dark. The fish feels the change of tide, and becomes more demoniacal than ever. For half an hour he is in one incessant fury, and at last, for the first time, except the single occasion when he jumped and showed himself, he rises to the surface, and through the dark night we can hear and see the huge splashes he makes as he rolls and beats the water. He must be near done, Jimmy thinks. As he is speaking the line comes slack. He's bolting towards the boat, and we reel up with the utmost rapidity. We reel on ; but no sign of resistance. Up comes the minnow minus the hooks ! Jimmy rows home without a word ; and neither he nor the fisherman will ever get over it.'

A large fish was taken in the nets at Newburgh the next year, which Dr. Browne identified as the same, by a mark where he had seen the tail hook of the minnow when the fish showed itself, and a peculiarity of the form of the shoulder. It was the largest salmon ever known to be taken, 'weighing

74 lb. as weighed at Newburgh, and 70 lb. in London the next day.' Mr. Frank Buckland took a cast of it, and I believe it may still be seen in his museum at South Kensington. This evidence of identity is not conclusive ; but very probably it was the very fish which escaped after so gallant a fight.

The Bishop tells me that he has often discussed with sportsmen the question of gaffing the fish by drawing him up to the blaze. 'At the time, I thought it unfair to the fish to entertain my boatman's suggestion, and I think so still' (December 1897), 'but I have never yet come across a man of sporting experience who has not said he would certainly have gaffed the fish by using the lantern to attract him.'

In my own opinion, the forbearance of the tired angler was sportsmanlike in the highest degree, but

> Video meliora, proboque
> Deteriora sequor,

and I do not think that if I had been in his position I should have resisted the temptation. In another place a fish, caught after a very prolonged fight, was taken in the end by a most ingenious contrivance, which some would consider unfair, but which I think thoroughly justifiable under the circumstances. Mr. Frederick Fowler, brother of Sir John Fowler of Braemore, hooked a fish in the Lynn pool on the

L

Broom at about twelve noon. The 'Lynn' I must
describe for the benefit of those who have not seen
it, as one of the most extraordinary pools to fish that
I have ever seen. A wild fall dashes into a deep
hole between two high rocks; and the fisherman
stands high above it on artificial steps cut in the
rock, and has to cast a long line to cover it. The
Braemore visitor's book contains a humorous sketch
by the late Sir John Everett Millais, of himself
fishing this pool, held by a gillie from above by
the gaff through his coat tail, labelled 'A necessary
precaution when fishing the Lynn pool.' At the time
of which I am writing it was possible for a gillie to gaff
a fish at one place in the pool, but since the great
flood of 1892 every fish hooked has to be led down
through the rapids into the pool below, the lower
Lynn; and a light wooden rail has been fixed
on the rocks beside the rapid to prevent the line
being cut by them, as the fisherman passes above at
a necessarily considerable distance. From this
description it will be seen that, although there are
difficulties in casting and landing the fish, the angler
is high above the pool and has great leverage if
required. Nevertheless, on this occasion referred to,
the fish refused to move far, and no strain was
sufficient to bring him to the surface. Hours passed,

dusk arrived, and with it assistance in the shape of
Mr. Arthur Fowler, but his efforts, like those of his
uncle, failed to bring the fish to the surface.   Many
were the conjectures as to the probable size of the
monster which had resisted a heavy strain in so
strong a stream for so long a period ; but when dusk
was rapidly changing to darkness desperate remedies
were called for.   A lantern was sent for and a second
rod, and Mr. Arthur Fowler, having rigged up an
impromptu triangle of three large flies and fastened it
to the new line, attached it to a key ring and sent it
down the other line to the fish 'like a kite messenger.'
Getting a second purchase on the salmon, he was
soon brought to the gaff and landed, when, to every
one's surprise and disappointment, he turned out to
be only about 16 lb., but hooked foul 'fair amid-
ships' in the side, half-way below the dorsal fin,
which accounted for his obstinate resistance.   Had
he also escaped, no doubt an addition would have
been made to the legends of lost monsters ; but it is
to be observed that in most recorded instances
opportunities are afforded for seeing the fish, which
did not occur here.   The contest lasted from noon
till nine o'clock.   I have endeavoured to obtain
authentic information of the size of fish taken with
the rod, but records are so unsatisfactorily kept, and

oral traditions so unreliable, that but for the kind assistance of Mr. Ffennell I could only have given a few sporadic instances. In small rivers the fish are usually smaller than in large, but in the Broom above referred to, narrow, rocky, and short as it is, there are an unusually large number of heavy fish. The records have been most accurately kept from 1867 to 1897, during which period of thirty years 1,061 salmon were taken with the rod, and nearly every year the heaviest fish was considerably over 20 lb., while on four occasions the record for the year was over 30 lb. The heaviest fish recorded was taken in 1884 and weighed 33 lb., but a much larger fish was hooked and lost by Sir John Fowler in the Lynn pool before referred to. It was seen several times during the struggle sufficiently plainly, and by a sufficiently accurate observer, to make it certain that it was much larger than the record fish of the river; and its fate may be conjectured from the fact that, after the spawning time in that same year, a fish was picked up which had been killed by an otter, which then, after the 'otter's piece' had been eaten and the season's waste had done its work, weighed no less than 36 lb. On the Add, of which I can speak from personal knowledge, a river similar in size and length, but of a much more sluggish character, I can only

remember the capture of two fish of about 20 lb. in a
similar period of thirty years, and the average weight
was about $7\frac{1}{2}$ lb. I should think that this may be
taken as more typical of the normal condition of
things in small Scotch rivers.

Many legends of big fish fail to stand the test of
careful examination ; but there are plenty of authentic
records of fish taken with the rod weighing 50 lb. and
over. These monsters do not always show such
desperate fight as in the historical encounter recorded
above. A fish of 56 lb. caught in the Cascapedia by
the Hon. Victor Stanley in 1892 gave very little
sport indeed. The record fish of 1897, a 53-pounder,
caught in the Gordon Castle water in the Spey by
Mr. W. Craven, although he fought gallantly, was
killed in a quarter of an hour. Mr. Craven, who was
fishing the Dallachy pool, not more than a mile from
the sea, with a small No. 4 Carron fly, with lemon body,
silver twist, and black hackle wing, tied on a double
hook, on a double gut cast with four feet of singie,
observed the fish rising behind a sunken stone, and
beyond the rapid stream from which he was casting,
the rise, as is frequently the case with very large fish,
being only indicated by the swirl of the water. From
this position he could only reach him by casting his
fly into the comparatively slack water beyond the

stream, and allowing it to be dragged past his nose in a manner 'quite contrary to the rules of casting.' Three times this was done without success ; but on the fourth occasion there was a wave on the water and a hard pull, and in a second away went 40 yards of line down stream. Mr. Craven was beginning to think of the boat 200 yards below, when the fish suddenly stopped and gave two or three unpleasant tugs ; but, being very firmly hooked, he allowed himself to be reeled slowly up, and enabled his captor to get ashore. He then made for his old resting-place and began to sulk, but not for long, for he quickly went up stream as fast as he had come down it, and it became a labour of difficulty to keep above him.

At this point a disagreeable grating feeling indicated that the line was rubbing against the edge of the shingle between the rod and the deep water, and it was necessary to take to the water again and get the line perpendicularly over him as he again stopped. At this point Mr. Craven first realised what a monster he had hooked, for although the rod was apparently pointing directly over the fish, the line suddenly ran out at full speed. This was because, having drowned the line under the heavy stream, the salmon was trying to ascend a small ' draw ' on the

far side of the river, and there he showed himself
struggling in about eight inches of water. The
strong tackle bore the strain well ; the sunken part of
the line was successfully reeled up, and, but for the
bend of the rod, the line was once more horizontal
between fish and angler. Now a slow steady pull
not only checked his career, but drew him back with
a splash into the deep, and the line was reeled up
short, so that when he had been carried a little way
down he came into the slack water, where fisherman
and gaffer were waiting him, but just out of reach.
This he repeated twice, but the third time, with two
or three feet more reeled up, he came well within
reach, and the steel went into him just above the
dorsal fin, the left hand came to the rescue of the
overtaxed right, and W. Davidson, who had not
uttered a syllable during the fifteen minutes' contest,
broke the silence with the exclamation : ' The biggest
fish I have ever taken out of the Spey.' After the
coup de grâce had been administered and the fly cut
out, both hooks of which were firmly fastened round
the lower jawbone, the handle of the gaff was passed
through the steelyard, and the salmon hoisted between
the shoulders of the exultant couple ; but the steelyard only indicating a maximum of 50 lb., his excess
weight was a matter of conjecture. This proved to be

3 lb. more. His length was four feet one and a half inches, and his girth two feet five ; a male fish, rather coloured, but perfect in shape and condition. The subsequent examination of the tackle showed that the risk of losing him had been considerable, as the reel line was cut a quarter through where it had grated against the shingle, and had to be removed as untrustworthy, and one strand of the double gut eye of the fly was severed and standing out at right angles.

The great authority on the size of salmon is Mr. Henry Ffennell, who has devoted much time and trouble to testing the accuracy of the alleged captures of large fish. Many such legends have been shattered in the process, but he has kindly supplied me with the following instances of fish of 50 lb. and over, taken with rod and line in the United Kingdom since 1870, which may be relied upon as strictly accurate. All of them appeared under Mr. Ffennell's name in the ' Times,' and were verified before publication.

1870. Mr. Haggard caught a fish of 61 lb. in the Stanley waters of the Tay.

1872. An angler landed a salmon of 58 lb. on the Shannon, and Dr. A. Peck took one of 51½ lb. in the Cumberland Derwent.

1873. A salmon of 53½ lb. was taken in the Tweed, and one of 57 lb. on the Suir in Tipperary.

1874. A salmon of 55½ lb. was caught in the Cumberland Derwent; one of 50 lb. in Loch Tay: one of 57 lb. in the Suir, Tipperary, by a professional angler. An amusing account of the capture of this fish, by the late Mr. Richard Bradford, a local inspector of fisheries, appeared in the 'Field' of February 9, 1895. It was to the following effect :—

The fish was caught on Longfield by Michael Maher. The river was reported coloured, and Maher left his flies at home and trusted to baits. When he reached the river he found the water was too clear for the Devon, and he was at his wits' end, as he had no flies. He, however, was a man of resource. He went into a farmhouse close by ; got some light orange silk from the farmer's daughter ; some hackles from a grizzled cock in the yard ; and with these and a little silver tinsel he formed the body. He could find nothing suitable for the wing, except some light orange goose feathers (dyed) in the farmer's daughter's hat. These made a decidedly clumsy fly ; but he tried it, and in a very few minutes was fast in the fish, which he landed in a very short time, and carried in triumph to Cashel. When asked what fly he used, he answered, 'That's a mystery.' This gave rise to the adoption of the name, and the combination thus accidentally arrived at is, with a few alterations, a standard fly on the Suir.

1877. Mr. T. B. Lawes killed a fish of 54 lb. on the Awe, near Dalmally.

1880. An angler killed a fish of 50 lb. on Loch Tay.

1884. The keeper on the Ardoe water of the Dee killed a fish of 57 lb.

1886. Mr. Pryor killed a salmon of $57\frac{1}{2}$ lb. on the Floors water of the Tweed.

1888. The late Mr. E. Frances killed a very handsome fish of $55\frac{1}{2}$ lb. on the Corby water of the Eden.

1889. Mr. Brereton, on Lord Polwarth's Mertoun water on the Tweed, killed a fish of 55 lb. on a small 'Wilkinson' with single gut. An angler on the Scotch Esk caught one of 50 lb. with a small grilse fly ; and Mr. Lowther Bridger also got one of 50 lb. with a small 'Bull Dog' fly and single gut.

1892. Mr. G. Mackenzie got one of 56 lb. on the Warwick Hall water of the Eden, on a small 'Jock Scott,' landing it in fifteen minutes. Colonel Home got one of $51\frac{1}{2}$ lb. on Lord Home's Birgham water on the Tweed, and Lord Winterton got one of 50 lb. on the Gordon Castle water on the Spey.

1893. Mr. Peter Loudon got one of 50½ lb. on the Annan.

1895. Lord Zetland got one of 55 lb. on the Tay.

In addition to these, Mr. Malloch, of Perth, mentions two caught on the Tay, one of 54 lb., caught by Lord Ruthven, and one of 50 lb. by Mr. Clark Jervoise. Mr. Ffennell also records a curious incident connected with a salmon of 51½ lb. taken in the nets on the Wye in 1887. A fly with some gut attached to it was found in his mouth. Dr. Norman of Ross identified this fly as one he had lost in a big fish which he had been playing for a long time some twelve days before. This is a most singular incident, as salmon usually get rid of flies and hooks very soon after they have broken them off.

Mr. Ffennell has certainly done great service to the cause of accuracy by investigating every alleged instance of exceptional weight at the time, and he really merits the title of 'giant killer.' As he rightly states, in a letter to the 'Times,' in April 1887, on a 'bogus' Shannon salmon of 72 lb., unless such false reports are contradicted immediately they appear, many mythical salmon would be handed down and placed on record. Some of the cases, exposed after paragraphs had gone the round of the papers, turned out to be pure invention; many more, hardly less culpable exaggeration. Thus 52 lb. dwindles on examination to 36 lb., 75 lb. to 45, and 51 lb. to 27 lb. This last was an Irish salmon, and the additional weight was tacked on between Banagher and Castle Connell !

CHAPTER VIII

POACHING

THE best friend of the salmon is undoubtedly the fair rod fisherman. Only a modest gleaning falls to his lot out of the ample harvest of the stream ; yet he does far more for the protection of the crop than the tenant of the net fishing, who, like a thriftless farmer who exhausts the soil of his fields, too often looks only to the immediate present, and leaves a wasted heritage to those who come after him. I have, however, said my say upon the legal destruction of our salmon fisheries, and will now devote a few pages to some of the many illegal methods by which fish are destroyed.

The time-honoured pastime of 'burning the water' is, I fear, by no means obsolete, although the law prevents its being carried on so openly as in the days of Scrope and Sir Walter Scott. The vivid description in 'Guy Mannering' must be familiar to most of my readers, and doubtless the 'shirra' had often taken part in proceedings which his successors punish with no undue severity. A salmon was a salmon in those days; and the object was to get them *quocunque modo.* Scrope says, 'A salmon is a fish of passage, and if you do not get him to-day he will be gone to-morrow. You may as well think of preserving herrings or mackerels as these delicious creatures, and there would be no objection to you taking 3,378 salmon at one haul if fortune would so favour you.'

The 'leister' or 'waster' is figured in his pages, and was a formidable weapon resembling a trident, but with five prongs instead of three, with only one barb to each prong, as two would tear the fish too much in extricating them. This weapon was fastened to a pole usually about sixteen feet long, and was used for 'canting' the boat up stream as well as for striking the fish. It was not grasped firmly, but sent loosely through the hands, its own weight in falling being more effective than a strong thrust. The stroke was aimed at the shoulders of the fish, from a vertical position, and the grip was then shortened and the fish lifted head foremost. The boat in use for the purpose was larger and steadier than a rod-fishing boat, and in the centre, near the side, was a pole fixed vertically, with a basket on the top to contain the combustibles, rags steeped in pitch and fragments of tar

barrels. There were 'three men in a boat'; one at
the head and one at the stern as boatmen and
leisterers, and the third in the centre to kill the fish
and trim the fire. A suitable evening was selected
when the water was low : half the country side assisted
as actors or spectators, and carts were brought to take
home the fish—a not unnecessary precaution, as
hundreds were massacred in the course of a single
evening. Our authority states, curiously enough, for the
benefit of the rod fisher, that salmon disturbed in the
night with boats and lights will draw up into the
streams above and take the fly all the better for this
disturbance the following morning. No doubt it must
have been a picturesque sight to see. 'The ruddy light
glared on the rough features and dark dresses of the
leisterers in cutting flames directly met by dark
shadows. Extending itself, it reddened the shelving
rocks above, and glanced upon the blasted arms of
the trees, slowly perishing in their struggle for existence among the stony crevices ; it glowed upon
the hanging wood, on fir, birch, broom, and
bracken, half veiled or half revealed, as they
were more or less prominent. The form of things
remote from the concentrated light was dark and
dubious ; even the trees on the summit of the brae
sank in obscurity.' Great numbers of fish were

taken in a night—more than a hundred is the
number given in 'Guy Mannering,' a 'hundred
and twa' in a portion of the evening described by
Scrope ; and in addition to this massacre no doubt
there were many others which got off the leister,
wounded, to perish miserably. The eels used to
follow the blood and eat the flesh out of the skin—
' You will see the eels by dozens hanging thick on him
like sticks in a bundle of faggots '; and altogether
I sympathise with the feelings of the spectator
described by Scott, who did 'not relish being so
near the agonies of the expiring salmon as they
lay flapping about in the boat, which they mois-
tened with their blood.' It seems to have been
a barbarous performance ; but *autres temps, autres
mœurs,* and it is only fair to add that I have heard
that so famous a rod fisher as the late Sir William
Scott of Ancrum said there was no sport like it. In
addition to these gregarious raids, many fish perished
on the spawning beds by the leisters of individual
poachers—such as Tom Purdie, Sir Walter's attendant, who was great with the ' clodding' or throwing
leister, and whose murder of a 'muckle kipper of
40 lb. on a big redd' is narrated in detail. All this
is of course unlawful now ; but I am afraid that it is
still a common enough method of poaching on the

Tweed and its tributaries, although paraffin is substituted for the tar barrel and ' heather lichts,' and the
' cleik ' or gaff for the leister. Many of the fish which
go up to the spawning beds never return ; and the
gangs who go out to ' burn the water ' are too often
prepared to use violence, and bailiffs and poachers
have met their death, like Grimes in the 'Water
Babies,' in the fierce encounters that have taken place.
Whether from hereditary instinct or traditional in-
struction, the sympathies of the Lowlander are rather
with the poacher than the water bailiff, and the
wanton destruction of fish is not easily punished or
prevented.

Nets of various kinds are used for poaching as
well as for legal fishing, in and out of season : splash
nets, which entangle the fish when they strike them ;
shove nets to take them under the banks or rocks ;
nets to catch them at the salmon leaps, and fine seines
to drag the pools at night from the bank, or a light
boat or coracle, often managed by a single skilful
hand. A poacher resident at Crinan was more than
once caught at night taking salmon in this manner
up the river Add, and his boat was for some time up at
the keeper's house at Poltalloch—a flat-bottomed skiff
with outriggers, rather like a duck shooter's punt ;
but although it certainly was never used for any

M

legitimate object, the authorities were unable to condemn it as an implement of poaching, and it had to be returned to its owner. He was fined rather heavily more than once ; but a single night's success, unfortunately, goes a long way towards providing the means of paying the legal penalties inflicted, and I hardly think the authorities are sufficiently severe on professional and systematic river marauders. I was rather amused at the description of his experience given me by a keeper in the Border country the other day. The poachers he had caught had, in his opinion, got off too lightly, until one night he came upon a man burning the water on his beat, who after a struggle was rescued by a second, who put my informant into the river. Far from being annoyed, he said to them, ' Now I know your faces, and I have got a good case against you.' What amused me most in his description was his threat to the fiscal. ' I told him that if he did not imprison them this time, *I would never bring a case before him again.*' Whether in consequence of this awful threat, or on the merits of the case, his assailants on the occasion referred to got three months' imprisonment.

Otters and cross-lines with a number of flies and minnows are objectionable, not only for the destruction they cause but for the number of fish they prick and

POACHING

frighten ineffectually. Another, and even worse method
of poaching, is snatching or stroke hauling. This
cruel and barbarous practice of sinking a weighted
triangle or triangles in some place where salmon lie
thick, and jerking it through the water till it catches
in some part of a fish, is, unfortunately, only too
common and well known. Numbers of fish escape,
lacerated and torn, and the tackle is usually so
strong that little play is given by the struggles of
those landed. Yet, in some parts of Ireland
especially, 'sportsmen' may be seen in rows manipu-
lating a bunch of weighted triangles through a shoal
of salmon—sometimes with a prawn or minnow
attached to them as a colourable pretext for the
proceeding. This is done, not occasionally and to
obtain a fish for the pot in low water, but in the
name of sport, and to provide amusement for the
perpetrators ! I confess I should like to see some of
these 'gentlemen' severely punished, as I sympathise
far more with the poor man who poaches for gain or
food than with such desecrators of the gentle name
of sport.

In Scrope's time these snatching implements were
known as rake-hooks, and he avers that 'most fishermen were provided with the tackle.' 'It consists of
two strong hooks about two or three inches long tied

back to back, and fastened to twisted gut, on which
are put five or six large shot at equal distances from
one another   The fisherman, with a strong rod,
throws the line with these bare hooks attached to it
about a foot beyond any salmon that he may discover
lying, and then with a sudden jerk draws the hook
into him if he can, and gets him to the land if he is
able.'   I fear the 'Rake's progress' was frequently
over the spawning beds, as he calmly adds : ' Clean
fish are *sometimes* taken in this manner.'   His method
of spearing fish in low water on a bright day is
elaborately described under the title of 'Sunlight ' in
the tenth chapter of his book.   Indeed, I hardly
know any sort of poaching which he does not describe
and countenance, except the curious practice of spearing salmon on horseback described in ' Red Gauntlet.'
He tells us that 'vast numbers are captured in this
manner, *i.e.* by "sunning," particularly in the upper part
of the Tweed,' but the scene of the raid which he
describes in detail is, as I have mentioned elsewhere,
the Craigover Boat hole on the Mertoun water, close
to Melrose. With a man clever with the leister standing
in the water at the head of the stream to strike the
fish which endeavour to pass out of it into another
cast, and nets spread about in every direction, just
avoiding the illegality of barring the river by stretch-

ing one quite across, they routed about and frightened
the fish till they lay half stupefied under or beside the
rocks and stones. The poor creatures were then
speared from a boat, not worked broadside in front as
in burning the water, for 'one artist is sufficient for the
amusement.' Many escaped wounded, for 'if you do
not strike a fish near the centre of his body, you are
never very sure of lifting him.' 'Begin at the lower
part of the river that belongs to you, so that you may
again come across those fish that escape upwards. If
the river continues low for some time, disturbed fish
will be continually coming forward, and you may go
over your water two or three times at different periods,
till you have caught nearly every fish that takes up
his seat in it.'

Here I take leave of Scrope, whom, but for the
allowance necessarily made for the times, I should
regard—much as I do Benvenuto Cellini after reading
his confessions of hardly less heinous iniquities—as a
delightful rogue, but one who richly merited the
gallows. However, as an Eton boy in my school-days
translated the line of Horace—'Delicta majorum
immeritus lues,' 'The delights of our ancestors were
unmitigated filth '—and I do not doubt that he was a
fair and even sportsmanlike product of the early part
of the century now drawing to an end. At the close

of the chapter just quoted, he gives the sound advice :
'Keep close time strictly ; kill no spawning fish ;
tamper not with foul ones of any sort ; preserve the
fry.'

A skilful poacher can sometimes gaff numbers of
fish in a narrow passage or by a fall. Many salmon
also fall victims to a variety of implements in the
upper pools of small rivers which speedily run low
even after a heavy spate. They are unable to escape,
and pitchforks, rakes, and even scythes suffice to
destroy them, as well as instruments of destruction
especially manufactured for the purpose. In deep
holes ruffled by the wind, a water telescope is sometimes employed to discover their whereabouts.

I am not concerned to defend any form of poaching, but the most venial form of that offence, in my
opinion, is the occasional capture of a fish with the
fly in low water in a river entirely your own—*volenti
non fit injuria* ; but I am here referring to a fly affixed
to the lips of the salmon by other methods than those
of mere coaxing and persuasion. No one is bound
to criminate himself, and I have 'hardly ever' been
guilty of such an offence. But I have heard of many
parties after a long drought irresistibly attracted to
the water side, and of deeds of doubtful legality
achieved with the luncheon-paper fly, so called

because a small piece of paper was attached to the barb of the ' Captain ' or ' Jock Scott ' to indicate its whereabouts. Frightened salmon, as Scrope mentions, take refuge under stones or clods, and I remember one noted fisherman, who ought to have known better, promising a certain lady that she should catch a fish, and actually with his fingers putting the hook attached to her line into the fish's mouth as it sheltered close to the bank. Sometimes such crimes were justly punished ; and one leader of society may recall an occasion when the bank gave way with her, and she was precipitated into a pool amid shouts of merriment from the unfeeling spectators, and the difficulties entailed by the process of drying her dripping garments and providing her with an impromptu rig-out. But I only mention these shocking occurrences in order to stamp them with my condemnation. We were young then, and the century, alas ! a good deal younger than it is now, and no doubt such things are never done by our more enlightened and respectable children.

A curious collection of salmon-poaching implements, exhibited at the International Fisheries Exhibition of 1883 by Mr. Henry Ffennell, was one of the great attractions of that successful show. Although it contained no models, all the implements shown

having been taken by water-bailiffs or keepers from
marauders taken red-handed, it numbered several hundred exhibits. Among these were quantities of spears
or leisters, with every number of prongs from nine to
two, some with barbs and some without. But the
favourite poaching weapon was shown to be the gaff or
' cleik,' which is easier to carry and conceal than the
leister, and quite as effective. The collection contained
no less than two hundred and forty of these implements,
all seized along the Usk and Ebbw. Some of these had
as many as eight barbed hooks upon them, and one,
used in the River Cleddy, had a handle 25 feet long.
There were also a large number of snatches, or rake-
hooks, one of which, shown from the Derwent River,
was worked by a rope between two men, and had an
oyster-shell at the end to attract the fish. A number
of lamps, from the most primitive dark lanterns to
an elaborate naphtha torch with a metal case, which
could be flared up, darkened, or extinguished with
great rapidity, formed part of the same interesting
collection. Several of these exhibits were figured and
described in the *Illustrated London News* of Aug. 18,
1883.

A poacher may sometimes be a friend in need.
My brother, Colonel C. Gathorne-Hardy, was once
fishing the Blackwater from a garden terrace, when he

hooked a salmon. He had no attendant, and had no chance to beach his fish, as he was four or five feet above the water. A man opposite, seeing his difficulty, shouted to him, 'Will I come across, your honour?' My brother remarked that it was a long way round, when the man swam across, dressed as he was, and producing a gaff from some mysterious recess in his dripping garments, soon landed the fish. 'Sure, I could see your honour was a true sportsman,' said Pat, 'and if it had been fifty thousand fathoms deep, I would have come across just the same.' He retreated by the same route, gladdened with a small donation, and no questions asked ; but I fear that he carried that pocket gaff for no legitimate purpose, and that it might well have formed an exhibit in the Ffennell museum.

CHAPTER IX

PISCATOR AND VENATOR

LOCHIEL, in the introductory chapter on deer-stalking
of the volume on the Red Deer, which he contributed
to this series, institutes a comparison between the
four pre-eminent British sports—deer-stalking, grouse-
shooting, salmon-fishing, and fox-hunting—naturally
to the advantage of his own favourite pursuit. Small
wonder that the Laird of Achnacarry, bred and nurtured
in the heart of the forest, should firmly hold and
stoutly maintain such an opinion ; but I think that he
hardly does justice to the votaries of the other sports
enumerated, by the arguments he puts into their
mouths. I should perhaps be going outside my subject
if I were to take up the cudgels for the fowler and fox-
hunter ; but it is quite in accordance with the precedent
of the earliest and most famous works on fishing that
Venator and Piscator should hold a conference on
paper, each commending his own recreation. In the
book of St. Albans, Dame Juliana Berners makes a

comparison of the various sports, giving the reasons for her preference of angling. 'Huntynge is toe laboryous, for the hunter must always renne and folowe his houndes : traueyllynge and swetynge full sore, and blowynge tyll his lyppes blyster.' 'Hawkynge is laboryous and noyouse also as me seemeth.' 'Fowlynge is greuous.' But the 'angler maye haue no cold nor dysease nor angre, but if he be causer hymself. For he may not lese at the moost, but a lyne or an hoke . . . and other greyffes may he not haue, sauynge but yf ony fysshe breke away after that he is take on the hoke, or elles that he catch nought.' A dialogue on the same topic forms the opening chapter of the 'Compleat Angler,' and, like my prototype, ' I accuse nobody ; for, as I would not make a watery discourse, so I would not put too much vinegar into it, nor would I raise the reputation of my own art, by the diminution or ruin of another's.'

Lochiel enumerates certain tests by which to try each of these sports separately, taking as the first 'the degree of pleasure derived from success.'

This test no doubt is a fair one, but the human temperament varies so infinitely that it is not very easy of application. There are some misguided individuals who enjoy a public dinner or a charity bazaar, and who would rather hear the sound of

their own voices than catch a salmon as big as the one
which got away from Mr. Bromley-Davenport on the
Rauma in Norway. But taking the test to be what
ought to give pleasure to reasonable beings, and
leaving such lost souls as I have referred to out of
the question, I submit that it is hardly fair to
compare the 'aggregate amount of pleasure derived
from capturing ten or a dozen salmon' to the
'supreme happiness of standing over a splendid
royal.' If you are going in for numbers, compare
ordinary fish with stags just worth a shot; if you go
in for quality, balance a record fish with the 'splendid
royal.' There are small stags as well as large ones,
and my limited experience tends to persuade me that
the ordinary stalker as a rule has to put up with
moderate animals. This no doubt enhances the
pleasure of a great and exceptional success in the
forest; but why should not the fortunate captor of a
monster fish be equally delighted with his triumph?
I not only admit the existence of the spirit of rivalry
to which Lochiel 'alludes in a whisper,' but assert
that it is the salt of sport, adding with diffidence that
it is as present in the forest as by the stream. The
deer-stalker likes to beat the record established by
his predecessors in quantity, weight, size, and quality
of head and number of points. A like ambition,

mutatis mutandis, actuates the fisherman, and, unless
it leads to any jealous and underhand advantages
taken over a competitor, it is surely justifiable and
even laudable. And it may be noted that it is much
easier to be sure that the conditions of the competition are fair in fishing than in deer-stalking. Such
salmon as his beat contains are at the disposal of the
angler to catch if he can ; but it is by no means so
certain that the stalker will give all visitors a chance
of shooting an exceptionally fine stag, even if he spies
one. Big salmon are 'here to-day and gone to-
morrow,' and an exceptionally large fish is never
specially preserved for a favoured guest or the Laird
himself ; but in some places it is not everyone who is
allowed a chance at the modern representatives of
Club-foot or the 'Muckle Hart of Benmore.' Again,
it is usually more difficult to land a very heavy fish
than one of moderate size. The mere weight and
bulk tell on the tackle and the hold, and it is not
only on account of the lying propensities of anglers
that the biggest salmon get away : but a monster stag
is no more difficult to approach than a small one,
and presents an even larger mark for the rifle.
Another advantage that I claim for fishing is that,
whereas it is always something gained to catch even
a very small grilse, it may be that when you have

somewhat doubtfully shot at a stag and killed him,
you may find that he is one that it would have been
better to have allowed to grow for another year or
two on the hill, and you return with your victim
strapped on the pony rather apologetic than
triumphant. Although it is the stalker's business to
settle whether you are to shoot at a stag or not when
you are in a friend's forest, he is generally amiably
anxious to give you a shot; and instances have been
known where infanticide has been the result of his undue confidence in the incapacity of a visitor to hold his
rifle straight. There is a well-known anecdote of a
guest at a forest who during his stay was almost daily
given a shot at a small beast which regularly frequented a particular corrie not very far from the
lodge. Later in the season a more skilful professor
had his day in the forest. He watched the stalker
spying the ground, and when the long and deliberate
survey was over and the glass shut up, asked if any
deer had been seen. 'Hoot,' was the answer, 'just
nothing but that wee bit deevil, "Charlie Blake."'
The little beast had acquired the name of the gentleman (not the one in the text) to whose inaccuracy
of aim he owed his life—but it might well have
happened that a chance bullet had ended his career.

It is always a pleasure to catch a fish at all; but

the great days are those on which you catch a larger
number of salmon, a greater aggregate weight, or a
bigger fish than you have ever caught before ; and if
you also have done better in any respect than anyone
has ever been known to do previously on the par-
ticluar water you are fishing, it undeniably adds zest
to your triumph.   The phrase 'beating the record ' is
of modern origin, and rather jars upon my ear, but
the desire

αἰὲν ἀριστεύειν καὶ ὑπείροχος ἔμμεναι ἀλλῶν

is at least as old as Homer. I have never myself
kept a formal fishing register, although I have from
time to time jotted down the weights and numbers
caught on special occasions, in my pocket Almanack,
and I am sorry for my neglect. Such sporting
memoranda are interesting to look back upon, and,
when they relate to the forest or the river, unobjec-
tionable.

    ' But,' says Lochiel, ' take as the next test the
disappointment resulting from a bad day. Here
salmon-fishing may be put out of court. No one
will deny that an absolutely blank day's fishing is a
disappointment unmitigated by any other circumstances attendant on the sport   The fisherman has
been engaged in monotonous exertion all day long,
and experiences the sensation of having wasted his

time as completely as if he had been using a pair of
dumb-bells.'

Here I join issue altogether. If it were true that
blank days deserved this sweeping condemnation it
would be almost fatal to the claims of salmon-fishing
as an amusement ; but I utterly deny it. Many a
time have I started for the river, sometimes with high
expectations, sometimes almost on a forlorn hope,
and come back empty-handed indeed, but having
thoroughly enjoyed my outing. Monotonous ! Why?
All day long the shifting panorama of nature passed
before my eyes ; the birds, the flowers, the ferns, like
living actors, played their parts for my edification ; or
if I must confine my attention to points more strictly
relating to the sport itself, no two pools, no two
motions of the rod—I had almost said, no two
sensations of the six or eight hours spent by the
water side—were the exact counterparts the one of
the other. But let me describe one or two ' blank
days.' I have many to choose from, and the reader
may judge whether it is true that they present no
features of interest, but merely a ' monstrous cantle '
carved from the too brief space of an autumn holiday.

Take first in order the instance which is most
antagonistic to my argument, namely, the day when
all conditions are apparently favourable, and I have

started in the morning with the highest hopes ; all
the previous afternoon the rain came down in torrents,
and I could hear the trickle of the water from
the eaves when I went to bed ; but when I rose in
the morning the sky was clear, with a few flying
clouds and a strong breeze ; the roofs were dry, and
it was evident that the storm moderated long before
the morning, and that by ten o'clock—quite late
enough for a start on such an occasion—the river
would have had seven or eight hours to run down.
Had I been the lessee of a beat on the Tweed, Tay,
or Dee, or any large river, I should have been con-
demned to inaction, or some other form of sport, for
a day or two after such a spate ; but the little West
Coast stream by whose banks fate had fixed my
residence for the time being was fed by mountain
torrents and deep sheep drains, and fell as rapidly as
it rose. The upper pools—and these were the most
interesting to fish, and when in order the most productive—were sometimes too high to fish one day
and too low the next ; but on this day I was in no
doubt whither to go, and all impatience to make a
start. What a long time the lazy servants seemed
bringing the breakfast ! But if I could not control
their movements, I was at all events master of my
own, and I gobbled down my food with a rapidity

N

which would have made my respected medical ad-
viser's hair stand on end, had he been there to see ;
but the next few hours would, at all events, be an
antidote against dyspepsia. Long before the dogcart
drove round I was 'booted and spurred' and cursing
the dilatory groom, although the poor man was not to
blame, as a reference to my watch and the stable
clock convinced me. The two or three miles which
divided me from the nearest point of the river were
finished at last ; and as I passed over the bridge I
saw by the stone on my left, over which the water
just broke, that the height was all right, and the
colour spoke for itself—of course also favourably.
Another mile, a second bridge, and another inspection, and we pulled up at last at a gate by a field,
opposite to which, about a hundred yards off, the
river took a sharp turn under the wooded brae of
Kirnan. I almost raced across the field—my little
terrier partaking of my eagerness,—and began to put
my rod together, taking rather longer than usual in
consequence of my hurry to commence operations ;
for certainly in fishing the proverb ' More haste, worse
speed,' holds good. At my feet the river ran dark
but clear ; a splash or two broke the surface while
my preparations were completing. I approached the
top of the pool—and now I let the curtain fal on

Act I. The fish might sulk, the sky might alter, the
river might wax, but nothing could deprive me of
those two hours of excitement and pleasant expecta
tion ; nor would they have been any pleasanter if
subsequently I had attained the greatest success. I
was on the brink of the unknown, but the past has
been irrevocably mine.

Act II.—The first few throws are more to wet
the line and straighten the cast than for any other
purpose. Of course, I begin higher up the stream
than any fish would be likely to go ; but, in such
high water, they may rise very near the head of the
pool, and, at any rate, I will make sure that I miss no
chance. How well the fly looks as it plays in the
dancing rapids ! Surely no sensible fish can decline
such a temptation. Now I am getting down to a
stone just under an overhanging alder bush, and my
heart beats quicker as I recognise the scene of many
past successes. How often has a salmon taken my
fly within a yard—nay, a foot—of that very spot ! It
is a little far, the wind is wrong, and the bush awkward, and if my hook catches in a bough I shall have
to break or go round nearly half a mile ; yet I must
venture all, for I know that the fish rises just under
the opposite bank. My next cast is a failure ; I have
miscalculated the distance or not allowed enough for

the wind ; but I just manage, by a quick movement
of the wrist, to save myself from catching the bush,
and the next time the ' Blue Doctor ' goes straight and
true, as I intended, and falls fairly lightly—not that
that signifies much – almost to an inch on the spot I
aimed at.   How carefully I bring the point of the rod
round, how cautiously I work it, how eagerly I watch
the spot where the fly circles across and down the
stream !   The fish does not come this time, nor the
next, nor at all ; but I have had the pleasure of my
successful casts.   I have overcome difficulties, small
ones it is true, but real for all that ; I have hoped
with good reason, and exercised memory and judgment.   Then I wander down the stream to the next
cast, noting, as I pass the shallow water, any pools
which seem in process of formation—for the course of
the river is by no means stereotyped—and trying a
cast or two where it looks as if there was a possible
chance.   At each regular pool my hopes revive, as I
cannot believe that the salmon will display the dis-
graceful apathy which has marked their conduct
hitherto.   Here a rock, there a bush, reminds me of
former successes and inspires me with renewed excitement.   At last, as I still fail to stir a fish, I try to
find a reason for their sluggishness.   Sky and water
have seemed all that I could desire when I came out ;

but it is hard if I cannot find something wrong in one
or other, when the event has proved that there must
be. It is too clear overhead, or there is a glare or
the mist is lower than it ought to be ; but it will be
better presently. At last, when I reach my destination,
and find the dogcart waiting for me at Dunadd Bridge,
I determine that there must be more bad weather
coming, and that I may look forward to a real big
flood and a record day to compensate me for the
blank one, which after all has passed the time
pleasantly enough.

Or take a day not so disappointing as the one
I have just described, because I never expected to
catch anything. There has been no rain, the sun is
shining and there is not even a strong breeze at
present, and the veriest tyro could see that there was
little chance, if any, of catching a salmon. What
then ! there is a magnetic attraction about the running water which somehow draws me to its banks.
It is so long since I have had a day's fishing that I
must wet a line and look at the pools, although I
know it is not much use. A trout rod will do all the
casting required, so I shall not have to break my back
or strain my arms ; and, with fine gut and small flies,
who knows but that the impossible may happen, as it
has done more than a few times in my experience ?

Nothing is more certain than that you will not catch fish unless you try ; but there are scarcely any conditions, except a really ' waxing' water after the first half-hour of the flood, under which an exceptional success has not occurred to baffle expectation and encourage perseverance.   But I am precluded by the rules of the argument from catching a salmon on the present occasion ; I hardly know whether I am justified in seeing one, but I cannot help it.   Here, as I pass the Herd-boy's pool, the water is like glass and I can see ten or a dozen shadowy forms flitting like ghosts over the bottom.   One or two of them are of exceptional size, and I feel a certain amount of complacency at resisting the temptation to acquire one by illegitimate means.   They will certainly not rise to-day ; but it would not be beyond the resources of science for an unconscientious man to get hold of one.   So I pass on, merely noting that the bottom has altered considerably since I fished it twelve months ago.   There is hardly a foot of water where I rose the 14-pounder, and what was a shallow a little lower down has deepened and washed out into a promising hole.   I shall not forget this when this part of the river is next in order, and fill my mental note-book with similar ground plans of the various pools as I pass down the river.   Here and there the stream runs fairly strong, or there is a good curl on the water just where the breeze catches it, and I try my luck without success : but I am quite at peace with mankind when I return in the evening, and I have acquired a stock of knowledge which I hope will serve me in good stead on some future and more auspicious occasion. Those who fish a West Highland river, with crumbling and undermined banks, cannot rely upon tradition to tell them where to cast their fly ; the fickle stream thinks nothing of filling a ten-foot hole with gravel, or bringing a few tons of peaty bank down with a splash to turn the current and make new resting-places for the salmon at the bottom of the water.

I have purposely abstained from any allusion to scenery or natural history in my brief sketch of two blank days, because I desired to combat the suggestion that even the most unsuccessful salmon-fishing at all resembled dumb-bell exercise ; but the true fisherman finds many delights in his occupation apart from the mere capture of fish. Like the deer-stalker, he takes his exercise 'in the purest of atmospheres, among the grandest scenery in Britain.'

Not very long ago it was my privilege to be a fellow guest with Lochiel himself, in perhaps the most beautiful place in all Scotland, where both pursuits can be carried out in perfection—Braemore, the

Highland home of Sir John Fowler. Certainly the
views from Ben Dearig Ben Lear, of the exquisitely
shaped Dundonell Hills, Loch Broom, and the
wilderness of fairy islands at its mouth, are a dream
of beauty : but a like charm attaches to the beautiful
river which dashes through gorges and over boulders
at the foot of the brae. How lovely are the slopes
above in all the glory of their autumn clothing of
bracken and birch !

From the beautiful pool where one first casts a
fly, to the place where the river joins the sea, there is
not a spot where it would not be a pleasure to loiter,
even without a rod in hand. There is to me a fascination in a rushing stream which justifies the old
legend that all evil things are powerless to pass across
running water—the very sight washes the cobwebs
from the brain ; and if one cannot watch the red deer
in a state of nature as one may do in the corries
above, the pugnacious stags and the sentinel hinds,
the eagles soaring round the peaks, and the ptarmigan
crooning among the stones, it is no slight pleasure to
study the habits of the more homely creatures which
haunt the river and its banks. One comes suddenly
right upon an old heron first motionless in a shallow,
then blundering off with hasty flight and discordant
cry when it realises the presence of an intruder ; the

ubiquitous dipper gives his jerky skirt-dancing performance. Occasionally one may still see the king-
fisher, even in the Highlands, dart away like a bar of
living turquoise ; the merganser convoys her numerous
progeny up the pool ; even that inveterate poacher,
the otter, shy though he be, occasionally permits me
to get a glimpse at his movements ; or the roe stands
to stare from some opening among the birches, while
far above tower the mist-capped peaks not less picturesque from below than when distance no longer lends
enchantment to the view.

Taking next the element of weather, Lochiel con-
tends that as regards the comfort or discomfort of
pursuing any particular form of sport in bad weather,
there is not much to choose. Here I again cannot
agree with him. I do not doubt from his high
authority, confirmed as it is by my own slight experience, that more deer are likely to be killed on a wet,
stormy day than upon a fine one ; but it requires
youth and enthusiasm to enjoy facing the discomforts
of a Highland storm on an exposed hillside, to crawl
through heather, bog, and grass wringing with mois-
ture, and then wait for the deer to rise, wet to the
skin, and with chattering teeth and frozen fingers, in a
bleak north-easter. I am far from saying that the
final triumph does not fully compensate one for these

drawbacks, but as a mere question of comfort, which
is all with which I am dealing at present, how far
preferable is the state of the salmon-fisher, supposing
him to be pursuing his craft under like conditions of
wind and rain? With mackintosh and waders he
laughs at the elements. Even on the coldest and
wettest day of early spring fishing he can keep himself warm and dry, if he has but taken the common-
sense precaution to suit his clothing to the requirements of the season—indeed, I am not sure that
there is not a satisfaction in the sensation that the
tempest is beating upon you in vain. Let me briefly
state a few more points in which Piscator has an
advantage over Venator. He is independent; he
need not, if he knows his river, take even a gillie with
him; at any rate he can pursue his own bent, and does
do so if he has had any considerable experience, without further deference to his attendant than a friendly
consultation as to flies, the best places to fish, and
the like. But in the forest, in ninety-nine cases out
of a hundred, you are a mere automaton in the hands
of a stalker. He it is who conceives the plan of
campaign, and executes it from start to finish, sometimes not even communicating to the novice the
reasons for the movements he has blindly imitated to
the best of his ability, until he withdraws the rifle

from its case, points out the stag, and tells him to
'take time.'   And then supposing that an easy chance
is missed, or, still worse, that a stag is wounded and
escapes to die a lingering death, what moment is
there in the fisherman's experience to compare with
the utter misery of such a failure ?   One may lose a
salmon and possibly suspect that it is one's own fault,
although it is not very often that one can trace one's
loss directly and certainly to any sin of omission or
commission ; but at least one has the assurance that the
fish is none the worse, that if he has taken your fly he
will have soon extracted the hook by a simple surgical
operation with the assistance of some rock at the
bottom of the pool, and will be ready for another
tussle in a day or two if you should have the good
luck to encounter him again.   It is a disagreeable
moment, no doubt, when the line comes back slack
after an hour or more with what is, of course, the fish
of the season, but I usually feel that it is *kismet*, and
recover my equanimity after a very brief interval of
lamentation.

Another advantage I claim for fishing is that
it can be, and is, pursued up to extreme old age.   A
few veterans like Horatio Ross have continued to
go deer-stalking very late in life ; but I have myself
known scores once devoted to that sport who have

entirely given it up at a comparatively early period.
There are not many in the sixties who can face all
weathers, and crawl among the peat hags and through
burns, regardless of possibilities of gout and rheumatism, or press up the brae face without a good
many sobs confessing their toil.   An occasional day
on the hill is enough for many for whom the brief
season was all too short a few years ago ; but I hardly
ever knew a true fisherman who did not become, if possible, more devoted to his sport with advancing years.
The skill and judgment which come with long practice
and ripe experience make up for a considerable
diminution of muscular activity and youthful energy.
The three typical fishermen of my own acquaintance,
whom I have celebrated in an earlier chapter, could
still hold their own on Tweed and Ness with almost
any competitors when the youngest of them was over
seventy, and were never so happy as with a rod in
their hands. Salmon have been caught from a
pony's back or a bath chair ; but although I have
read of a paralysed sportsman who succeeded in killing
deer from a litter carried by two bearers, I have always
thought it rather an example of cheerful perseverance
under difficulties than actually representative of deer-
stalking in any true sense of the word.

     But enough of argument, which, like Lochiel, I

have rather used as a means of urging the merits of one form of sport than with any hope of converting the devotees of others. There are so many enthusiasts already competing for the limited amount of fishing still to be had for love, money, or trouble, that I have no desire to dragoon any reluctant sportsman into their ranks. Nor do I wish to depreciate the grand sport of deer-stalking, which fully deserves all the praise bestowed upon it. To be candid, what I really believe is that the great charm of sport is variety, and that the ideal place for an autumn holiday is one where hardly two consecutive days are spent alike, but where you can go from the river to the moor, from the moor to the forest, and from the forest to the yacht, deriving health, distraction, and recreation from each form of sport in turn.

CHAPTER X

THE salmon is the king of fresh-water fishes, though
it is run hard by its cousin the sea-trout. Nor are we
concerned to settle, the question of precedence with
the turbot, the prince of the pure fishes of the sea,
which Brillat-Savarin has glorified in the memorable
anecdote, when he cooked a monster in a washing-
house boiler, to the delight of a select gathering of
gourmets. It is true that Russians swear by the
sterlet, a miniature edition of the mighty sturgeon, the
pièce de prédilection of the Nijni Novgorod restaurants,
when the commerce of the East gathers thither for the
Fair. We remember how the magnificent Monte
Cristo, with the somewhat vulgar ostentation of a
nouveau riche, showed his guests the tanks in which
his sterlets had travelled from the Volga to the Seine,
at the famous banquet at Auteuil, which was the pre-

lude to the tragedy of revenge. But the sterlet, though rich, is rare—a local delicacy limited to the affluents of the Caspian and Black Seas, and all the Westerns generally know of it is by the periodical remittances of caviare. As for the salmon, it is to be found in abundance wherever there are cold waters and cool climates. Indeed, it is almost as prolific as the herring ; and though it does not swim about in shoals, it would multiply so as to become a nuisance were it not for the hosts of finned and feathered enemies that prey voraciously on the spawn and the smolts. As it is, in the lower waters of Alaskan rivers the banks are malarious through the short, hot summers, with the piles of decaying salmon cast up by the floods. Yet the Indians do their utmost to abate the plague by gorging on them when they come in fresh-run from the sea and half-starving, on them when smoked, through the long, dark winters. Canning factories on the shores of Alaska and Labrador give an air of busy industry to oases in that bleak desolation ; and through the provision merchants and co-operative stores, the salmon of the sub-Arctic floods is made as cheap and common as the board-like *bacalao* which taxes the *dura ilia* of the Portuguese.

Yet, though we are glad to think that the salmon has become a luxury of the poor, he is likewise, and

will always be, a delicacy of the rich.   We are far from
saying that size is in itself a recommendation.   On
the contrary, in our opinion, he is never in greater
perfection than in 6 lb. or 8 lb. grilse.   But whenever a portentous fish comes to town, he not only
figures on the slabs of some fashionable fishmonger,
but is glorified in special paragraphs in the journals,
as if he were some star of song or a Christianised
heathen potentate.   When the papers are chronicling
the events of the past year, the monster salmon have
their obituary memorials with statesmen and the
distinguished lights of science.   For the most part
the mighty departed have been netted in Tweed or
Tay ; and Scotland, the land of the mountain and the
flood, is *par excellence* among European countries the
home of the salmon.   Indeed, Scotland would be the
ideal Paradise of the fish were it not for the cruives,
which blockade the upper waters and deny him fair
play with the angling sportsman.   Even the alderman
and gourmand may sympathise with his wrongs, for
the firmness and richness of the flaky flesh comes of
constant exercise and hard condition.   Naturally he is
an athlete in highest training, and his vaulting ambition might take *Excelsior* for its motto.   The most
affectionately domesticated of all living creatures, his
marvellous instincts bring him ever back to his birth-

place. Nothing short of sheer impossibility will bar
the rush of his homely affections. Follow him in his
progress up some rapid Scottish stream. He will wait
in fretted impatience in some stagnant back-water till
the sluices in the cruives are opened of a Sunday.
Then unsabbatically he spends what should be the
day of rest in super-salmonic efforts to make up for
lost time. He splashes up shallows in sun or starlight,
making the water fly behind him in silvery spray. He
faces the foaming and flashing cascades ; and he
climbs artificial ladders, let down to assist him, with
the agility of a monkey. See him in low water below
the half-submerged reef, locally known as the 'Salmon
Leap.' He makes the effort to bound over again and
again, bending himself together tail to head, like a bird
shooting arrow-like upwards from the bow's elasticity.
Of course, if the efforts are indefinitely baulked by
protracted drought and the shrinking water, he falls
back in the sulks, losing heart and condition. Consequently he is only in prime order when he is coming
in clean-run from the sea, or coasting the stake nets
in his quest for the natal stream, when he is
striving to rid himself of the parasitical sea lice which
are the sure signs of his excellence. Later in the
season, after idling away existence in pools that are
prisons, with no serious pre-occupation but family

O

cares, the silvery sea rover that shot up beneath the
bridges at Perth or Berwick ; that faced the swift rush
of the Spey or surmounted the raging cataracts of
Findhorn, losing spirit, subsides into a moping kelt,
with scales as ruddy as a fox's fur, and becomes altogether unfit for human food.

England has good rivers as well as Scotland ; and
Ireland would have another undeniable grievance if
the salmon of the Erne, the Shannon, and the Blackwater were ranked beneath the fish from the sister
islands. There are connoisseurs and salesmen who
profess to discriminate ; but we greatly question a
subtlety of palate which reminds one of the rival
wine-tasters in ' Don Quixote.' We understand
drawing the broad and easy distinctions between fish
from the rapid rivers of the North and the clear waters
of West Ireland, and those caught in the streams that
meander through muddy lowlands. But we doubt
whether the finest expert can discriminate between
the salmon of the Severn and that taken in the Avon
at Christchurch. The question is complicated by considerations of season, condition, packing, and keeping.
What we do know is that in England, and even in the
Tay and Tweed, industry and commercial activity have
been injurious or fatal to salmon breeding for the
table. The fish that clings to hereditary haunts must

often pay the inevitable penalty. The pools he must
pass above the harbour mouth have been converted
by sewage and the shipping into cesspools. As he
ascends, he swallows the diluted products of iron-
works, dyeworks, paper mills, and pestilential alkali
factories. In fact, when brought to bank by rod or
net, he is an animated filter, having assimilated,
thanks to a sound constitution, all manner of dele-
terious abominations. Still, like a disreputable pro-
digal, he may keep up a decent appearance, and the
wary buyer may be let in, unless he can trust his fishmonger ; but happily these medicated fish are much
in the minority, so that there are long odds against
blood-poisoning or unpleasant but less serious con-
sequences.   .

There is little to be said about foreign salmon,
though not a few are imported from Holland, and
many more from Sweden, Norway, and Russia.
Scandinavian salmon run to a great size and are
decidedly coarser than our own. The Rhine salmon
are, or used to be, very good, but the Rhine has been
foully polluted, like Thames or Tyne, with the industrial expansion of Imperial Germany. The pools
below the romantic rocks of the legendary Lurlei
used to yield 6,000 lb. a year to the fishermen of
St. Goar and Goarhausen. Now, we believe, the annual

produce is barely a third of that. But the so-called Rhine salmon is greatly appreciated on the Continent; the innumerable hotels keep up the price, and it commands nearly half-a-crown a pound. We confess to having very pleasant associations with it, enjoying it on each annual arrival on the Continent, looking out on the ' exulting and abounding river ' from a window in the old Englischer Hof or the Hôtel de Hollande, before the great caravanserai of the Nord had engulphed the rush of English. We always associate it there with the apposite *sauce Hollandaise,* and with that queer topaz-coloured vinegar in the cruets which seems to be a *spécialité* of Germany. Though, by the way, unless the salmon were somewhat stale, it would be sacrilege to taint the silky *sauce Hollandaise* with vinegar. We have eaten salmon in Paris often enough, though never in perfection. Still, the accompanying *sauce verte* at Lédoyen's in the Champs Elysées will always linger a haunting memory.

But after all, as good wine needs no bush, so good salmon should be served sauceless, and only with the water in which it is boiled. The veritable *sauce piquante* is memory and association. The cut or cutlet sends you back on the old tracks of sport or touring. To the classic Tweed, from Clovenford, dear to the Ettrick Shepherd, down to the long bridge

of Berwick, past Ashestiel and Abbotsford, Dryburgh
and Melrose, with all the phantom forms fancy
summons up, from Scott and Scrope down to Tom
Purdie and Rob Kerse. On the Tay from Taymouth,
where Eachin MacIan was inaugurated chief of the
Clan Quhele, when, by the way, the Tay salmon
figured in barbaric profusion, down to the Palace of
Scone, and past Campsie Linn, where Lord Hunting-
don wished himself back when sick of playing the
courtier. To the Spey, that too often flows crystal-
clear, though draining half the watershed of the
Grampians, perpetually shifting pools and gravel-
banks towards the estuary, or to the still swifter
Findhorn with its heronry and single-arched bridges,
a smaller but more unbridled torrent than the Loire,
for its rushes after heavy rainfall would burst any
barrier of cruives. Or to the Aberdeenshire Dee, with
its gravelly bed, sweeping round the royal residence
of Balmoral, and beneath the clean-stemmed giants
skirting the Forest of Ballochbuie. So we might
follow the fancy to Ireland—to Gweedore, beneath
the glistening cone of Errigal and beyond the sugges-
tively named Bloody Foreland ; to famed Ballyshannon
on the beautiful Erne, where Lord Castlereagh was
scared by the spectral apparition ; to Galway town,
where the passing pedestrian sees the salmon jostling

each other below the bridge ; to the Shannon at
Castle Connel and Killaloe, the birthplace of Phineas
Phinn : and by a coincidence Trollope's brilliant
political *parvenu* bears the name of a celebrated
Edinburgh rod-maker. Nor dare we go on to the
Blackwater or cross over to the Severn, although the
ingredients of that ' memory sauce ' are inexhaustible,
and in them is a *prononcé* flavour of the actual and
prosaic. We recall the simple *impromptu menu* of
many an unpretentious hostelry in the Highlands.
Salmon, venison or grouse, cranberry tart with ' the
rich plain cream,' so heartily appreciated by Dr.
Redgill when he dined with the Nabob of St.
Ronan's—all corrected by the Glenlivet or Tal-
lisker, undiluted or in tumblers of steaming toddy.
Also ' we have memory,' as M. Beaujeu of the
Ordinary remarked to Lord Glenvarloch, of the crisp,
crimped, curdy slices, which used to be a speciality
of the breakfasts at Perth Railway Station before it
became more bustling than Paddington or King's
Cross, and when the morning express from the South
steamed in about 8.30. We know not if we have ever
enjoyed anything so much, save the matutinal cup
of *café au lait* when the fast night train from Paris to
Neuchâtel pulled up on the heights of the Jura beyond
Pontarlier.   . . .   . .

The salmon was an inestimable boon to the Church when pious monks with nothing particular to do had to reconcile religion with gourmandise. When their lines had fallen to them in the pleasantest places on Tay or Tweed, Severn or Thames, there was small hardship in supping *au maigre* when the salmon came swimming to their doors. The cloistered orders of the Midlands might mortify the flesh on the pike from their moats and the carp from their ponds, as the fathers of the Fenland fattened on their eels. But in all the riverain or seaward convents, the rights of net and coble were highly appreciated and rigidly maintained. We believe the Venerable Bede gave as little thought to his dinner as most people, yet perhaps he would never have accomplished his stupendous historical works had he not been nourished on the Tynemouth salmon. For the salmon is remarkable in this respect, that though full flavoured almost to excessive richness, the veritable devotee does not easily tire of it. With eels, for example, it is a different thing : we have sometimes been inclined to pity the priests of the Fens, nor have we ever envied the townsfolk of Biggleswade. We would say, ' Eels in moderation, but salmon *à discrétion*,' and discretion with us runs into indiscretion. If any *gourmand* in fiction ever knew

what was good, it was the kindly Abbot of Kennaquhair. He must have had salmon every day of his
life when Tweed salmon was in season. Yet when
he suddenly taxes the hospitality of Glendearg, the
convent miller undertakes to send back to that tower
in the wilderness a noble fish to furnish out Dame
Elspeth's table. And look at the drawing in Scrope's
' Days and Nights of Salmon-fishing,' by Charles
Landseer, of 'The Pretty Kettle of Fish.' Doubtless
it perpetuates time-honoured tradition. The portly
priest, probably an abbot sitting in the House of
Lords, stands with beaming smiles of sharp-set
expectancy over the caldron, into which the fresh-
caught salmon are being passed. Long use and an
indolent life had never staled his appetite. To come
down to a humbler degree, Scrope tells a capital
story of a water-bailiff whose mouth watered for the
forbidden delicacies he was paid to preserve. When
dinner was served, his wife brought in a platter of
potatoes and a napkin. The napkin was tied over
his eyes. Then came the salmon, nor was the
napkin taken off till all the *débris* was removed.
It is a good story, and yet we doubt it. Try
sipping Château Lafitte in the dark, or smoking
the choicest *puro* of the Vuelta Abajo, and we fancy
most men will say that they might as well have

swallowed small beer, or been inhaling bird's-eye or niggerhead.

But there is no doubt that Scott, the most trustworthy of social antiquaries, did perpetuate that tradition of the Tweed kettle. Next to the Abbotsford Hunt, which one of the border farmers, wishing he might sleep on to the next anniversary, declared was the only thing in life worth living for, came what Lockhart describes as a solemn bout of salmon-fishing for the neighbouring gentry and their families. After the day's sport, 'the whole party assembled to regale on the newly caught prey, boiled, grilled, and roasted in every variety of preparation beneath a grand old ash.' Something of the sort was anticipated in the picturesque scene of the 'burning the water' in 'Guy Mannering' when Dandie was doing the honours of Charlie's Hope to Captain Brown. 'The sportsmen returned laden with fish, upwards of one hundred salmon having been killed. The best were selected for the use of the principal farmers, the others divided among their shepherds, cottagers, dependants, and others of inferior rank. These fish, dried in the turf smoke of their cabins or shielings, formed a savoury addition to the mess of potatoes mixed with onions which were a principal part of their winter food.'

That passage suggests the subject of kipper, a delicacy by no means confined to the cotters or shepherds, thanks to a process by which the fish is conserved for use through the close season. In the introductory epistle to 'The Monastery,' where the honest landlord of the 'George' at Kennaquhair comes to wile Captain Clutterbuck out of his lodgings late at eve, to sup with the learned Benedictine, David dresses the hook with a lure he knows will take. 'That's right, Captain; button weel up, the night's raw, but the water's clearing for a' that ; we'll be in't next night wi' my Lord's boats, and we'll hae ill luck if I dinna send you a kipper to relish your ale at e'en.' But there is kipper and kipper. The first thing is to select the best material, and then there are secrets in the scientific smoking and drying, only known to the elect. Morell's branch establishment in Inverness used to be an intelligent and munificent patron of the local industry. But the most renowned artist in kippers was a hairdresser of Dingwall, whose wares always fetched the highest prices in every shooting-box and forest lodge between the Garve and Strome Ferry.

We remarked that, rich as it is, and speaking personally, salmon does not easily pall on one. But then with the palate, as in graver matters, free will

acts very differently from the sense of constraint.
Ramsay of Ochtertyre, who left interesting social
memoirs, says that a hundred years ago Scottish
servants on the banks of *salmreich* rivers invariably
stipulated that they should not be compelled to
dine on the fish more than thrice in the week. An
early traveller who visited the North in the middle of
the seventeenth century tells precisely the same story.
Richard Frank writes that 'the Firth of Forth
relieves the country with her plenty of salmon, where
the burgomasters (as in many other parts of Scotland)
are compelled to enforce an ancient statute that
compels all masters not to force any servant or
apprentice to feed upon salmon more than thrice in
the week.' The salmon swarmed. The adventurous
travellers who had preceded Franck tell similar tales.
Don Pedro de Ayala, who got as far as the Beauly
and Spey in 1498, says it is impossible to describe
the immense quantity of fish, which sufficed for
Flanders, France, Italy, and England. He adds
when he had gone back to Dunbar, that nothing
was scarce in the kingdom save money, but that
the salmon was specially abundant. So says Fynes
Morrison, when he entered Scotland at Berwick in
1598. So said Taylor, the water poet, who put up
at the border city just twenty years later, when

starting to seek hospitality and tips among his
generous Scottish patrons. Moreover, he mentions
that the municipality had great difficulty in enforcing
Sabbath observance, and preventing the townsfolk
from fishing for the pot or gridiron on the holy day.
Brereton, who followed closely upon Taylor's heels,
neard of miraculous draughts at a single haul—of as
many salmon as there were days in the year ; and, by
the way, Brereton must have travelled economically
enough, for at the 'Crown' he had 'great entertain-
ment and good lodging, with a respective host,' for
eightpence a day. Well might Evan dhu Macombich
declare to Waverley that no Highlander thought
shame to take a deer from the hill or a salmon from
the stream. The most arbitrary chief never dreamed
of taking action against poachers when there were
more than enough for all. It seems odd that Scott
does not mention salmon at the great banquet of
Glennaquoich ; but we know that Simon Fraser, of
Lovat, when he kept open house for his clan at
Beaufort, relied greatly upon the fish swimming
beneath his fall, where they are said, when they
failed of the leap, to have dropped back into suspended
caldrons. And in England the importance of the
salmon was recognised when the peasants, who did
not follow their lords to the field, lived in chronic

semi-starvation, when agriculture and pasturing were in their infancy. When the cruel Norman forest laws were enforced by the Angevin kings, and before the Barons had compelled John to set his hand to the Great Charter, the common law prohibited the monopoly of salmon fishings by the Crown or its grantees, and ordered the suppression of all weirs or obstructions. Now, perhaps the nearest locality where salmon are to be taken in profusion is Iceland. There the natives hunt them towards the nets or traps as if they were driving a cover for hares and pheasants, and you may see some half-hundred fine fish taken out of a box—the produce of the single twenty-four hours.

The most distinguished southern anglers who have visited Scotland in modern days were Scrope and Sir Humphry Davy. Both were familiar friends of Scott, and frequent guests at Abbotsford, and both have been immortalised in the biography. Sir Humphry, in his old hat, festooned with casting lines, was a conspicuous figure at the morning meet on the lawn, which, Lockhart said, should have been painted by Wilkie. Sir Humphry's 'Salmonia' was sharply criticised by Wilson in an essay—perhaps for the reason that two of a trade can never agree. Yet the personal fishing feats of the Professor should have made him

superior to jealousy. Possibly the contempt of the
President of the 'Noctes' was provoked by the
chemist's narrow-minded ideas on dinners and drink.
Rather the drink than the dinners, for Sir Humphry
appreciated a noble grilse, and scientifically supervised the preparation. He gives excellent instructions
for crimping. After landing his fish, he directs
Poietes, whose wits were apt to go a-woolgathering :
'Give him a transverse cut just below the gills, and
crimp him by cutting to the bone on each side, so as
almost to divide him into slices ; and now hold him
by the tail that he may bleed. There is a small
spring, I see, which I daresay has the mean temperature of the atmosphere in this climate, and is much
under 60 degrees—place him there and let him
remain for ten minutes, and then carry him to the
pot, and let the water and salt boil furiously before
you put in a slice, and give time to the water to
recover its heat before you throw in another, and so
on with the whole fish, and throw in the thickest pieces
first.' We have often practised similar methods in
less philosophical fashion, sending the last grilse of
the day up to the lodge by a swift-footed gillie to be
crimped in the kitchen, for a brief delay makes but
slight difference, and it is wise not to trench on the
province of the hot-tempered cook. But if Sir

Humphry's science made him an intelligent *gourmet*, his views on the liquor question were sadly heterodox. The party of Southerners had gone through a day of tremendous exertion in the bracing air of Loch Maree. Honest Ornither, satiated with the salmon and having neglected to correct it with a quaich of mountain dew, moves for another bottle of claret, modestly remarking that a pint a man is not too much. Whereupon Halieus is down on him like a hammer. 'You have made me president, and I forbid it. A half-pint of wine for young men in perfect health is enough.' The force of asceticism could hardly have gone farther, in such seducing circumstances. A well-spent day, bodies slightly fagged, sociable company, and a long evening to kill. So might St. Simeon Stylites have spoken had he stepped down from his column to take a day's fishing in the Nile and then invited some clerical friends to a frugal supper.

Naturally Wilson's gorge was roused by the passage. The *convives* of the imaginary revels at Ambrose's might have pledged each other in Odin's bottomless horn, and the salmon at their feasts was always, in the words of Morris's drinking song, 'a reason fair' for a caulker. The Shepherd once declared that, though men of good and even great appetites, they were neither gluttons nor wine-bibbers,

which illustrates the wide diversity of opinion and
the marvellous elasticity of the conscience. They
were no gluttons ; but *apropos* to salmon, here is the
poet's notion of an insufficient supper. ' Ye dinna
mean to say, Mr. Aumrose, that that's a'? Only the
roun, the cut o' saumon, beefsteaks and twa broods o'
eisters ! This 'ill never do, Aumrose. Remember
there's a couple o' us, and that a sooper that may be
no' amiss for one may be little better than starvation
to twa.' The Homeric feasting in Gabriel's Road
was play of the fancy, though there was a fair foundation for the romantic superstructures. Neither
Christopher nor the Shepherd could say with the
town clerk in 'The Antiquary,' that they were nae
glass-breakers, and both Wilson and Hogg played a
capital knife and fork. But for actual and authentic
performances we should be inclined to back the
annual salmon dinners which used to celebrate—as
probably they do still—the opening of the fishing
season in some of the Scotch boroughs. When a
party of the town bailies, with their chosen friends,
sit down to solid eating and steady drinking, it was hard
indeed to beat them. We have seen slice upon slice
vanishing like snow-flakes, and cutlet fast following
cutlet, like the cut and carve again at a round of beef
set down before a famishing beggar. The steaks, hot

and hot, dear to the gormandising of the Beef Steak Club, are undeniably solid, but the devotees of the salmon, like the Solan geese of the Bass and Ailsa, have unlimited and well-founded faith in the facility of digestion. They aver, and we have seen no reason to doubt it, that the secret of sound slumbers after a Gargantuan repast is the absorption of a super-sufficiency of strong whisky toddy.

Thanks to the habits of the salmon, some of our rivers are opened so early that the Metropolitan market is supplied for the best part of the year. We believe fishing in the Ness begins in December; in the Severn in the previous month, and towards April all the streams are in full swing. Scotch servants and apprentices have no longer to complain of being sated with a luxury they seldom taste. Swift trains, with admirable arrangements for icing and packing, have brought even the remote Brora and the Laxford into speedy communication with Leadenhall. Prices are regulated by the supply, and to some extent by the rise or fall of the thermometer, but in the beginning of the salmon season and of the London season they are always high. For no London dinner *menu* is deemed complete without salmon in one shape or another, till at last the inevitable appearance is expected like that of turkey on

P

Christmas day or pancakes on Shrove Tuesday. And the salmon has one special recommendation, not only for the lessees of net fishings, but for the epicures who regale on him. It is true that to be eaten in perfection he should be freshly caught, crimped and cooked. But for the many who must miss that blissful moment, he rather improves with a brief delay, unlike the sea fish, who can only have full justice done them on the day and at the hour when the boats come in. We do not pretend to explain the matter philosophically, but Sir Humphry, speaking as Halieus, concludes 'that the fat of salmon between the flakes is mixed with much albumen of gelatine, and extremely liable to decompose,' that by keeping it cool decomposition is retarded, and that by the application of boiling salt and water at a high heat, the albumen again coagulates, and the preserved curdiness comes out.

We may be sure that the cooking in semi-barbaric days was by the boiling or the broiling, and it is impossible really to improve on those simple methods. It is noteworthy that the earliest recipe we have happened upon, which is in the 'Noble Book of Cookery,' of the sixteenth century, goes as far towards spoiling the noble fish as perverted ingenuity could devise. The hot spicing and general bedevilling would

have done injustice to pike or tench. 'To mak
samon rost in sauce '—'Tak a samon and cutt him in
round (?) peces and rost him on a gredirne, and tak
wyn and pouder of canelle and draw them through a
stren, and mynce onyans smalle, and do ther to boilen,
then ther tak vergices pouder of peper and guinger
and salt and do ther to the samon in a difshe and
pour on the ceripe and service it.' After that aggrava-
tion of the temper, it is refreshing to turn to the
modern precepts for boiling. There is no great
divergence on the subject, but Megg Dodds, as
an enlightened Scotchwoman, is as safe an authority
as any.

'Scale or clean the fish without unnecessary
washing or handling, and without cutting it too much
open. Have a roomy and well-scoured fish kettle, and
if the salmon be large or thick, when you have placed
it on the strainer or in the kettle, fill up and amply
cover it with cold spring water that it may heat
gradually. Throw in a handful of salt. If a jowl or
quarter is boiled, it may be put in with warm water.
In both cases take off the scum carefully and let the
fish boil slowly, allowing twelve minutes to the
pound. The minute the boiling of any fish is
completed, the fish strainer must be lifted and laid
across the pan to drain the fish. Throw a soft cloth

or flannel in several folds over it. Dish on a hot
fish plate under a napkin.' Mrs. Dodds remarks,
that it is difficult to estimate the boiling time,
nor can anything but sage experience be trusted.
Twelve minutes to the pound is a rough calculation.
Cre-fydd professes to be more exact. She says, ' A
slice weighing one pound will require a quarter of
an hour ; two pounds, twenty-three minutes, five
pounds for a very large thick fish, thirty minutes ;
the same weight for a small fish twenty-five minutes ;
four pounds of a split fish twenty minutes ; a whole
fish weighing seven to eight pounds, thirty minutes.'
These rules, on the other hand, are rather arbitrary,
and as Mrs. Dodds observes, it is experience that
does it. And when the salmon is sent up, the carving
must be carefully attended to, the thin slices which
have the more delicate lusciousness being duly ap-
portioned to the thicker.   Lemons or thinly sliced
cucumbers may be the accompaniments ; personally,
we prefer to dispense with them.   As we have said,
with a fresh-killed salmon it is sacrilege to serve anything but the salted water in which it was boiled,
with perhaps a faint addition of Chili, enough to
elicit without deadening the characteristic flavour.
Christopher North never scandalised us more, though
the recent 'Annals of the Blackwoods' show the

culpable recklessness of his criticism, than when he
called on the waiter for the cruets, the mustard, etc.,
when sitting down to a noble Tay salmon. But
when the fish has lost something even of its second
day freshness, we are open to consolation, for it gives
a chance to the *sauce Hollandaise* or the *Tartare*.
With salmon cold, whether plain or dressed, the
Tartare comes naturally, and indeed it may be
almost identified with the *sauce Mayonnaise*.

'Broiling is best,' sings Southey in a Pindaric Ode,
when beef and mutton were looming in the poetic eye.
If he had been singing of the salmon, a good many
connoisseurs would have been inclined to agree with
him. Partly, perhaps, because after coming home
from a long day's sport, or when kindling a camp
fire at the bivouac in the sheltered open, the salmon
sliced and broiled is most quickly served with the
sauce piquante of ravenous appetite. Mrs. Dodds
asserts that fresh salmon grilled is 'the way in which
the solitary epicure best relishes this luxury.' 'Split
the salmon and take out the bones'—they may be
subsequently devilled—'cut fillets of from three to
four inches in breadth'—too thick, we think—'dry
them in the folds of a cloth, but do not beat or press
them. Have a clean fire and a bright, barred
gridiron, rubbed with chalk to prevent the fish from

sticking; turn with steak-tongs, and serve piping hot.'

Mrs. Margaret Sims, in her clever 'Cookery Book,' agrees with us as to the thickness. She suggests cutting the salmon in slices of an inch, rubbing them with salad oil or fresh butter—so that the chalk may be dispensed with—and basting frequently with the butter or oil. As for the thinner slicing, it recommends itself to common sense, for the object is to cook thoroughly yet quickly.

We can have no great opinion of baked salmon, though we must confess we never tried it. It is baked in a deep pan with abundance of butter. But as it is to be seasoned with sauce or other spices, it resembles the counsels of adulterating imperfection in the 'Noble Book,' and suggests that the relics of some former meal have got beyond a creditable resurrection.

Braising is a more pleasing alternative, for it gives opportunity for artistic seasoning. This is Crefydd's recipe: 'Spread some strong white paper thickly with butter: wipe the salmon dry and fold it in the paper: place it in a drainer over the warm water and steam for three-quarters of an hour. Take off the paper, put the fish in a hot dish, and pour the following sauce over it: mix half a pint of stock, a table spoonful of capers, a dessert spoonful of soy'—

we should have fancied the sickening soy was a thing of the past, did it not appear still in the quadrangular cruets of certain old-fashioned clubs — 'a teaspoonful of anchovy sauce, a teaspoonful of fresh-made mustard, and half a grain of cayenne. Boil ten minutes. Knead together three ounces of butter and a tablespoonful of baked flour, and stir in for eight minutes. Add the strained juice of a lemon and a wineglassful of Marsala or Madeira.'

We like Cre fydd's confident affectation of precision, as exemplified in her instructions for boiling and in these eight minutes for stirring the sauce. Nevertheless, we daresay if she stirred for ten the sauce would not perceptibly suffer. And as she has made her mixture somewhat strong, she may be justified in adding the Marsala or Madeira. But we take the opportunity of hinting that *in nostro arbitrio*, in the words of the Antiquary, the wine to drink with salmon is sound Rhenish, though champagne will always serve at a pinch. Even in Rhineland—and setting questions of cost aside—we have no great faith in Johannisberg beyond the Metternich cellars. But Rudesheimer Berg, Rauenthaler, and the Liebfraumilch of Worms are all passable second growths, and will do well enough.

Fillets are dressed in various ways. To *à*

l'Indienne, as in curry, there is, of course, the objection that the tropical heat of the ingredients burns the edge off the flavour, yet somehow the essential essences struggle through; they do not when the fish is smothered in mace and other spices. 'Cut the fish into neat squares, about a quarter of an inch thick : dip in beaten eggs and roll in bread crumbs : fry to a light brown in lard, previously made very hot for the purpose, and then serve up with Indian sauce, sprinkling the fillets with shred green gherkins.' The Indian dressing is made of half a pint of tomato-sauce, a dessert spoonful of curry paste, with a little anchovy. The Dutch sauce is simple : 'Make some butter sauce rather thin : stir in the yolk of an egg, lemon juice, pepper and salt : add a little cream : beat all together with a whisk and heat.' It must not be boiled after the egg is added, as in that case it would curdle.

This is a good direction for *Mayonnaise* sauce. ' Boil five eggs for twelve minutes, and when cold pound the yolks to powder. Mix a saltspoonful of salt, a teaspoonful of flour of mustard, and a quarter of a grain of cayenne, beat the yolks of two fresh eggs and stir in till smooth, then add, drop by drop, seven spoonfuls of the finest salad oil, three teaspoonfuls of Tarragon vinegar, and three table spoonfuls of

French vinegar, set the mortar in a cold place or on
ice for an hour, then stir in a teaspoonful of finely
chopped chives or shalot.'

Mayonnaise and other artistic arrangements of
cold salmon are of course in favour for ball suppers,
the wedding breakfasts which are going out of
fashion, and other festivities of the kind. For some
of these *plats de luxe* we may turn to Urban Dubois,
who supervised for many years the Court banquets at
Berlin. Always an enthusiast in his art, he rises to
raptures over the salmon. 'Among the most distinguished and delicious fishes, the salmon is one
possessing the most appreciable qualities. From a
gastronomic point of view the salmon is a real
treasure, being always exquisite, whether fried,
smoked, or salted. In whatever way it is dressed, it
will always be tempting.' He adds that in the
benighted south of Europe, from Marseilles to Constantinople, he never saw a fresh salmon in the
market, and says that the salmon most esteemed by
epicures are unquestionably those of Scotland and the
Rhine. He pronounces boiling in a *court-bouillon*
the most fitting mode of cooking, though in that case
it is to be eaten hot as may be. Briefly, the fish is
boiled in slices as we have described, and then
pieced together in the original form. It is to be

garnished with gratinated lobster-shells and sprigs of
parsley, and served with *sauce Espagnole*, flavoured
with lemon. We need hardly add that in that dish
of high ceremony, essentials must be somewhat
sacrificed to appearances. Indeed M. Dubois assents
to that when writing of 'slices of salmon with jelly.'
He says, 'It is not generally the custom to serve
salmon in slices on a ball buffet, but experience has
taught that it is a good plan.' He goes on, 'I have
endeavoured to serve the salmon in slices, without
the least detracting from its pleasing appearance.'
This is his recipe for salmon sliced *à la Royale*, and
he remarks that the piece, simple and easy of execution, is not without its attractions as a variation from
the usual masses of fish.

' Two thick slices must be cut from the broadest
part of a large salmon, placed in the drainer of a fish
kettle, just covered with a good cold *court-bouillon*
with wine, in order to cook them according to the
method applied to salmon, that is to say, at the first
boiling of the liquid the kettle is removed to the side
of the fire, to be kept there for twenty-five or thirty
minutes. When the slices are well-drained and have
become cold, the skin is taken off, then dished on a
pain-vert of a long shape, masked on the top with white
paper, and then fixed on a dish. They are then en-

tirely masked with Parisian butter, very slightly coloured
with green or red, either with spinach green or crayfish butter.'

When the slices are placed on the *pain-vert* they
are decorated with *Mayonnaise* or with frothy butter
squeezed through a cornet, and with fillets of anchovy,
gherkins, and chervil leaves. Then the *plat* is
surrounded with halves of hard-boiled eggs, bedecked
with crayfish, skewered and grouped, according to
the artist's fancy, and sent up with *Mayonnaise.*

Middle-piece (*tronçon*) of salmon *à la Parisienne*
is a pleasing variation. The centre piece is cut out,
boiled, cooled and carefully drained. Then it is
trimmed and 'set on a *plateau historié*,' and
masked with the butter *à la Parisienne.* For the
butter : 'Six yolks of eggs are put in a stewpan,
mixed with a table spoonful of flour, and a piece of
crayfish butter—then the whole is dissolved with a
gill of fresh mushroom liquor. When on the fire it
is stirred like cream, and when it has got some con-
sistence it is removed and passed through a sieve.
Should it happen not to be quite smooth when cold,
then a pound of butter in little bits is introduced.
The preparation must be well worked till it is light,
then finished with a few spoonfuls of mustard and
as many of essence of anchovies.' The piece is

garnished with salad, and the sides are decorated with bottoms of artichokes filled with vegetables. It is decorated with skewers of truffles and prawns, and *sauce Mayonnaise* may be sent up as well.

To come down from the heights of ostentatious luxury to frugal housekeeping, there are many ways of using up salmon for a second dressing. It may be done in potato paste, with salt, cayenne, white pepper and three table spoonfuls of shrimp sauce or melted butter. It may be made into a pudding. 'Boil three ounces of bread crumbs in a third of a pint of milk till it becomes smooth, and turn out to cool. Beat as many ounces of fresh butter to a cream, pound half-a-pound of boiled salmon to paste; beat the yolks of four, and the whites of two, eggs for ten minutes. Mix well together. Add a clove of garlic, a salt-spoonful of salt, a salt-spoonful of anchovy sauce, half a salt-spoonful of white pepper, and half a grain of cayenne. Pound till the seasoning is well mixed; roll into lobster shape, dredge with baked flour, and wrap in foolscap paper, spread with butter. Roll in a cloth, and place it in a steamer over *fast* boiling water for thirty-five minutes. Turn it out and serve with sauce.'

Or you may *souse* the salmon in half a pint of

vinegar, with salt, pepper, cayenne, peppercorns, clove, mace, and a shred or two of garlic. Boil for ten minutes, then let it cool. Strain the vinegar on it, leave it in pickle for twelve hours, and serve with fresh fennel. For salmon *au gratin*, put the cold pieces in a flat dish, season with salt and pepper, and a little ketchup : sprinkle with grated Parmesan. Take a frying pan, put it on a slow fire ; put a small piece of butter into it, with fine bread crumbs ; make them a light brown ; pour a little butter sauce over the fish and cheese, and sprinkle bread crumbs over them. Put it into the oven to heat, and brown with a red-hot salamander. For kedgeree, boil half a pound of rice : dry before the fire : boil two eggs for ten minutes, peel and mince them. Heat a stewpan : with a piece of butter put in the salmon, then the rice and eggs. Season with salt and pepper : mix lightly with a fork, and serve as hot as possible. Tinned salmon comes in usefully for cakes, *Mayonnaise*, curries, or kedgeree. And finally we may say a good word for the lax, a Norwegian variation of Scotch kipper, sent over in oil and hermetically sealed tins. With slices of toast split and frizzled before a slow fire, it makes a capital addition to a light luncheon.

CHAPTER XI

THE LAW AS TO SALMON-FISHING

By Claud Douglas Pennant

SINCE the days when Sir John Hawkins, Knight, wrote his 'short discourse touching the laws of angling by way of Postscript' to Walton's 'Compleat Angler,' many changes have taken place. In compiling a statement of the law as to the salmon, as it at present stands, the chief difficulty of the writer has been to compress within the space at his disposal all that might be said upon so wide a subject, and at the same time to render such statement clear and comprehensive—at best it can only be instructive : to make it light or even interesting reading is beyond his hope or power. This difficulty is due to the fact that the law varies in England (which country will be taken in this chapter to include Wales), in Scotland, and in Ireland, not to mention the districts of the Tweed and Solway ; and although the policy of the legislature, in recent times at any rate, has been to assimilate the various systems, wide differences still exist.

The treatment of the matter naturally falls under two heads.

I. *The right to fish for salmon :* in whom it vests and upon what it rests.

·II. *The legislation* in favour of the salmon.

I. The right to fish for salmon is vested throughout the United Kingdom in the Crown or in subjects who have acquired that right from the Crown. In England and Ireland the Crown holds the right, where it has retained it, on behalf of the public. In Scotland the Crown holds it for its own benefit and as a source of revenue. Thus we have in England and Ireland a division of the right to fish for salmon into a public and private right.

In those countries there is in ancient navigable rivers as far as the tide ebbs and flows, in estuaries and on the sea-coast, a *primâ facie* public right to fish for salmon. This right may, however, be overridden by the existence of some private right which an individual may enjoy by virtue of grant or charter from the Crown or by immemorial usage ; the onus lying on the individual claiming such right to prove its existence. In rivers made navigable by statute, the public have no such right, nor have they in ancient navigable rivers above where the tide ebbs and flows, although this latter point has only been

decided in recent years.   Nor, again, can the public
acquire such right by user during any length of time.

There is a *primâ facie* private right to fish for
salmon in all waters where no public right exists.
Many distinctions have been drawn in English law
between the different kinds of private rights of
fishing, and much confusion has been caused thereby
in the past ; but the better and more recent opinion
as expressed by Willes J. in the case of Malcolmson
v. O'Dea, 10 H. L. C. 593, seems to be that for
practical purposes there are only two kinds of
private rights to be distinguished, viz. (1) a Several,
(2) a Common of Fishery, and of these the former is
by far the more important.

A *Several Fishery* is an exclusive individual right
of fishing *primâ facie* existing (*a*) in all non-navigable
rivers, (*b*) in all non-navigable rivers above the tide-
way, and (*c*) in rivers made navigable by statute.   It
may exist in navigable rivers below the tide-way, in
the sea and in estuaries under a grant or charter,
actual or presumptive, from the Crown made before
Magna Charta.   A grant, however, which has been
created before that time, and has been resumed by
the Crown for forfeiture or otherwise, can be re-
granted by the Crown ; and a grant subsequent to
Magna Charta, coupled with proof of long enjoyment,

is good evidence to prove that the Crown was entitled to make such grant to confirm a several fishery
which existed before the time of legal memory. If
the right to a several fishery is once proved, no act on
the part of the public can divest the owner of that right
or transfer it to the public. The right may be shortly
described as riparian, since it attaches to the owners of
the soil adjoining the river on either bank, or to persons
deriving their title from such owners. Where the opposite banks are in different ownership, the right extends
' *ad medium filum*,' *i.e.* to a line drawn over the centre of
the main channel of the river. This right, as has been
said, attaches to the soil, and so, should the river
change its course, the owner of a several fishery in
the old channel cannot claim a right in the new
channel, if it has left his lands. With regard to the
right extending only ' *ad medium filum*,' an obvious
difficulty suggests itself, in cases where the water is at
all narrow and the catch is in a single channel, which
renders it impossible effectively to fish with rod or
net without passing the line in mid-stream. In strict
law, to do so is an encroachment ; but, as a matter of
custom, this difficulty is adjusted in practice by
arrangement between the adverse owners.

In England a several fishery can be granted or
leased only by deed, in order to be effective. This

Q

was formerly the case in Ireland; but, since the passing of the Landlord and Tenant Amendment Act of 1860, a fishery can be let by mere word of mouth for a year or from year to year, and for a longer period, by a note in writing without seal.

A grant of a fishery is *primâ facie* a grant of a several fishery, and an action for trespass will lie for entering the same.

II. A *Common of Fishery* is like other rights of common, *e.g.* of pasture belonging to tenants of a particular manor, and can only exist in waters within the manor.   It can only be transferred by deed.

With regard to Scotland, the different position in which the Crown stands towards the public has already been noticed.   All salmon-fishings in Scotland, whether in rivers, estuaries, or in the sea, in so far as fishing is carried on there in connection with the land, were of original right vested in the Crown, and, where not granted away, are under the management of the Commissioners of Woods and Forests. No grant has ever been made to confer upon the public of any locality a right of salmon-fishing, though doubtless in many places the public have · enjoyed such right as a privilege ; nor will the duration of such enjoyment for any length of time confer upon them such right as against the Crown.

The rights of salmon-fishing which the Crown has granted away to individuals are separate heritable estates, distinct from the ownership of the adjoining lands, and vested in individuals by express grant in terms of 'salmon-fishing' (*cum piscatione salmonum*)—although, if the words *cum piscatione* alone are found in the grant, a long practice and enjoyment of salmon-fishing may extend them to imply a grant of 'salmon' fishing. The view once held, that a right to 'angle' for salmon accompanied the ownership of the soil in Scotland, despite a grant of salmon-fishing to another, has, since the case of Anderson *v.* Anderson, decided in 1867, perhaps unfortunately been rejected, and so it happens that while one individual owns the adjoining lands, another sometimes has the right of fishing in the river.

LEGISLATION

The Salmon Fishery Acts

From very early times salmon have been protected by various Acts of Parliament, both general and local, throughout the United Kingdom. It is not, however, until the present century that we find the subject generally treated in a practical manner, and attempts made to check the abuses then existing. We may take as the foundations of our modern salmon-fishery laws, the Acts of 1861 for England, 1862 for Scotland, 1842 for Ireland, and 1857 for the Tweed, which last river has always been the subject of independent legislation. From those times onwards, the legislature has endeavoured to promote the welfare of the salmon through the various enactments passed, by—

1. Affording him a free and unpolluted course from the sea to the spawning grounds;

2. Putting a check on the rapacity of individual proprietors and illegal capture.

The course pursued to attain these ends has been practically the same in all the countries mentioned.

Below we have appended a table [1] of the more

[1] ENGLAND

1861.	24, 25 V. c. 96, ss. 24, 26.		Larceny.
1861.	24, 25 V. c. 97, ss. 32, 57–78.		Malicious injuries.
1861.	24, 25 V. c. 109	. .	Salmon.
1863.	26, 27 V. c. 10 .	. .	Salmon, export.
1865.	28, 29 V. c. 121	. .	Salmon.
1870.	33, 34 V. c. 33 .	. .	Export.
1873.	36, 37 V. c. 71 .	. .	Salmon.
1877.	40, 41 V. c. 65 .	. .	Dynamite.
1878.	41, 42 V. . .	. .	Dynamite.
1886.	49, 50 V. c. 39 .	. .	Salmon.
1892.	55, 56 V. c. 50 .	. .	Salmon.

SCOTLAND

1828.	9 Geo. IV. c. 39	. .	Salmon.
1844.	8, 9 V. c. 95	. .	Salmon.
1862.	25, 26 V. c. 97 .	. .	Salmon.
1863.	26, 27 V. c. 50 .	. .	Salmon.
1864.	27, 28 V. c. 118	. .	Salmon.

important Acts of Parliament, passed during the present century, which affect the question. It would be

SCOTLAND (continued)

1865.	28, 29 V. c. 121, 363 .	.	Salmon, Esk.
1867–8.	31, 32 V. c. 123	. .	Salmon.
1870.	33, 34 V. c. 33 .	. .	Export.
1873.	36, 37 V. c. 71, s. 12	.	Esk.
1877.	40, 41 V. c. 65 .	. .	Dynamite.
1878.	41, 42 V. .	. .	Dynamite.
1882.	45, 46 V. c. 78 .	. .	Fishery Board.
1884–5.	48, 49 V. c. 6, s. 5 .	.	Secretary for Scotland.
1887.	50, 51 V. c. 52 .	. .	Secretary for Scotland.

IRELAND

1842.	5, 6 V. c. 106 .	. .	Salmon.
1844.	7, 8 V. c. 108 .	. .	Salmon.
1845.	8, 9 V. c. 108 .	. .	Salmon.
1846.	9, 10 V. c. 86, ss. 3, 4	.	Public works.
1847–8.	11, 12 V. c. 92 .	. .	Salmon.
1850.	13, 14 V. c. 88 .	. .	Salmon.
1861.	24, 25 V. c. 96, ss. 24, 26 .		Larceny.
1861.	24, 25 V. c. 97, ss. 32, 57–78		Malicious injuries.
1863.	26, 27 V. c. 10 .	. .	Salmon, export.
1863.	26, 27 V. c. 114	. .	Salmon.
1868–9.	32, 33 V. c. 9 .	. .	Salmon.
1868–9.	32, 33 V. c. 9 .	. .	Inspector.
1868–9.	32, 33 V. c. 92 .	. .	General.
1870.	33, 34 V. c. 33 .	. .	Export.
1877.	40, 41 V. c. 68 .	. .	Dynamite.
1895.	58, 59 V. c. 29 .	. .	Salmon.

Tweed 1857. 20, 21 V. c. 148.

,, 1859. 22, 23 V. c. 70.

Solway 1804. 44 Geo. III. c. 45.

,, 1877. 40, 41 V. c. 240.

Annan 1841. 4 V. c. 18.

impossible, within the limits of this chapter, to inquire at any length into the reason for this mass of legisla tion upon this one particular subject. Briefly stated, it was the decline of the salmon fisheries throughout the United Kingdom, due to the increase of pollu tions and obstructions such as weirs, mill-dams, or nets ; the abstraction of water for waterworks, factories, and other purposes ; and the inefficiency and evasion of the laws then in force. The increase of rod and line fishing for salmon as a sport during the present century may also have directed attention to the subject, and been the cause of a good deal · of legislation which would not otherwise have been passed had the sport not attained to that prominent position which it now holds.

The Act of 1861 in England, founded upon the report of the Commissioners appointed to inquire into the salmon fisheries of England and Wales in 1860, repealed, in whole or in part, thirty-three Acts of Parliament then in force, and placed the superinten dence of the salmon fisheries in those countries under the Home Office, with power to appoint two inspec tors for a period of three years. This superintendence is now transferred to the department of the Board of Trade, in accordance with the report of the select committee of the House of Commons appointed in

1870 to inquire into the subject. The Board of Trade now exercises all the powers conferred by the Salmon Fishery Acts upon the Home Office, and the appointment of inspectors has been continued from time to time by various Acts of Parliament.

By the Act of 1861, certain modes of taking fish were prohibited, and the minimum size of the mesh of nets to be legally used was fixed at two inches from knot to knot, or eight inches measured all round, when wet. Fixed engines were prohibited, close seasons established, fish passes were ordered to be erected in obstructions, and free gaps in certain instances made.

Two years later the Act of 1863 made the export of salmon illegal from any part of the United Kingdom if caught during close time in any district.

The year 1865 saw some very important changes in the law, not the least of which was the formation of fishery districts and boards of conservators for the protection of the fish. These matters were further dealt with by the Act of 1873, and the present state of the law with regard to them is as follows :—

The county council of any county can apply to the Board of Trade to form into a fishery district or districts all or any of the salmon rivers lying wholly or partly within the county, and the Board of Trade may include in any district so formed any river or rivers or parts thereof, although not situated in the county on behalf of which the application is made. The limits of a river are to be defined and a fishery district formed by a certificate from the Board of Trade, and such district may be altered by the Board of Trade upon the application of the conservators. Where a fishery district lies wholly within any one county, the county council elect certain of their number to act as members of the Board of Conservators for that district : in addition to these there are two classes of conservators, (1) *ex officio*, (2) representative.

1. Everyone comes within the first class who is the owner or occupier of a fishery in the district which is assessed to the poor rate on a gross estimated rental of 30*l.* per annum, or is the owner of lands within the district of an annual value of not less than 100*l.* having a frontage of not less than a mile to any salmon river, and has the right to fish there, and has paid license duty for fishing for salmon within the district in the preceding year.

2. The second class are the elected representatives of fishermen duly licensed to fish for salmon (otherwise than with rod and line) during the last

preceding season in public or common waters—one
member being eligible for every 50*l.* of license duty
paid. That there are defects in the system is apparent. County councillors do not necessarily
possess any knowledge of, or have any interest in,
fishery matters, yet some of their number have seats
on the board, while rod and line fishermen, on the
other hand, are not adequately represented. It would
also be desirable that some change in the law should
be made to prevent anyone who has been convicted
of an offence against the Salmon Fishery Acts from
being eligible as a conservator.

When a fishery district does not lie wholly within
the limits of one county, the county council of any
county within which any part of such district lies may
apply to the county council of every other county in
the district to appoint a fishery committee, consisting
of three of their number to form, with the fishery
committee of the same number to be appointed by
the county council making the application, a joint
fishery committee for the district. Such joint fishery
committee, together with the *ex officio* and representative members, form the board of conservators. A
board of conservators thus formed are a body cor-
porate, having perpetual succession and a common
seal, and invested with the following powers :—

1. To make contracts.

2. To issue licenses.

3. To purchase by agreement and compulsorily (under the Lands Clauses Acts), for the purpose only of removal, fishing weirs, fishing mill-dams, and fixed engines.

4. To take legal proceedings against persons offending against the Salmon Fishery Acts.

5. To make bye-laws subject to the approval of the Board of Trade.

6. To alter the commencement and termination of the close time, annual and weekly as to the whole or part of a district (with limitations which will be noticed).

7. To determine the length and size of nets and the manner in which they may be used (but no hang or draft net may be limited by bye-law to less than two hundred yards).

8. To determine the size of the mesh of nets (but the mesh is not to be decreased to less than one and a half inches from knot to knot, nor extended to more than two and a half inches all round when wet).

9. To determine the form of licenses.

10. To vary the rate of license duty in different parts of the district.

11. To determine what marks or labels are to be fixed to nets or painted on boats used in fishing.

12. To prohibit the use of nets within a certain distance of a river mouth, and of the confluence of rivers in any part of the district not being a several fishery.

13. To determine the time during which it may be lawful to use a gaff in connection with rod and line.

14. To determine where gratings are to be placed during certain times of the year across the head and tail race of mills and across artificial channels leading into or out of a river.

15. To regulate during the annual and weekly close times the use within any river of nets for fish other than salmon.

16. To prohibit the use in any inland water of any net except a landing net, or a net for taking eels, between sunset and sunrise.

17. To impose a penalty not exceeding 5*l.* for an offence against a bye-law.

(*N.B.*—No bye-law to come into operation until confirmed by the Board of Trade.)

18. To adopt such means, with the consent of the Board of Trade, for preventing the ingress of salmon into streams in which they or their spawning beds

are, from the nature of the channel, liable to be destroyed.

19. Generally to do everything for the protection of the salmon fisheries within their district.

Turning now to Scotland, in which country greater attention seems always to have been given to the salmon fisheries than in England, due no doubt to their relatively greater value, the Act of 1862 is the foundation of modern legislation upon the subject.

All fishery matters are under the Fishery Board of Scotland, which is again under the Secretary for Scotland. The Board consists of seven members, viz. three members (of whom one is chairman, one a sheriff of a county, and one a person skilled in the branches of science concerned with the habits and food of fishes) and four representative members of the various sea fishing interests in Scotland. The Board has the appointment of one inspector of salmon fisheries.

The Act of 1862, unlike the corresponding English Act of 1861, is rather a re-enacting than a repealing statute. The first point we may notice is the formation of fishery districts. Under section 4, every river in Scotland flowing into the sea, and every tributary stream or lake flowing into or connected with such river and the sea-coast adjoining thereto, divided into such portions as may be fixed and defined by the Commissioners under the Act, shall form a fishery district. For this purpose three Commissioners were appointed for a period of three years, with further power to determine the close season and to make general regulations for its observance and for the construction and use of cruives, the construction and alteration of mill-dams, lades, or water-wheels, so as to afford reasonable means for the passage of salmon ; for the meshes of nets and obstructions in rivers and estuaries to the free passage of salmon, with power to summon witnesses and take evidence upon these matters.

In accordance with these powers the Commissioners, by bye-law made in January 1863, divided Scotland into districts and settled their annual close times respectively. By a further bye-law of May 1864 the size of the mesh of nets was fixed at one and three-quarters inches from knot to knot, and the use of two nets, one behind the other, or nets made of canvas, was prohibited.

Further bye-laws passed in May 1864 and July 1865 regulate the use of cruives and mill-dams, while a salmon pass was ordered to be affixed to every dam, weir, or cauld.

Upon a district being constituted, a list of the upper and lower proprietors has to be made, the qualification being the ownership of a fishery entered in the valuation roll as of the yearly rent or value of 20*l.*, and in the former case also the ownership of half a mile frontage to the river with a right of salmon-fishing. From these two classes the members of the district board are elected. By a further Act of 1868, if a district board had not been so constituted in any district, any two proprietors of salmon-fishings in the district can petition the sheriff to form one, and the factor of any proprietor of a fishing can be elected a member.

A district board continues in office for three years.

A district board

1. May sue or be sued in the name of its clerk.

2. May appoint constables, water-bailiffs, and watchers.

3. May impose and has power to collect an assessment, called the 'fishery assessment,' on the several fisheries in the district according to their yearly rent or value as entered in the valuation roll.

4. May petition the Secretary for Scotland to vary the close seasons, annual or weekly, and to alter the regulations with regard to them.

5. May petition the Secretary for Scotland to alter the regulations with respect to the construction and use of cruives, cruive dykes, or weirs.

6. May purchase by agreement, for the purpose only of removal, any weir, dam, cruive, or other fixed engine for the benefit of the fisheries in the district.

7. May remove all natural obstructions to the passage of fish in the bed of a river.

8. May attach a fish-pass to any waterfall.

9. May generally do all things within their district for the protection of salmon.

IRELAND

Modern legislation upon the salmon started in Ireland some few years sooner than in other parts of the United Kingdom, and the Act of 1842 is the foundation of the law as it at present stands. Under that and the succeeding Acts, all fishery matters are placed in the hands of three inspectors of Irish fisheries, appointed by and under the control of the Lord-Lieutenant. For the formation of fishery districts, Special Commissioners were appointed as in Scotland, and each district so formed was placed under conservators, of whom there are two classes, (1) *Ex officio*, (2) Elected. Class 1 comprises owners, lessees, or occupiers of a several fishery of the yearly value of 100*l.* or upwards ; Class 2 are the representatives of the licensees, elected triennially. No person is eligible for the office of conservator in any electoral division in which he does not reside or possess real property. Certain powers are given to conservators, but not to the same extent as in England. Such are

1. To fix the license duty for all methods of taking salmon, and to fix the rate to be paid (but subject to the approval of the inspectors of fisheries) in respect of several fisheries in the district.

2. To appoint water-bailiffs and inspectors.

3. To apply such funds as they possess to make fish passes over weirs, to remove or make passes over natural obstructions, and to inspect passes and ladders at all times.

Close Time. —The regulations as to close time, annual and weekly, vary somewhat in the different fishery districts throughout the United Kingdom. In England and Wales the annual close time was fixed by the Act of 1861 from September 1 to February 1 following, for all methods of fishing other than with rod and line ; and for rod and line fishing, from November 2 to February 1 following ; the weekly close time, from noon on Saturday to 6 A.M. on

Monday for all fishing except with rod and line, for which there is no weekly close time in England. Power is however given to boards of conservators under the Act of 1873 to alter both annual and weekly close times, as to the whole or part of a district, but so that the former shall not be less than one hundred and fifty-four days for all modes of fishing other than with rod and line, and shall not begin later than November 1; and as regards rod and line fishing, that the close time shall not be less than ninety-two days nor commence later than December 1. As to weekly close time boards have power to alter it, but so that it does not commence before 6 P.M. on Friday nor terminate earlier than midnight on the Sunday following, nor continue later than twelve o'clock noon on Monday nor exceed forty-eight hours. In Whitaker's Almanack may be found the variations in the close times in the different districts throughout the United Kingdom, it being impossible within this chapter to set them out.

A close time has been imposed in Scotland for salmon from a very early date. About the year 1200 it was ordained that a free passage should be given to salmon in various rivers from Saturday night to Monday morning. This was called 'Satterday's

R

stoppe.' From 1424 to 1828 the annual close time
for salmon-netting was one hundred and seven days.
In 1828 the Home Drummond Act was passed, the
preamble of which is interesting reading upon this
point, and runs as follows : 'Whereas by an Act
passed in the Parliament of Scotland in the year
1424 it was forbidden that any salmon be slain from
the feast of the Assumption of Our Lady until the
feast of St. Andrew in winter' (*i.e.* from August 15 to
November 30), 'and whereas sundry other laws and
Acts were made and passed at divers times by the
Parliament of Scotland anent the killing of salmon,
kippers, red and black fish in forbidden times, and
the killing and destroying of the fry and smolts of
salmon, which laws were ratified and confirmed and
approved by an Act passed in the said parliament in
the year 1696 intituled an Act against Killers of Black
Fish and Destroyers of the Fry and Smolts of Salmon,
and whereas it is expedient . . . that sundry other
regulations should be made : be it therefore enacted
by the King's most excellent Majesty that no salmon,
grilse, sea trout, nor other fish of the salmon kind,
shall be taken in or from any river, stream, lake,
water or estuary whatsoever, or on any part of the
sea-coast, between the 14th day of September and the
1st of February following on any year by any person or

persons, any law, statute, or practice to the contrary notwithstanding . . . '

Such became the law in 1828, and so it remained until 1862, when the annual close time for every district was fixed at one hundred and sixty-eight days, and the weekly (except for rod and line fishing) from 6 P.M. on Saturday to 6 A.M. on Monday following, power being given to the Commissioners (now the Fishery Board of Scotland) to alter the close times, but so that the annual shall not be less than one hundred and sixty-eight days nor the weekly less than thirty-six hours (except for rod and line fishing, the weekly close time for which is Sunday). The Fishery Board have also power to determine at what periods after the commencement and prior to the termination of the annual close time it may be lawful to fish for salmon with rod and line.

In Ireland the duration of the annual close time, which under the Act of 1842 was fixed as from August 20 to February 12, and not less than one hundred and twenty-four days, was extended by the Act of 1863 to one hundred and sixty-eight days for all fishing except with rod and line, the close time for which is from November 1 to February 1, and may not be less than ninety-two days. The weekly close time for all fishing except with rod and line (for which, as in England, there is no weekly close time) is from 6 A.M. on Saturday to 6 A.M. on Monday following. Further regulations in force in Ireland upon this matter are that no fish of the salmon kind may be taken on the sea-coast, in any estuary, in any river, or in the tide-way from September 1 to January 31, nor in any lake or river above the tide-way between September 18 and the last day of February. Owners, however, of fishing weirs held under grant, charter, prescription, or Act of Parliament above the tide-way, within two miles of where the tide ceases to ebb and flow, if no other fishing weir is interposed between them and the tide-way, may use them for catching salmon in February.

The inspectors of Irish fisheries have similar powers to the Fishery Board of Scotland for the alteration of the close time in rivers.

Fixed Engines.—The use and abuse of what are termed fixed engines, *i.e.* any stationary contrivance for catching salmon or other fish, seems to be of very early date, and we find many laws passed for their suppression. They were in use in the form of ' kiddels and wears ' in the time of King John, for they are referred to in Magna Charta as then existing in the Thames ; while in a later statute we are told that

the reason for their suppression in that river was not
only on the account of the obstructions which they
caused to navigation, but also on account of the
numbers of fry which they were the means of destroying. It was ordained in a statute passed in the
reign of Henry VI. that 'standing nets and engines
called "trinks," and all other nets which are wont to
be fastened and hanged continually day and night to
great posts, boats, and anchors overthwart the river
Thames and other rivers of the realm, which standing
is a cause of as great and more destruction of the
brood and fry of fish and disturbance of the common
passage of vessels, as be the wears and kyddels or any
other engines, be wholly defended for ever; provided
always, that it shall be lawful to the possessors of the
said "trinks" to fish with them, drawing and pulling
them by hand as other fishers do with other nets, and
not fastening or tacking the said nets to posts, boats,
or anchors continually to stand as aforesaid.' Again,
in the reign of Henry VIII., the use of certain
engines, composed of 'stakes, piles, and other things,'
was forbidden in the Ouse and Humber 'by persons
studying only for their own private lucre, not regarding the Common weal, by reason whereof not only
ships and boats were daily in jeopardy, but also broode
and fry of fishe in those rivers be commonly thereby

destroyed and putrified.' We find similar enactments
applying to the rivers of Lancashire and elsewhere,
and Commissioners and Conservators appointed even
in ancient days to put them down, a practice which,
as we shall see, has been followed by modern legislation.

In Scotland, fixed engines have been prohibited
from a very early period, especially in rivers and
estuaries. The old law, and the statutes applicable
to them, was discussed at great length by the Lord
Justice Clerk in the case of Kintore *v*. Forbes, 4 S. 641
(1826), the conclusion derived, after a careful examination of the various Acts of Parliament from the time
of Alexander II., being that stake nets (a form of
fixed engine) were not illegal in the sea, but that
it was settled law that if set in rivers or in estuaries,
to the fullest extent of their limits, they were
illegal.

The first Act of Parliament dealing with the
matter in Ireland is that passed in 28 Henry VIII.,
against the erection of weirs and other engines
for catching fish upon the Barrow and other rivers.

As the law now stands, fixed engines are illegal in
England in inland and tidal waters. The term 'fixed
engine' has been defined by the Salmon Fishery Acts
to mean 'any net or other instrument for taking fish,

fixed to the soil or made stationary in any way (not being a fishing weir or fishing mill-dam), or any net placed or suspended in any inland or tidal waters, unattended by the owner, used for the purpose of catching or facilitating the catching of salmon, or detaining or obstructing the passage of salmon, and all engines, devices, machines, or contrivances, whether floating or otherwise, for placing or suspending such nets, or maintaining them in working order and making them stationary.' Fishing weirs and fishing mill-dams are not illegal if lawfully in use at the time of the passing of the Salmon Fishery Act, 1861, and if they comply with certain requirements contained in the subsequent Salmon Acts as to free gaps and fish passes. The legality of all fixed engines was inquired into by Special Commissioners appointed for that purpose by the Act of 1865, and power was given to them by that Act to abate all those found to be illegal. Their general superintendence is now placed in the hands of the inspector of salmon fisheries. In Scotland the old law is not affected by recent legislation. It should, however, be noticed that cruives are in a different position from other fixed engines in that country. The right to fish with cruives is not carried by a general grant of salmon-fishing, but is itself the subject of an express grant;

or else requires a prescriptive possession of cruive-
fishing following upon a general grant. The legal
use of cruives by various statutes is permitted in, but
limited to, that part of the river which is above the
tide-way—'All cruives and yairs (weirs) set in wateris
quhair the sea fillis and ebbis be put away and
destroyed for ever mair.' Cruives had also, from early
days, to comply with certain conditions whereby
smolts and fry should not be taken in them. ' It was
Statute and ordanit be King Alexander at Perth, on
Thursday before the feist of St. Margaret, with consent
of the Erlis, Baronis, and Judges of Scotland, that the
midst of the water should be fre, sa mekill than ane
swine of three zeir auld and well fed is of length and
may turn him within it in sic manner that nather
his grunzie nor his tail tuich any of the sides of the
cruives that are biggit on each side of the water.'
The Commissioners for Scotland, in accordance with
their powers, have in more recent times, by a bye-law
dated July 28, 1865, made certain regulations with
regard to cruives.

The law in Ireland has undergone some changes
with regard to fixed engines in tidal waters in modern
times. As defined by the Act of 1850, they are
practically the same as those included in the defini-
tions under the English law. By the Act of 1842 the

settlement of this vexed question was attempted by the bold experiment of permitting owners of several fisheries in, and lessees of, land adjoining tidal waters or estuaries to erect fixed engines, subject to certain restrictions. They were not to impede navigation, nor were they to be placed in or near the mouths of narrow rivers, nor might they extend beyond high or low water mark, nor be capable of taking under-sized fish. Stake weirs, established for twenty years before the passing of the Act, and head weirs were not affected by these provisions. A rapid increase in the number of bag nets followed upon this, and a consequent decrease in the number of salmon. Therefore, in 1863, the Act was amended, and bag nets rendered illegal in inland and tidal waters and within three miles of a river's mouth ; other fixed engines in use in 1862—and only those—were for the future to be recognised as legal. Free gaps or Queen's shares, under the Act of 1842, were made compulsory in all cases of obstructions extending more than half-way across a river, while in many cases, upon the application of a fishery proprietor, the Commissioners had power to make the same. Special Commissioners were appointed under the Act to inquire into the legality of all fixed nets, and to order the removal of those found to be illegal or, in their opinion, injurious to navigation. They were also empowered to inquire into the legality of all fishing weirs with regard to which new regulations were imposed as to free gaps.

OFFENCES AGAINST THE SALMON FISHERY ACTS

1. *Poisoning Fish.*—Causing or knowingly permitting any liquid or solid matter to flow into water containing salmon, or into any tributaries thereof, to such an extent as to cause the waters to poison salmon.

In England and Scotland no person is guilty of this offence if he proves he has used the best practical means, within a reasonable cost, to render such matter harmless. It is a further offence in Ireland to be found on or near a salmon river in possession of poisonous matter with intent to use it for the destruction of fish.

2. *Using Illegal Instruments.*—Using any light, leister, spear, otter, stroke-haul, gaff (except as an auxiliary to rod and line, when not forbidden by bye-law, or when used for removing fish from boxes or cribs), or other instrument for the purpose of taking salmon.

In England and Scotland it is an offence to be

found, at any time, in possession of these instruments
with intent to kill salmon.   In Ireland it is an offence
only to be found in possession of them between
sunset and sunrise.

3. *Fishing with Roe.*—Using any fish roe for
fishing. Buying, selling, or exposing for sale or
possessing salmon roe.   But this does not apply to
any person in England or Scotland who possesses
roe for scientific purposes or for artificial propagation.

The prohibition in Ireland is limited to possessing
salmon roe.

4. *Killing Smolts.*—Wilfully taking or destroying
smolts or salmon fry, or buying, selling, exposing for
sale, or possessing the same.

Placing any engine or device for obstructing the
same or wilfully injuring the same.

Wilfully injuring or disturbing any salmon spawn,
or spawning bed on which the salmon may be.

5. *Killing Unclean Salmon.*—Wilfully taking, fishing for, or attempting to take unclean or unseasonable salmon.   But no person is guilty of an offence
in England and Scotland if he takes the same for
scientific purposes or for artificial propagation.   In
England the consent of a conservancy board is
necessary to do this.

6. *Selling Unclean Salmon.*—Buying, selling, or exposing for sale unclean or unseasonable salmon.

7. *Killing Salmon in Close Time.*—Fishing for, taking, or attempting to take, or aiding or assisting in fishing for, taking, or attempting to take, salmon during the close time, annual or weekly, as fixed by Act of Parliament or bye-law.

8. Buying, selling, exposing for sale, or possessing for the purposes of sale, salmon or part of any salmon in annual close time.

9. *Exporting Salmon.*—Exporting unclean or unseasonable salmon, or salmon caught during the time at which its sale is prohibited in the district in which it is caught, from any part of the United Kingdom. The burden of proving that any salmon entered for exportation, between the third of September and the thirtieth of April, is not entered in infringement of the Act, lies upon the person exporting the salmon.

10. Sending salmon in England by carrier without conspicuously marking the package containing the same between September 3 and February 1.

11. *Not removing Nets in Close Time.*—Neglecting to remove from a fishery all engines, spears, hand nets and other nets, planks and temporary obstructions, inscales, hecks, and rails of cruives, boxes, and

cribs, all boats and oars (except those used for angling), within thirty-six hours after the commencement of the annual close time.

12. Neglecting to keep open a clear passage for salmon through nets, cribs, boxes, cruives, and other engines during weekly close time.

13. Doing any act or using any device for the purpose of preventing the free passage of salmon through the same during the close times (annual or weekly).

14. *Fish Passes and Free Gaps.*—Neglecting to erect or maintain, or injuring and thereby rendering less efficient, when erected, a free gap, Queen's share, or fish pass, in dams, dykes, weirs, or other obstructions, as and where required by law.

15. Doing any act for the purpose of preventing the free passage of salmon through the same.

16. *Using Illegal Nets and other Engines.*—Using a net whose mesh in England is less than 2 inches, measured from knot to knot or 8 inches all round when wet; in Scotland and Ireland, whose mesh is less than one and three-quarter inches from knot to knot or seven inches all round when wet; or in the United Kingdom, a net whose mesh is of a smaller size than is sanctioned in a particular locality by bye-law.

17. Using a box, crib, or cruive which does not comply with the regulations imposed by the Acts in England and Ireland, or with any bye-law affecting the same in Scotland.

18. Using any fixed engine not privileged, or declared to be illegal, for the purpose of catching or facilitating the catching of salmon.

19. *Fishing near a Dam.* — Fishing, except with rod and line, near a weir, dam, or artificial obstruction which is not provided with a fish pass, or in the waters of a mill. In England the limit is 50 yards above, and 100 below. In Scotland it is an offence to fish at a dam, but no limit is fixed. In Ireland the limit is 50 yards above and below.

20. *Obstructing Water-bailiffs.* — Refusing to allow a water-bailiff, inspector, or person appointed by a board of conservators or district board to have access to a weir, dam, fishing weir, fishing mill-dam, fixed engine, obstruction, or water-course.

21. Refusing to allow water-bailiffs and others to search, or obstructing them in their search of, any boat, barge, cot, coracle, or other vessel used in fishing, or which they may suspect contains salmon.

22. Refusing to allow water-bailiffs and others to search, or obstructing them in searching, nets,

baskets, or instruments used in fishing or carrying fish.

23. *Breach of Bye-laws.*—Infringing any bye-law sanctioned by the Board of Trade, Fishery Board of Scotland, or Lord-Lieutenant of Ireland as the case may be.

24. *Gratings and Sluices.*—Neglecting to erect or maintain, or injuring when erected, gratings at the points of divergence from and return to the main river of all artificial streams, cuts, or water-courses used for conveying water to towns, mills, or factories.

25. Neglecting to keep shut the sluices in mill-streams during the time prescribed by the Acts or by bye-law, or when the water is not used for milling purposes.

26. Fishing for salmon with rod and line without a license. (This does not apply to Scotland or to places in England and Ireland where no board of conservators has been formed.)

27. Fishing for salmon by means of a putt, putcher, fishing weir, fishing mill-dam, net, instrument or device (not being a rod and line) without a license. (This does not apply to Scotland or to England and Ireland as above mentioned.)

28. Refusing to produce a license upon the

application of a licensee, conservator, water-bailiff, constable, or officer of a board.

29. *Draft Net across a River.*—Shooting draft net for salmon across the whole width of a river. This does not apply to Scotland, nor to Ireland in the case of the owner of a several fishery in the whole of a river or its tributaries.

30. Using baskets or traps for catching eels in England between January 1 and June 24, in Ireland between January 10 and July 1.

31. *Trespass.*—Trespassing upon lands in Scotland or Ireland for the purpose of fishing.

32. *Duty of Clerk of Peace.*—The clerk of the peace neglecting to send the names and addresses of conservators appointed by different counties, when the district comprises more than one county, to the clerk of the board within fourteen days of the appointment. (This only applies to England.)

33. *Duty of Clerk to Justices.*—The clerk of the justices neglecting to send a certificate of a conviction against the Salmon Fishery Acts to the clerk to the board of conservators within a month. (This only applies to England.)

34. *Placing Device upon Weir.*— Placing upon the apron of a weir any basket or device for taking fish

except wheels and leaps for taking lamperns between August 1 and March 1. (This only applies to England.)

35. *Night Poaching.*—If three or more persons, acting in concert, or being together between the expiration of the first hour after sunset and the beginning of the last hour before sunrise, enter or are found upon any land adjacent to a river, estuary, or sea-coast with intent illegally to kill salmon, or in possession of illegal nets or instruments, they commit an offence.   (This only applies to Scotland.)

36. *Salmon Leaping at a Fall.*—Setting or using a net or other engine for the capture of salmon when leaping at or trying to ascend a fall, or when falling back from the same.   (This only applies to Scotland.)

37. *Pollution.*—Wilfully putting, or neglecting to take reasonable precautions to prevent the discharge of, any sawdust, chaff, or shelling corn into a river. (This only applies to Scotland.)

The following do not apply to England or Scotland :—

38. *Obstructing Fishermen.*—Obstructing any fisherman, or persons employed by him, in entering upon, and using for the purpose of drawing their nets or landing their fish, any beach, land, or wastes,

S

except gardens and lands with a growing crop upon
them.

39. *Discharging Ballast.*—Discharging ballast
from any vessel within an estuary harbour, or place
not sanctioned by the Commissioners or local regulations.

40. *Netting in Narrow Estuaries.*—Shooting or
using a net for salmon at the mouth of a river (the
inland part of which is frequented by salmon), or
within half a mile of the mouth when the breadth of
the mouth is less than a quarter of a mile. This
does not apply to the owner of a several fishery,
except as to bag nets.

41. *Netting in Fresh Waters.*—Using a haul, draft,
seine, or other net in inland waters. This does not
apply (except as to bag nets) to the owner of a several
fishery, nor to cases where a common of piscary has
been enjoyed for twenty years before 1842.

42. *Nets generally.*—Using in tidal waters a net
covered with canvas, or in fresh waters a net formed
with a false bottom, or two nets placed one behind
the other.

43. *Cross Lines.*—Using cross lines in any river.
(This does not apply to the owner of a several
fishery or to any person authorised by him in
writing.)

44. Removing or using any cot or boat without the owner's permission.

45. *Intimidation.*—To be found to the number of three or more together by an officer of the Navy, coastguard, water-bailiff, or peace officer, by violence or intimidation obstructing persons lawfully fishing.

46. *Eel Weirs.*—Taking salmon in an eel weir.

47. *Bag Nets.*—Placing or using a bag net in a river or estuary, or within three miles of a river's mouth. But this does not apply to the owner of a several fishery in the whole of a river and its tributaries.

48. *Fishing at Night.*—Using any net, except a landing net, for catching salmon in fresh water between 8 P.M. and 6 A.M., except so far as the same has been used within the limits of a several fishery next above the tidal flow, and held under grant, charter, or immemorial usage.

This is not a complete list of offences, nor technically expressed, but it comprises the most important under the Salmon Fishery Acts.

In addition to the above-mentioned offences, by the Fisheries (Dynamite) Act of 1877 it is an offence to use dynamite or other explosive to catch or destroy fish in a public fishery in the United Kingdom.

This was extended to private fisheries in England by an Act of the following year.

By the Malicious Injuries to Property Act, 1861, s. 32, it is an offence unlawfully and maliciously to put any lime or noxious material into any salmon river with intent to destroy fish therein. This Act extends to England and Ireland, and by s. 24 of the Larceny Act, 1861, it is an offence unlawfully and wilfully to take or destroy any fish in any water, which shall run through or be in any land adjoining to or belonging to the dwelling house of any person being the owner of such water or having a right of fishery therein, or to destroy or attempt to destroy fish in a private fishery. This applies to England and Ireland.

By the Gas Works Clauses Act, 1847, it is an offence if the persons authorised to construct gasworks cause or suffer to be brought or flow into any stream or place for water, or into any drain communicating therewith, any washing or other substance produced in making or supplying gas, or do any act whereby the water in such stream or place may be fouled.

Similar provision is made in the Rivers Pollution Act, 1878, with regard to the refuse from factories, quarries, and mines, and to sewage. No one, however, will be guilty of an offence under this Act if he proves that he has taken the best means to render the refuse or sewage harmless.

LEGAL PROCEDURE

The legal procedure with regard to the prosecution of offences against the Salmon Fishery Acts is almost identical in England, Scotland, and Ireland. Proceedings are taken in England before two Justices at Petty Sessions; in Scotland, before a Sheriff or two Justices; in Ireland, before one or more Justices. In England and Ireland there is an appeal to Quarter Sessions; in Scotland to the next Circuit Court, or, where no Circuit Court exists, to the Court of Justiciary in Edinburgh. No Justice is disqualified from hearing a case by reason of his being a conservator or member of a district board, provided he deals with no case arising out of an offence committed upon his own fishing. A *bonâ fide* claim of right ousts the jurisdiction of Justices. Proceedings are to be taken within six months of the alleged offence having been committed. Offences committed upon the sea-coast, or at sea beyond the ordinary jurisdiction of any Justice, may be tried by a Justice having jurisdiction on the land abutting on the sea-coast, and offences committed upon water forming the boundary between two counties may be prosecuted in either county.

For the detection and prevention of offences, water-bailiffs and officers appointed by conservancy or district boards are invested with special powers. In England a water-bailiff may

1. Seize without warrant any person putting noxious matter into a salmon river with intent to destroy fish, or illegally taking salmon, or found on or near a salmon river with intent to take salmon between the expiration of the first hour after sunset and the beginning of the last hour before sunrise, or found during those hours in possession of an illegal instrument.

2. May apply to a Justice for a warrant to remain on land near a salmon river, and make search if he has good reason to suspect a breach of the Acts is about to be or has been committed.

3. May, under a special order in writing from the chairman of the conservancy board for a period not exceeding two months, go upon any land (except a decoy) near any salmon river in the district.

4. May examine weirs, dams, fixed engines, and obstructions and artificial water-courses.

5. May stop and search boats, coracles, or vessels used in fishing, or which there is reason to suspect

contain salmon, and all nets and baskets and other instruments.

6. May seize all salmon illegally caught, and all instruments illegally used.

In Scotland, any person employed in the execution of the Salmon Fishery Acts may seize and detain all fish illegally taken, and all boats, tackle, nets, and other engines illegally used. Water-bailiffs and officers of district boards have power, as in England, to enter upon land if they have reason to suspect a breach of the Acts to have been or may be committed. But no special order or warrant is necessary. Similar powers are also given to them to examine dams, weirs, cruives, etc., as in England.

The Irish Acts confer upon water-bailiffs almost identical powers as do the English Acts ; one point only may be noticed, viz. that under a warrant they may enter a garden or a dwelling house. For the further protection of the fisheries in Ireland, officers and men of the Navy and Coastguard, and the Royal Irish Constabulary, are empowered to carry out and enforce the provisions of the Salmon Fishery Acts.

Under the Larceny Act, 1861, above mentioned, private individuals in England and Ireland may arrest persons offending against its provisions, except for angling in the daytime, and if any person is found unlawfully fishing in a private fishery, the owner of the ground, water, or fishery, his servant, or any person authorised by him, may demand from the offender any rod, line, hook, net, or other instrument for taking or destroying fish, and in case such offender shall not immediately deliver up the same, may seize and take the same. But any person angling in the daytime, from whom such implement is taken, is exempted from the payment of any damages or penalty. This section, it will be seen, gives no such power to a lessee, nor any power to seize fish which a poacher may have in his possession.

By the Irish Act of 1842, any person interested in a fishery, who finds any person fishing with any illegal net or engine, may require him to desist, and give his name and address, and upon refusal to do so may arrest him.

In Scotland the law is somewhat different. There any person may seize without warrant, detain, and give into custody persons committing the following offences :—

Against the Act of 1828.

1. Trespassing for salmon or neglecting to observe the law as to ' Satterday's Stop.'

Under the Act of 1868.

2. Fishing during annual or weekly close time.

3. Fishing with a net contrary to bye-law.

4. Using a net or other engine for catching salmon leaping at a fall.

5. Preventing salmon passing through a fish pass.

6. Using a light, spear, leister or other illegal instrument.

7. Using fish roe.

8. Destroying smolts or fry, or disturbing the spawning grounds.

9. Taking or selling unseasonable salmon or salmon caught in close time.

10. Illegally exporting salmon.

THE TWEED AND SOLWAY

Although it is impossible to enter into the matter in detail, some reference must now be made to the Tweed and the rivers flowing into the Solway, with regard to which special legislation has from time to time been passed, the reason for which is not far to seek. The Tweed on the east, the rivers and Firth of Solway on the west, form the boundary between England and Scotland, and while the two kingdoms

T

were in different hands different laws were in force, and little regard was shown to those existing *ex adverso*. Consequently we find certain exemptions in favour of these rivers, or some of them, in many instances in old Scottish Acts of Parliament. By the Act of 1424, a special exemption for Tweed and Solway from the penalties of killing fish in close time, ' quhilkis sall be reddie to Scottismen at all times of the zeir als lang as Berwick and Roxburgh are in English mennis hands.' Again in 1563 the Solway was exempted from the prohibition against ' cruives and yairs.' Again in 1600 killing salmon in forbidden times was declared to be theft, 'except in Annand and Tweed, because the said rivers devyded at many parts the bounds of Scotland and England adjacent to them, whereby the forbearance upon the Scots' part of the slauchter of salmon in forbidden time or of kipper, smolts, and black fish at all times, would not have made salmond any mair to abound in these waters if the like order had not been observed on the English side.'

Special legislation upon the Tweed commenced in 1771, and was followed by various Acts down to 1857 and 1859, bringing the law upon that river to its present condition, the management of the river being put in the hands of local Commissioners. Solway

legislation commenced in 1804, and all the fisheries
of the Solway and its Scotch tributaries, except the
Annan and Esk, were regulated by an Act passed in
that year. In 1861 the English Act repealed the
Solway Act in so far as it related to English waters,
and in 1865 the whole of the Esk was put under
English law. In 1862 the English law as to fixed
engines was made to apply to the whole of the
Solway Firth. The Annan was placed under a special
Act in 1841, which Act extends to its tributaries, and
to that portion of the sea-coast lying between the
rivers Sark on the east and Lochar on the west.

To the state of affairs which must have existed
in olden days, when the hand of everyone was against
the salmon in these waters, and it became necessary
by united legislation to prevent their extermination, we
find an almost parallel instance in the condition of
affairs and destruction of the seals in the Behring Sea
by Canadian and United States fishermen at the
present time.

Spottiswoode & Co. Printers, New-street Square, London.

MESSRS. LONGMANS, GREEN, & CO.'S
CLASSIFIED CATALOGUE
OF
WORKS IN GENERAL LITERATURE.

History, Politics, Polity, Political Memoirs, &c.

Abbott.—A HISTORY OF GREECE. By EVELYN ABBOTT, M.A., LL.D.
Part I.—From the Earliest Times to the Ionian Revolt. Crown 8vo., 10s. 6d.
Part II.—500-445 B.C. Cr. 8vo., 10s. 6d.

Acland and Ransome.—A HANDBOOK IN OUTLINE OF THE POLITICAL HISTORY OF ENGLAND TO 1896. Chronologically Arranged. By A. H. DYKE ACLAND, M.P., and CYRIL RANSOME, M.A. Crown 8vo., 6s.

ANNUAL REGISTER (THE). A Review of Public Events at Home and Abroad, for the year 1896. 8vo., 18s.
Volumes of the ANNUAL REGISTER for the years 1863-1895 can still be had. 18s. each.

Arnold (THOMAS, D.D.), formerly Head Master of Rugby School.
INTRODUCTORY LECTURES ON MODERN HISTORY. 8vo., 7s. 6d.
MISCELLANEOUS WORKS. 8vo., 7s. 6d.

Baden-Powell.—THE INDIAN VILLAGE COMMUNITY. Examined with Reference to the Physical, Ethnographic, and Historical Conditions of the Provinces; chiefly on the Basis of the Revenue-Settlement Records and District Manuals. By B. H. BADEN-POWELL, M.A., C.I.E. With Map. 8vo., 16s.

Bagwell.—IRELAND UNDER THE TUDORS. By RICHARD BAGWELL, LL.D. (3 vols). Vols. I. and II. From the first Invasion of the Northmen to the year 1578. 8vo., 32s. Vol. III. 1578-1603. 8vo., 18s.

Ball.—HISTORICAL REVIEW OF THE LEGISLATIVE SYSTEMS OPERATIVE IN IRELAND, from the Invasion of Henry the Second to the Union (1172-1800). By the Rt. Hon. J. T. BALL. 8vo., 6s.

Besant.—THE HISTORY OF LONDON. By Sir WALTER BESANT. With 74 Illustrations. Crown 8vo., 1s. 9d. Or bound as a School Prize Book, 2s. 6d.

Brassey (LORD).—PAPERS AND ADDRESSES.
NAVAL AND MARITIME, 1872-1893. 2 vols. Crown 8vo., 10s.
MERCANTILE MARINE AND NAVIGATION. from 1871-1894. Cr. 8vo., 5s.
IMPERIAL FEDERATION AND COLONISATION FROM 1880-1894. Crown 8vo., 5s.
POLITICAL AND MISCELLANEOUS, 1861-1894. Crown 8vo., 5s.

Bright.—A HISTORY OF ENGLAND. By the Rev. J. FRANCK BRIGHT, D.D.
Period I. MEDIÆVAL MONARCHY: A.D. 449-1485. Crown 8vo., 4s. 6d.
Period II. PERSONAL MONARCHY: 1485-1688. Crown 8vo., 5s.
Period III. CONSTITUTIONAL MONARCHY: 1689-1837. Cr. 8vo., 7s. 6d.
Period IV. THE GROWTH OF DEMOCRACY: 1837-1880. Crown 8vo., 6s.

Buckle.—HISTORY OF CIVILISATION IN ENGLAND AND FRANCE, SPAIN AND SCOTLAND. By HENRY THOMAS BUCKLE. 3 vols. Crown 8vo., 24s.

Burke.—A HISTORY OF SPAIN, from the Earliest Times to the Death of Ferdinand the Catholic. By ULICK RALPH BURKE, M.A. 2 vols. 8vo., 32s.

Chesney.—INDIAN POLITY: a View of the System of Administration in India. By General Sir GEORGE CHESNEY, K.C.B. With Map showing all the Administrative Divisions of British India. 8vo. 21s.

Corbett.—DRAKE AND THE TUDOR NAVY, with a History of the Rise of England as a Maritime Power. By JULIAN CORBETT. With Portraits, Illustrations and Maps. 2 vols. 8vo.

Creighton.—A HISTORY OF THE PAPACY FROM THE GREAT SCHISM TO THE SACK OF ROME (1378-1527). By M. CREIGHTON, D.D., Lord Bishop of London. 6 vols. Cr. 8vo., 6s. each.

Cuningham.—A SCHEME FOR IMPERIAL FEDERATION: a Senate for the Empire. By GRANVILLE C. CUNINGHAM of Montreal, Canada. Cr. 8vo., 3s. 6d.

History, Politics, Polity, Political Memoirs, &c.—*continued.*

Curzon.—PERSIA AND THE PERSIAN QUESTION. By the Right HON. GEORGE N. CURZON, M.P. With 9 Maps, 96 Illustrations, Appendices, and an Index. 2 vols. 8vo., 42s.

De Tocqueville.— DEMOCRACY IN AMERICA. By ALEXIS DE TOCQUE-VILLE. 2 vols. Crown 8vo., 16s.

Dickinson.—THE DEVELOPMENT OF PARLIAMENT DURING THE NINE-TEENTH CENTURY. By G. LOWES DICKINSON. M.A. 8vo. 7s. 6d.

Eggleston.—THE BEGINNERS OF A NATION : A History of the Source and Rise of the Earliest English Settlements in America, with Special Reference to the Life and Character of the People. By EDWARD EGGLESTON. With 8 Maps. Crown 8vo., 7s. 6d.

Froude (JAMES A.).

THE HISTORY OF ENGLAND, from the Fall of Wolsey to the Defeat of the Spanish Armada. 12 vols. Crown 8vo., 3s. 6d. each.

THE DIVORCE OF CATHERINE OF ARA-GON. Crown 8vo., 3s. 6d.

THE SPANISH STORY OF THE ARMADA, and other Essays. Cr. 8vo., 3s. 6d.

THE ENGLISH IN IRELAND IN THE EIGHTEENTH CENTURY. 3 vols. Crown 8vo., 10s. 6d.

ENGLISH SEAMEN IN THE SIXTEENTH CENTURY. Crown 8vo., 6s.

THE COUNCIL OF TRENT. Cr.8vo.,3s.6d.

SHORT STUDIES ON GREAT SUBJECTS. 4 vols. Cr. 8vo., 3s. 6d. each.

CÆSAR : a Sketch. Cr. 8vo., 3s. 6d.

Gardiner (SAMUEL RAWSON, D.C.L., LL.D.).

HISTORY OF ENGLAND, from the Ac-cession of James I. to the Outbreak of the Civil War, 1603-1642. 10 vols. Crown 8vo., 6s. each.

A HISTORY OF THE GREAT CIVIL WAR, 1642-1649. 4 vols. Cr. 8vo., 6s. each.

A HISTORY OF THE COMMONWEALTH AND THE PROTECTORATE, 1649-1660. Vol. I., 1649-1651. With 14 Maps. 8vo., 21s. Vol. II., 1651-1654. With 7 Maps. 8vo., 21s.

WHAT GUNPOWDER PLOT WAS. With 8 Illustrations and Plates. Crown 8vo., 5s.

Gardiner (SAMUEL RAWSON, D.C.L., LL.D.)—*continued.*

CROMWELL'S PLACE IN HISTORY. Founded on Six Lectures delivered in the University of Oxford. Crown 8vo., 3s. 6d.

THE STUDENT'S HISTORY OF ENGLAND. With 378 Illustrations. Cr. 8vo., 12s.
Also in Three Volumes, price 4s. each.

Vol. I. B.C. 55-A.D. 1509. 173 Illus-trations.

Vol. II. 1509-1689. 96 Illustrations.

Vol. III. 1689-1885. 109 Illustrations.

Greville.—A JOURNAL OF THE REIGNS OF KING GEORGE IV., KING WILLIAM IV., AND QUEEN VICTORIA. By CHARLES C. F. GREVILLE, formerly Clerk of the Council. 8 vols. Crown 8vo., 3s. 6d. each.

HARVARD HISTORICAL STUDIES.

THE SUPPRESSION OF THE AFRICAN SLAVE TRADE TO THE UNITED STATES OF AMERICA, 1638-1870. By W. E. B. DU BOIS, Ph.D. 8vo., 7s. 6d.

THE CONTEST OVER THE RATIFICA-TION OF THE FEDERAL CONSTITU-TION IN MASSACHUSETTS. By S. B. HARDING, A.M. 8vo., 6s.

A CRITICAL STUDY OF NULLIFICATION IN SOUTH CAROLINA. By D. F. HOUSTON, A.M. 8vo., 6s.

NOMINATIONS FOR ELECTIVE OFFICE IN THE UNITED STATES. By FRED-ERICK W. DALLINGER, A.M. 8vo., 7s. 6d.
*** *Other Volumes are in preparation.*

Gross.—A BIBLIOGRAPHY OF BRITISH MUNICIPAL HISTORY, including Gilds and Parliamentary Representation. By CHARLES GROSS, Ph.D., Assistant Pro-fessor of History in Harvard University. 8vo., 12s.

Historic Towns.—Edited by E. A. FREEMAN, D.C.L., and Rev. WILLIAM HUNT, M.A. With Maps and Plans. Crown 8vo., 3s. 6d. each.

Bristol. By Rev. W. Hunt.

Carlisle. By Mandell Creighton, D.D.

Cinque Ports. By Montagu Burrows.

Colchester. By Rev. E. L. Cutts.

Exeter. By E. A. Freeman.

London. By Rev. W. J. Loftie.

Oxford. By Rev. C. W. Boase.

Winchester. By G. W. Kitchin, D.D.

York. By Rev. James Raine.

New York. By Theo-dore Roosevelt.

Boston (U.S.). By Henry Cabot Lodge.

History, Politics, Polity, Political Memoirs, &c.—*continued.*

Joyce (P. W., LL.D.).

A SHORT HISTORY OF IRELAND, from the Earliest Times to 1608. Crown 8vo., 10s. 6d.

A CHILD'S HISTORY OF IRELAND, from the Earliest Times to the Death of O'Connell. With Map and 160 Illustrations. Crown 8vo., 3s. 6d.

Kaye and Malleson.—HISTORY OF THE INDIAN MUTINY, 1857-1858. By Sir JOHN W. KAYE and Colonel G. B. MALLESON. With Analytical Index and Maps and Plans. 6 vols. Crown 8vo., 3s. 6d. each.

Knight.—MADAGASCAR IN WAR TIME: the Experiences of *The Times* Special Correspondent with the Hovas during the French Invasion of 1895. By E. F. KNIGHT. With 16 Illustrations and a Map. 8vo., 12s. 6d.

Lang (ANDREW).

PICKLE THE SPY, or, The Incognito of Prince Charles. With 6 Portraits. 8vo., 18s.

ST. ANDREWS. With 8 Plates and 24 Illustrations in the Text by T. HODGE. 8vo., 15s. net.

Laurie.—HISTORICAL SURVEY OF PRE-CHRISTIAN EDUCATION. By S. S. LAURIE, A.M., LL.D. Crown 8vo., 12s.

Lecky (WILLIAM EDWARD HARTPOLE).

HISTORY OF ENGLAND IN THE EIGHTEENTH CENTURY.
Library Edition. 8 vols. 8vo., £7 4s.
Cabinet Edition. ENGLAND. 7 vols. Cr. 8vo., 6s. each. IRELAND. 5 vols. Crown 8vo., 6s. each.

HISTORY OF EUROPEAN MORALS FROM AUGUSTUS TO CHARLEMAGNE. 2 vols. Crown 8vo., 16s.

HISTORY OF THE RISE AND INFLUENCE OF THE SPIRIT OF RATIONALISM IN EUROPE. 2 vols. Crown 8vo., 16s.

DEMOCRACY AND LIBERTY. 2 vols. 8vo., 36s.

THE EMPIRE: its Value and its Growth. An Inaugural Address delivered at the Imperial Institute, November 20, 1893. Crown 8vo., 1s. 6d.

Lowell.—GOVERNMENTS AND PARTIES IN CONTINENTAL EUROPE. By A. LAWRENCE LOWELL. 2 vols. 8vo., 21s.

Macaulay (LORD).

THE LIFE AND WORKS OF LORD MACAULAY. '*Edinburgh*' *Edition.* 10 vols. 8vo., 6s. each.
Vols. I.-IV. HISTORY OF ENGLAND.
Vols. V.-VII. ESSAYS; BIOGRAPHIES; INDIAN PENAL CODE; CONTRIBUTIONS TO KNIGHT'S 'QUARTERLY MAGAZINE'.
Vol. VIII. SPEECHES, LAYS OF ANCIENT ROME; MISCELLANEOUS POEMS.
Vols. IX. and X. THE LIFE AND LETTERS OF LORD MACAULAY. By the Right Hon. Sir G. O. TREVELYAN, Bart.
This Edition is a cheaper reprint of the Library Edition of LORD MACAULAY'S *Life and Works.*

COMPLETE WORKS.
Cabinet Edition. 16 vols. Post 8vo., £4 16s.
'*Edinburgh*' *Edition.* 8 vols. 8vo., 6s. each.
Library Edition. 8 vols. 8vo., £5 5s.

HISTORY OF ENGLAND FROM THE ACCESSION OF JAMES THE SECOND.
Popular Edition. 2 vols. Cr. 8vo., 5s.
Student's Edit. 2 vols. Cr. 8vo., 12s.
People's Edition. 4 vols. Cr. 8vo., 16s.
Cabinet Edition. 8 vols. Post 8vo., 48s.
'*Edinburgh*' *Edition.* 4 vols. 8vo., 6s. each.
Library Edition. 5 vols. 8vo., £4.

CRITICAL AND HISTORICAL ESSAYS, WITH LAYS OF ANCIENT ROME, in 1 volume.
Popular Edition. Crown 8vo., 2s. 6d.
Authorised Edition. Crown 8vo., 2s. 6d., or 3s. 6d., gilt edges.
'*Silver Library*' *Edition.* Crown 8vo., 3s. 6d.

CRITICAL AND HISTORICAL ESSAYS.
Student's Edition. 1 vol. Cr. 8vo., 6s.
People's Edition. 2 vols. Cr. 8vo., 8s.
'*Trevelyan*' *Edit.* 2 vols. Cr. 8vo., 9s.
Cabinet Edition. 4 vols. Post 8vo., 24s.
'*Edinburgh*' *Edition.* 4 vols. 8vo., 6s. each.
Library Edition. 3 vols. 8vo., 36s.

History, Politics, Polity, Political Memoirs, &c.—continued.

Macaulay (LORD).—continued.

ESSAYS which may be had separately, price 6d. each sewed, 1s. each cloth.

Addison and Wal-pole.	Ranke and Gladstone.
Croker's Boswell's Johnson.	Milton and Machiavelli.
Hallam's Constitutional History.	Lord Byron.
Warren Hastings.	Lord Clive.
The Earl of Chatham (Two Essays).	Lord Byron, and The Comic Dramatists of the Restoration.
Frederick the Great.	

MISCELLANEOUS WRITINGS.

People's Edition. 1 vol. Cr. 8vo., 4s. 6d.

Library Edition. 2 vols. 8vo., 21s.

Popular Edition. Cr. 8vo., 2s. 6d.

Cabinet Edition. Including Indian Penal Code, Lays of Ancient Rome, and Miscellaneous Poems. 4 vols. Post 8vo., 24s.

SELECTIONS FROM THE WRITINGS OF LORD MACAULAY. Edited, with Occasional Notes, by the Right Hon. Sir G. O. Trevelyan, Bart. Cr. 8vo., 6s.

MacColl.—THE SULTAN AND THE POWERS. By the Rev. MALCOLM MAC-COLL, M.A., Canon of Ripon. 8vo., 10s. 6d.

Mackinnon.—THE UNION OF ENGLAND AND SCOTLAND: a Study of International History. By JAMES MAC-KINNON, Ph.D., Examiner in History to the University of Edinburgh. 8vo., 16s.

May.—THE CONSTITUTIONAL HISTORY OF ENGLAND since the Accession of George III. 1760-1870. By Sir THOMAS ERSKINE MAY, K.C.B. (Lord Farnborough). 3 vols. Crown 8vo., 18s.

Merivale (THE LATE DEAN).

HISTORY OF THE ROMANS UNDER THE EMPIRE. 8 vols. Cr. 8vo., 3s. 6d. each.

THE FALL OF THE ROMAN REPUBLIC: a Short History of the Last Century of the Commonwealth. 12mo., 7s. 6d.

GENERAL HISTORY OF ROME, from the Foundation of the City to the Fall of Augustulus, B.C. 753-A.D. 476. With 5 Maps. Crown 8vo., 7s. 6d.

Montague.—THE ELEMENTS OF ENGLISH CONSTITUTIONAL HISTORY. By F. C. MONTAGUE, M.A. Cr. 8vo., 3s. 6d.

Richman.—APPENZELL: Pure Democracy and Pastoral Life in Inner-Rhoden. A Swiss Study. By IRVING B. RICHMAN, Consul-General of the United States to Switzerland. With Maps. Crown 8vo., 5s.

Seebohm (FREDERIC).

THE ENGLISH VILLAGE COMMUNITY Examined in its Relations to the Manorial and Tribal Systems, &c. With 13 Maps and Plates. 8vo., 16s.

THE TRIBAL SYSTEM IN WALES: being Part of an Inquiry into the Structure and Methods of Tribal Society. With 3 Maps. 8vo., 12s.

Sharpe.—LONDON AND THE KINGDOM: a History derived mainly from the Archives at Guildhall in the custody of the Corporation of the City of London. By REGINALD R. SHARPE, D.C.L., Records Clerk in the Office of the Town Clerk of the City of London. 3 vols. 8vo. 10s. 6d. each.

Smith.—CARTHAGE AND THE CARTHAGINIANS. By R. BOSWORTH SMITH, M.A., With Maps, Plans, &c. Cr. 8vo., 3s. 6d.

Stephens.—A HISTORY OF THE FRENCH REVOLUTION. By H. MORSE STEPHENS, 3 vols. 8vo. Vols. I. and II., 18s. each.

Stubbs.—HISTORY OF THE UNIVERSITY OF DUBLIN, from its Foundation to the End of the Eighteenth Century. By J. W. STUBBS. 8vo., 12s. 6d.

Sutherland.—THE HISTORY OF AUSTRALIA AND NEW ZEALAND, from 1606-1890. By ALEXANDER SUTHERLAND, M.A., and GEORGE SUTHERLAND, M.A. Crown 8vo., 2s. 6d.

Taylor.—A STUDENT'S MANUAL OF THE HISTORY OF INDIA. By Colonel MEADOWS TAYLOR, C.S.I., &c. Cr. 8vo., 7s. 6d.

Todd.—PARLIAMENTARY GOVERNMENT IN THE BRITISH COLONIES. By ALPHEUS TODD, LL.D. 8vo., 30s. net.

History, Politics, Polity, Political Memoirs, &c.—*continued.*

Wakeman and Hassall.—ESSAYS INTRODUCTORY TO THE STUDY OF ENGLISH CONSTITUTIONAL HISTORY. By Resident Members of the University of Oxford. Edited by HENRY OFFLEY WAKEMAN, M.A., and ARTHUR HASSALL, M.A. Crown 8vo., 6s.

Walpole.—HISTORY OF ENGLAND FROM THE CONCLUSION OF THE GREAT WAR IN 1815 TO 1858. By SPENCER WALPOLE. 6 vols. Crown 8vo., 6s. each.

Wood-Martin.—PAGAN IRELAND: an Archæological Sketch. A Handbook of Irish Pre-Christian Antiquities. By W. G WOOD-MARTIN, M.R.I.A. With 512 Illustrations. Crown 8vo., 15s.

Wylie.—HISTORY OF ENGLAND UNDER HENRY IV. By JAMES HAMILTON WYLIE, M.A., one of H.M. Inspectors of Schools. 3 vols. Crown 8vo. Vol. I., 1399-1404, 10s. 6d. Vol. II. 15s. Vol. III. 15s. [Vol. IV. *in the press.*

Biography, Personal Memoirs, &c.

Armstrong.—THE LIFE AND LETTERS OF EDMUND J. ARMSTRONG. Edited by G. F. SAVAGE ARMSTRONG. Fcp. 8vo., 7s. 6d.

Bacon.—THE LETTERS AND LIFE OF FRANCIS BACON, INCLUDING ALL HIS OCCASIONAL WORKS. Edited by JAMES SPEDDING. 7 vols. 8vo., £4 4s.

Bagehot. — BIOGRAPHICAL STUDIES. By WALTER BAGEHOT. Cr. 8vo., 3s. 6d.

Blackwell.—PIONEER WORK IN OPENING THE MEDICAL PROFESSION TO WOMEN: Autobiographical Sketches. By Dr. ELIZABETH BLACKWELL. Cr. 8vo., 6s.

Boyd (A. K. H.). (**'A.K.H.B.'**).
TWENTY-FIVE YEARS OF ST. ANDREWS. 1865-1890. 2 vols. 8vo. Vol. I., 12s. Vol. II., 15s.
ST. ANDREWS AND ELSEWHERE: Glimpses of Some Gone and of Things Left. 8vo., 15s.
THE LAST YEARS OF ST. ANDREWS: September, 1890, to September, 1895. 8vo., 15s.

Buss.—FRANCES MARY BUSS AND HER WORK FOR EDUCATION. By ANNIE E. RIDLEY. With 5 Portraits and 4 Illustrations. Crown 8vo., 7s. 6d.

Carlyle.—THOMAS CARLYLE: a History of his Life. By JAMES ANTHONY FROUDE. 1795-1835. 2 vols. Crown 8vo., 7s. 1834-1881. 2 vols. Crown 8vo., 7s.

Digby.—THE LIFE OF SIR KENELM DIGBY, *by one of his Descendants*, the Author of 'The Life of a Conspirator,' 'A Life of Archbishop Laud,' etc. With 7 Illustrations. 8vo., 16s.

Erasmus.—LIFE AND LETTERS OF ERASMUS. By JAMES ANTHONY FROUDE. Crown 8vo., 6s.

FALKLANDS. By the Author of 'The Life of Sir Kenelm Digby,' 'The Life of a Prig,' etc. With Portraits and other Illustrations. 8vo., 10s. 6d.

Fox.—THE EARLY HISTORY OF CHARLES JAMES FOX. By the Right Hon. Sir G. O. TREVELYAN, Bart.
Library Edition. 8vo., 18s.
Cabinet Edition. Crown 8vo., 6s.

Halifax.—THE LIFE AND LETTERS OF SIR GEORGE SAVILE, BARONET, FIRST MARQUIS OF HALIFAX. With a New Edition of his Works, now for the first time collected and revised. By H. C. FOXCROFT. 2 vols. 8vo.

Hamilton.—LIFE OF SIR WILLIAM HAMILTON. By R. P. GRAVES. 8vo. 3 vols. 15s. each. ADDENDUM. 8vo., 6d.

Havelock.—MEMOIRS OF SIR HENRY HAVELOCK, K.C.B. By JOHN CLARK MARSHMAN. Crown 8vo., 3s. 6d.

Haweis.—MY MUSICAL LIFE. By the Rev H. R. HAWEIS. With Portrait of Richard Wagner and 3 Illustrations. Crown 8vo., 7s. 6d.

Holroyd.—THE GIRLHOOD OF MARIA JOSEPHA HOLROYD (Lady Stanley of Alderly). Recorded in Letters of a Hundred Years Ago, from 1776-1796. Edited by J. H. ADEANE. With 6 Portraits. 8vo., 18s.

Biography, Personal Memoirs, &c.—*continued.*

Jackson.—THE LIFE OF STONEWALL JACKSON. By Lieut.-Col. G. F. HENDERSON, York and Lancaster Regiment. With Portrait, Maps and Plans. 2 vols. 8vo.

Lejeune.—MEMOIRS OF BARON LEJEUNE, Aide-de-Camp to Marshals Berthier, Davout, and Oudinot. Translated and Edited from the Original French by Mrs. ARTHUR BELL (N. D'ANVERS). 2 vols. 8vo., 24*s.*

Luther.—LIFE OF LUTHER. By JULIUS KÖSTLIN. With Illustrations from Authentic Sources. Translated from the German. Crown 8vo., 3*s.* 6*d.*

Macaulay.—THE LIFE AND LETTERS OF LORD MACAULAY. By the Right Hon. Sir G. O. TREVELYAN, Bart., M.P.
Popular Edit. 1 vol. Cr. 8vo., 2*s.* 6*d.*
Student's Edition. 1 vol. Cr. 8vo., 6*s.*
Cabinet Edition. 2 vols. Post 8vo., 12*s.*
Library Edition. 2 vols. 8vo., 36*s.*
'*Edinburgh Edition.*' 2 vols. 8vo., 6*s.* each.

Marbot.—THE MEMOIRS OF THE BARON DE MARBOT. Translated from the French. 2 vols. Crown 8vo., 7*s.*

Nansen.—FRIDTJOF NANSEN, 1861-1893. By W. C. BRÖGGER and NORDAHL ROLFSEN. Translated by WILLIAM ARCHER. With 8 Plates, 48 Illustrations in the Text, and 3 Maps. 8vo., 12*s.* 6*d.*

Place.—THE LIFE OF FRANCIS PLACE. By GRAHAM WALLAS.

Rawlinson.—A MEMOIR OF THE LATE SIR HENRY RAWLINSON, BART., K.C.B., F.R.S., D.C.L., ETC. Written chiefly by his brother, the Rev. GEORGE RAWLINSON, Canon of Canterbury. With Contributions by the late Sir Henry's eldest son, and by Field-Marshal LORD ROBERTS.

Reeve.—THE LIFE AND LETTERS OF HENRY REEVE, C.B., late Editor of the 'Edinburgh Review,' and Registrar of the Privy Council. By J. K. LAUGHTON, M.A.

Romanes.—THE LIFE AND LETTERS OF GEORGE JOHN ROMANES, M.A., LL.D., F.R.S. Written and Edited by his Wife. With Portrait and 2 Illustrations. Cr. 8vo., 6*s.*

Seebohm.—THE OXFORD REFORMERS—JOHN COLET, ERASMUS AND THOMAS MORE : a History of their Fellow-Work. By FREDERIC SEEBOHM. 8vo., 14*s.*

Shakespeare.—OUTLINES OF THE LIFE OF SHAKESPEARE. By J. O. HALLIWELL-PHILLIPPS. With Illustrations and Facsimiles. 2 vols. Royal 8vo., £1 1*s.*

Shakespeare's TRUE LIFE. By JAS. WALTER. With 500 Illustrations by GERALD E. MOIRA. Imp. 8vo., 21*s.*

Verney.—MEMOIRS OF THE VERNEY FAMILY.
Vols. I. and II. DURING THE CIVIL WAR. By FRANCES PARTHENOPE VERNEY. With 38 Portraits, Woodcuts and Facsimile. Royal 8vo., 42*s.*
Vol. III. DURING THE COMMONWEALTH. 1650-1660. By MARGARET M. VERNEY. With 10 Portraits, &c. Royal 8vo., 21*s.*

Wakley.—THE LIFE AND TIMES OF THOMAS WAKLEY, Founder and First Editor of the 'Lancet,' Member of Parliament for Finsbury, and Coroner for West Middlesex. By S. SQUIRE SPRIGGE, M.B. Cantab. With 2 Portraits. 8vo., 18*s.*

Wellington.—LIFE OF THE DUKE OF WELLINGTON. By the Rev. G. R. GLEIG, M.A. Crown 8vo., 3*s.* 6*d.*

Travel and Adventure, the Colonies, &c.

Arnold.—SEAS AND LANDS. By Sir EDWIN ARNOLD. With 71 Illustrations. Cr. 8vo., 3*s.* 6*d.*

Baker (Sir S. W.).
EIGHT YEARS IN CEYLON. With 6 Illustrations. Crown 8vo., 3*s.* 6*d.*
THE RIFLE AND THE HOUND IN CEYLON. With 6 Illustrations. Cr. 8vo., 3*s.* 6*d.*

Bent.—THE RUINED CITIES OF MASHONALAND : being a Record of Excavation and Exploration in 1891. By J. THEODORE BENT. With 117 Illustrations. Crown 8vo., 3*s.* 6*d.*

Travel and Adventure, the Colonies, &c.—*continued.*

Bicknell.—TRAVEL AND ADVENTURE IN NORTHERN QUEENSLAND. By ARTHUR C. BICKNELL. With 24 Plates and 22 Illustrations in the text. 8vo., 15*s.*

Brassey.—VOYAGES AND TRAVELS OF LORD BRASSEY, K.C.B., D.C.L., 1862-1894. Arranged and Edited by Captain S. EARDLEY-WILMOT. 2 vols. Cr 8vo., 10*s.*

Brassey (The late LADY).

A VOYAGE IN THE 'SUNBEAM'; OUR HOME ON THE OCEAN FOR ELEVEN MONTHS.

Cabinet Edition. With Map and 66 Illustrations. Crown 8vo., 7*s.* 6*d.*

Silver Library Edition. With 66 Illustrations. Crown 8vo., 3*s.* 6*d.*

Popular Edition. With 60 Illustrations. 4to., 6*d.* sewed, 1*s.* cloth,

School Edition. With 37 Illustrations. Fcp., 2*s.*cloth, or 3*s.*white parchment.

SUNSHINE AND STORM IN THE EAST.

Cabinet Edition. With 2 Maps and 114 Illustrations. Crown 8vo., 7*s.*6*d.*

Popular Edition. With 103 Illustrations. 4to., 6*d.* sewed, 1*s.* cloth.

IN THE TRADES, THE TROPICS, AND THE 'ROARING FORTIES'.

Cabinet Edition. With Map and 220 Illustrations. Crown 8vo., 7*s.* 6*d.*

Popular Edition. With 183 Illustrations. 4to., 6*d.* sewed, 1*s.* cloth.

THREE VOYAGES IN THE 'SUNBEAM'. Popular Edition. With 346 Illustrations. 4to., 2*s.* 6*d.*

Browning.—A GIRL'S WANDERINGS IN HUNGARY. By H. ELLEN BROWNING. With Map and 20 Illustrations. Crown 8vo., 3*s.* 6*d.*

Froude (JAMES A.).

OCEANA : or England and her Colonies. With 9 Illustrations. Crown 8vo., 2*s.* boards, 2*s.* 6*d.* cloth.

THE ENGLISH IN THE WEST INDIES : or the Bow of Ulysses. With 9 Illustrations. Cr. 8vo., 2*s.* bds., 2*s.* 6*d.* cl.

Howitt.—VISITS TO REMARKABLE PLACES, Old Halls, Battle-Fields, Scenes illustrative of Striking Passages in English History and Poetry. By WILLIAM HOWITT. With 80 Illustrations. Crown 8vo., 3*s.* 6*d.*

Jones. — ROCK CLIMBING IN THE ENGLISH LAKE DISTRICT. By OWEN GLYNNE JONES, B.Sc. (Lond.), Member of the Alpine Club. With 30 Full-page Illustrations and 9 Lithograph Plate Diagrams of the Chief Routes. 8vo., 15*s.* net.

Knight (E. F.).

THE CRUISE OF THE 'ALERTE': the Narrative of a Search for Treasure on the Desert Island of Trinidad. With 2 Maps and 23 Illustrations. Crown 8vo., 3*s.* 6*d.*

WHERE THREE EMPIRES MEET: a Narrative of Recent Travel in Kashmir, Western Tibet, Baltistan, Ladak, Gilgit, and the adjoining Countries. With a Map and 54 Illustrations. Cr. 8vo., 3*s.* 6*d.*

THE 'FALCON' ON THE BALTIC: a Voyage from London to Copenhagen in a Three-Tonner. With 10 Full-page Illustrations. Cr. 8vo., 3*s.* 6*d.*

Lees and Clutterbuck.—B. C. 1887: A RAMBLE IN BRITISH COLUMBIA. By J. A. LEES and W. J. CLUTTERBUCK. With Map and 75 Illustrations. Cr. 8vo., 3*s.* 6*d.*

Max Müller.—LETTERS FROM CONSTANTINOPLE. By Mrs. MAX MÜLLER. With 12 Views of Constantinople and the neighbourhood. Crown 8vo., 6*s.*

Nansen (FRIDTJOF).

THE FIRST CROSSING OF GREENLAND. With numerous Illustrations and a Map. Crown 8vo., 3*s.* 6*d.*

ESKIMO LIFE. With 31 Illustrations. 8vo., 16*s.*

Oliver.—CRAGS AND CRATERS : Rambles in the Island of Réunion. By WILLIAM DUDLEY OLIVER, M.A. With 27 Illustrations and a Map. Cr. 8vo., 6*s.*

Quillinan. — JOURNAL OF A FEW MONTHS' RESIDENCE IN PORTUGAL, and Glimpses of the South of Spain. By Mrs. QUILLINAN (Dora Wordsworth). New Edition. Edited, with Memoir, by EDMUND LEE, Author of 'Dorothy Wordsworth.' etc. Crown 8vo., 6*s.*

Travel and Adventure, the Colonies, &c.—*continued.*

Smith.—CLIMBING IN THE BRITISH ISLES. By W. P. HASKETT SMITH. With Illustrations by ELLIS CARR, and Numerous Plans.

Part I. ENGLAND. 16mo., 3*s*. 6*d*.

Part II. WALES AND IRELAND. 16mo., 3*s*. 6*d*.

Stephen. — THE PLAYGROUND OF EUROPE. By LESLIE STEPHEN. New Edition, with Additions and 4 Illustrations. Crown 8vo., 6*s*. net.

THREE IN NORWAY. By Two of Them. With a Map and 59 Illustrations. Cr. 8vo., 2*s*. boards, 2*s*. 6*d*. cloth.

Tyndall.—THE GLACIERS OF THE ALPS: being a Narrative of Excursions and Ascents. An Account of the Origin and Phenomena of Glaciers, and an Exposition of the Physical Principles to which they are related. By JOHN TYNDALL, F.R.S. With numerous Illustrations. Crown 8vo., 6*s*. 6*d*. net.

Vivian.—SERVIA: the Poor Man's Paradise. By HERBERT VIVIAN, M.A. 8vo., 15*s*.

Sport and Pastime.

THE BADMINTON LIBRARY.

Edited by HIS GRACE THE DUKE OF BEAUFORT, K.G., and

A. E. T. WATSON.

Complete in 28 Volumes. Crown 8vo., Price 10*s*. 6*d*. each Volume, Cloth.

*** *The Volumes are also issued half-bound in Leather, with gilt top. The price can be had from all Booksellers.*

ARCHERY. By C. J. LONGMAN and Col. H. WALROND. With Contributions by Miss LEGH, Viscount DILLON, &c. With 2 Maps, 23 Plates, and 172 Illustrations in the Text. Crown 8vo., 10*s*. 6*d*.

ATHLETICS AND FOOTBALL. By MONTAGUE SHEARMAN. With 6 Plates and 52 Illustrations in the Text. Crown 8vo., 10*s*. 6*d*.

BIG GAME SHOOTING. By CLIVE PHILLIPPS-WOLLEY.

Vol. I. AFRICA AND AMERICA. With Contributions by Sir SAMUEL W. BAKER, W. C. OSWELL, F. C. SELOUS, &c. With 20 Plates and 57 Illustrations in the Text. Crown 8vo., 10*s*. 6*d*.

BIG GAME SHOOTING—*continued.*

Vol. II. EUROPE, ASIA, AND THE ARCTIC REGIONS. With Contributions by Lieut.-Colonel R. HEBER PERCY, Major ALGERNON C. HEBER PERCY, &c. With 17 Plates and 56 Illustrations in the Text. Crown 8vo., 10*s*. 6*d*.

BILLIARDS. By Major W. BROADFOOT, R.E. With Contributions by A. H. BOYD, SYDENHAM DIXON, W. J. FORD, &c. With 11 Plates, 19 Illustrations in the Text, and numerous Diagrams. Crown 8vo., 10*s*. 6*d*.

BOATING By W. B. WOODGATE. With 10 Plates, 39 Illustrations in the Text, and 4 Maps of Rowing Courses. Crown 8vo., 10*s*. 6*d*.

Sport and Pastime—*continued.*

THE BADMINTON LIBRARY—*continued.*

COURSING AND FALCONRY. By HARDING COX and the Hon. GERALD LASCELLES. With 20 Plates and 56 Illustrations in the Text. Crown 8vo., 10s. 6d.

CRICKET. By A. G. STEEL, and the Hon. R. H. LYTTELTON. With Contributions by ANDREW LANG, W. G. GRACE, F. GALE, &c. With 12 Plates and 52 Illustrations in the Text. Crown 8vo., 10s. 6d.

CYCLING. By the EARL OF ALBEMARLE, and G. LACY HILLIER. With 19 Plates and 44 Illustrations in the Text. Crown 8vo., 10s. 6d.

DANCING. By Mrs. LILLY GROVE, F.R.G.S. With Contributions by Miss MIDDLETON, The Honourable Mrs. ARMYTAGE, &c. With Musical Examples, and 38 Full-page Plates and 93 Illustrations in the Text. Crown 8vo., 10s. 6d.

DRIVING. By His Grace the DUKE OF BEAUFORT, K.G. With Contributions by other Authorities. With 12 Plates and 54 Illustrations in the Text. Crown 8vo., 10s. 6d.

FENCING, BOXING, AND WRESTLING. By WALTER H. POLLOCK, F. C. GROVE, C. PREVOST, E. B. MITCHELL, and WALTER ARMSTRONG. With 18 Plates and 24 Illustrations in the Text. Crown 8vo., 10s. 6d.

FISHING. By H. CHOLMONDELEY-PENNELL.

Vol. I. SALMON AND TROUT. With Contributions by H. R. FRANCIS, Major JOHN P. TRAHERNE, &c. With 9 Plates and numerous Illustrations of Tackle, &c. Crown 8vo., 10s. 6d.

Vol. II. PIKE AND OTHER COARSE FISH. With Contributions by the MARQUIS OF EXETER, WILLIAM SENIOR, G. CHRISTOPHER DAVIES, &c. With 7 Plates and numerous Illustrations of Tackle, &c. Crown 8vo., 10s. 6d.

GOLF. By HORACE G. HUTCHINSON. With Contributions by the Rt. Hon. A. J. BALFOUR, M.P., Sir WALTER SIMPSON, Bart., ANDREW LANG, &c. With 25 Plates and 65 Illustrations in the Text. Cr. 8vo., 10s. 6d.

HUNTING. By His Grace the DUKE OF BEAUFORT K.G., and MOWBRAY MORRIS. With Contributions by the EARL OF SUFFOLK AND BERKSHIRE, Rev. E. W. L. DAVIES, G. H. LONGMAN, &c. With 5 Plates and 54 Illustrations in the Text. Crown 8vo., 10s. 6d.

MOUNTAINEERING. By C. T. DENT. With Contributions by Sir W. M. CONWAY, D. W. FRESHFIELD, C. E. MATHEWS, &c. With 13 Plates and 95 Illustrations in the Text. Crown 8vo. 10s. 6d.

POETRY OF SPORT (THE).—Selected by HEDLEY PEEK. With a Chapter on Classical Allusions to Sport by ANDREW LANG, and a Special Preface to the Badminton Library by A. E. T. WATSON. With 32 Plates and 74 Illustrations in the Text. Crown 8vo., 10s. 6d.

RACING AND STEEPLE-CHASING. By the EARL OF SUFFOLK AND BERKSHIRE, W. G. CRAVEN, the HON. F. LAWLEY, ARTHUR COVENTRY, and ALFRED E. T. WATSON. With Frontispiece and 56 Illustrations in the Text. Crown 8vo., 10s. 6d.

RIDING AND POLO. By Captain ROBERT WEIR, the DUKE OF BEAUFORT, the EARL OF SUFFOLK AND BERKSHIRE, the EARL OF ONSLOW, &c. With 18 Plates and 41 Illustrations in the Text. Crown 8vo., 10s. 6d.

SEA FISHING. By JOHN BICKERDYKE, Sir H. W. GORE-BOOTH, ALFRED C. HARMSWORTH, and W. SENIOR. With 22 Full-page Plates and 175 Illustrations in the Text. Crown 8vo., 10s. 6d.

Sport and Pastime—*continued.*

THE BADMINTON LIBRARY—*continued.*

SHOOTING.

Vol. I. FIELD AND COVERT. By LORD WALSINGHAM and Sir RALPH PAYNE-GALLWEY, Bart. With Contributions by the Hon. GERALD LASCELLES and A. J. STUART-WORTLEY. With 11 Plates and 94 Illustrations in the Text. Crown 8vo., 10s. 6d.

Vol. II. MOOR AND MARSH. By LORD WALSINGHAM and Sir RALPH PAYNE-GALLWEY, Bart. With Contributions by LORD LOVAT and LORD CHARLES LENNOX KERR. With 8 Plates and 57 Illustrations in the Text. Crown 8vo., 10s. 6d.

SKATING, CURLING, TOBOGGANING. By J. M. HEATHCOTE, C. G. TEBBUTT, T. MAXWELL WITHAM, Rev. JOHN KERR, ORMOND HAKE, HENRY A. BUCK, &c. With 12 Plates and 272 Illustrations in the Text. Cr. 8vo., 10s. 6d.

SWIMMING. By ARCHIBALD SINCLAIR and WILLIAM HENRY, Hon. Secs. of the Life-Saving Society. With 13 Plates and 106 Illustrations in the Text. Cr. 8vo., 10s. 6d.

TENNIS, LAWN TENNIS, RACQUETS, AND FIVES. By J. M. and C. G. HEATHCOTE, E. O. PLEYDELL-BOUVERIE, and A. C. AINGER. With Contributions by the Hon. A. LYTTELTON, W. C. MARSHALL, Miss L. DOD, &c. With 12 Plates and 67 Illustrations in the Text. Crown 8vo., 10s. 6d.

YACHTING.

Vol. I. CRUISING, CONSTRUCTION OF YACHTS, YACHT RACING RULES, FITTING-OUT, &c. By Sir EDWARD SULLIVAN, Bart., THE EARL OF PEMBROKE, LORD BRASSEY, K.C.B., C. E. SETH-SMITH, C.B., G. L. WATSON, R. T. PRITCHETT, E. F. KNIGHT, &c. With 21 Plates and 93 Illustrations in the Text, and from Photographs. Crown 8vo., 10s. 6d.

Vol. II. YACHT CLUBS, YACHTING IN AMERICA AND THE COLONIES, YACHT RACING, &c. By R. T. PRITCHETT, THE MARQUIS OF DUFFERIN AND AVA, K.P., THE EARL OF ONSLOW, JAMES MCFERRAN, &c. With 35 Plates and 160 Illustrations in the Text. Crown 8vo., 10s. 6d.

FUR, FEATHER AND FIN SERIES.

Edited by A. E. T. WATSON.

Crown 8vo., price 5s. each Volume.

₊ *The Volumes are also issued half-bound in Leather, with gilt top. The price can be had from all Booksellers.*

THE PARTRIDGE. *Natural History,* by the Rev. H. A. MACPHERSON; *Shooting,* by A. J. STUART-WORTLEY; *Cookery,* by GEORGE SAINTSBURY. With 11 Illustrations and various Diagrams in the Text. Crown 8vo., 5s.

THE GROUSE. *Natural History,* by the Rev. H. A. MACPHERSON; *Shooting,* by A. J. STUART-WORTLEY; *Cookery,* by GEORGE SAINTSBURY. With 13 Illustrations and various Diagrams in the Text. Crown 8vo., 5s.

THE PHEASANT. *Natural History,* by the Rev. H. A. MACPHERSON; *Shooting,* by A. J. STUART-WORTLEY; *Cookery,* by ALEXANDER INNES SHAND. With 10 Illustrations and various Diagrams. Crown 8vo., 5s.

THE HARE. *Natural History,* by the Rev. H. A. MACPHERSON; *Shooting,* by the Hon. GERALD LASCELLES; *Coursing,* by CHARLES RICHARDSON; *Hunting,* by J. S. GIBBONS and G. H. LONGMAN; *Cookery,* by Col. KENNEY HERBERT. With 9 Illustrations. Cr. 8vo., 5s.

Sport and Pastime—*continued.*

FUR, FEATHER AND FIN SERIES—*continued.*

RED DEER. *Natural History*, by the Rev. H. A. MACPHERSON; *Deer Stalking*, by CAMERON OF LOCHIEL. *Stag Hunting*, by Viscount EBRINGTON; *Cookery*, by ALEXANDER INNES SHAND. With 10 Illustrations by J. CHARLTON and A. THORBURN. Cr. 8vo., 5*s.*

THE RABBIT. By J. E. HARTING, &c. With Illustrations. [*In preparation.*

WILDFOWL. By the Hon. JOHN SCOTT MONTAGU. With Illustrations. [*In preparation.*

THE SALMOM. By the Hon. A. E. GATHORNE-HARDY. With Illustrations. [*In preparation.*

THE TROUT. By the MARQUIS OF GRANBY, &c. With Illustrations. [*In preparation.*

André.—COLONEL BOGEY'S SKETCH-BOOK. Comprising an Eccentric Collection of Scribbles and Scratches found in disused Lockers and swept up in the Pavilion, together with sundry After-Dinner Sayings of the Colonel. By R. ANDRE, West Herts Golf Club. Oblong 4to., 2*s.* 6*d.*

BADMINTON MAGAZINE (THE) OF SPORTS AND PASTIMES. Edited by ALFRED E. T. WATSON ('Rapier'). With numerous Illustrations. Price 1*s.* Monthly. Vols. I.-V., 6*s.* each.

DEAD SHOT (THE): or, Sportsman's Complete Guide. Being a Treatise on the Use of the Gun, with Rudimentary and Finishing Lessons on the Art of Shooting Game of all kinds. Also Game-driving, Wildfowl and Pigeon-shooting, Dog-breaking, etc. By MARKSMAN. With numerous Illustrations. Crown 8vo., 10*s.* 6*d.*

Ellis.—CHESS SPARKS; or, Short and Bright Games of Chess. Collected and Arranged by J. H. ELLIS, M.A. 8vo., 4*s.* 6*d.*

Folkard.—THE WILD-FOWLER: A Treatise on Fowling, Ancient and Modern; descriptive also of Decoys and Flight-ponds, Wild-fowl Shooting, Gunning-punts, Shooting-yachts, &c. Also Fowling in the Fens and in Foreign Countries, Rock-fowling, &c., &c., by H. C. FOLKARD. With 13 Engravings on Steel, and several Woodcuts. 8vo., 12*s.* 6*d.*

Ford.—THE THEORY AND PRACTICE OF ARCHERY. BY HORACE FORD. New Edition, thoroughly Revised and Rewritten by W. BUTT, M.A. With a Preface by C. J. LONGMAN, M.A. 8vo., 14*s.*

Francis.—A BOOK ON ANGLING: or, Treatise on the Art of Fishing in every Branch; including full Illustrated List of Salmon Flies. By FRANCIS FRANCIS. With Portrait and Coloured Plates. Crown 8vo., 15*s.*

Gibson.—TOBOGGANING ON CROOKED RUNS. By the Hon. HARRY GIBSON. With Contributions by F. DE B. STRICKLAND and 'LADY-TOBOGGANER'. With 40 Illustrations. Crown 8vo., 6*s.*

Graham.—COUNTRY PASTIMES FOR BOYS. By P. ANDERSON GRAHAM. With 252 Illustrations from Drawings and Photographs. Crown 8vo., 3*s.* 6*d.*

Lang.—ANGLING SKETCHES. By A. LANG. With 20 Illustrations. Crown 8vo., 3*s.* 6*d.*

Lillie.—CROQUET: its History, Rules, and Secrets. By ARTHUR LILLIE, Champion Grand National Croquet Club, 1872; Winner of the 'All-Comers' Championship,' Maidstone, 1896. With 4 Full-page Illustrations by LUCIEN DAVIS, 15 Illustrations in the Text, and 27 Diagrams. Crown 8vo., 6*s.*

Longman.—CHESS OPENINGS. By FREDERICK W. LONGMAN. Fcp. 8vo., 2*s.* 6*d.*

Madden.—THE DIARY OF MASTER WILLIAM SILENCE: A Study of Shakespeare and of Elizabethan Sport. By the Right Hon. D. H. MADDEN, Vice-Chancellor of the University of Dublin. 8vo., 16*s.*

Sport and Pastime—*continued*.

Maskelyne.—SHARPS AND FLATS: a Complete Revelation of the Secrets of Cheating at Games of Chance and Skill. By JOHN NEVIL MASKELYNE, of the Egyptian Hall. With 62 Illustrations. Crown 8vo., 6s.

Park.—THE GAME OF GOLF. By WILLIAM PARK, Junr., Champion Golfer, 1887-89. With 17 Plates and 26 Illustrations in the Text. Crown 8vo., 7s. 6d

Payne-Gallwey (Sir RALPH, Bart.). LETTERS TO YOUNG SHOOTERS (First Series). On the Choice and Use of a Gun. With 41 Illustrations. Cr. 8vo., 7s. 6d.

LETTERS TO YOUNG SHOOTERS (Second Series). On the Production, Preservation, and Killing of Game. With Directions in Shooting Wood-Pigeons and Breaking-in Retrievers. With Portrait and 103 Illustrations. Crown 8vo., 12s. 6d.

LETTERS TO YOUNG SHOOTERS (Third Series). Comprising a Short Natural History of the Wildfowl that are Rare or Common to the British Islands, with Complete Directions in Shooting Wildfowl on the Coast and Inland. With 200 Illustrations. Cr. 8vo., 18s.

Pole (WILLIAM).
THE THEORY OF THE MODERN SCIENTIFIC GAME OF WHIST. Fcp. 8vo., 2s. 6d.

THE EVOLUTION OF WHIST: a Study of the Progressive Changes which the Game has undergone. Crown 8vo., 2s. 6d.

Proctor.—HOW TO PLAY WHIST: WITH THE LAWS AND ETIQUETTE OF WHIST. By RICHARD A. PROCTOR. Crown 8vo., 3s. 6d.

Ribblesdale.—THE QUEEN'S HOUNDS AND STAG-HUNTING RECOLLECTIONS. By LORD RIBBLESDALE, Master of the Buckhounds, 1892-95. With Introductory Chapter on the Hereditary Mastership by E. BURROWS. With 24 Plates and 35 Illustrations in the Text, including reproductions from Oil Paintings in the possession of Her Majesty the Queen at Windsor Castle and Cumberland Lodge, Original Drawings by G. D. GILES, and from Prints and Photographs. 8vo., 25s.

Ronalds.—THE FLY-FISHER'S ENTOMOLOGY. By ALFRED RONALDS. With 20 Coloured Plates. 8vo., 14s.

Thompson and Cannan. HAND-IN-HAND FIGURE SKATING. By NORCLIFFE G. THOMPSON and F. LAURA CANNAN, Members of the Skating Club. With an Introduction by Captain J. H. THOMSON, R.A. With Illustrations. 16mo., 6s.

Wilcocks. THE SEA FISHERMAN: Comprising the Chief Methods of Hook and Line Fishing in the British and other Seas, and Remarks on Nets, Boats, and Boating. By J. C. WILCOCKS. Illustrated. Crown 8vo., 6s.

Veterinary Medicine, &c.

Steel (JOHN HENRY).
A TREATISE ON THE DISEASES OF THE DOG. With 88 Illustrations. 8vo., 10s. 6d.

A TREATISE ON THE DISEASES OF THE OX. With 119 Illustrations. 8vo., 15s.

A TREATISE ON THE DISEASES OF THE SHEEP. With 100 Illustrations. 8vo., 12s.

OUTLINES OF EQUINE ANATOMY: a Manual for the use of Veterinary Students in the Dissecting Room. Crown 8vo., 7s. 6d.

Fitzwygram.—HORSES AND STABLES. By Major-General Sir F. FITZWYGRAM, Bart. With 56 pages of Illustrations. 8vo., 2s. 6d. net.

Schreiner. — THE ANGORA GOAT (published under the auspices of the South African Angora Goat Breeders' Association), and a Paper on the Ostrich (reprinted from the *Zoologist* for March, 1897). By S. C. CRONWRIGHT SCHREINER. 8vo.

'Stonehenge.'—THE DOG IN HEALTH AND DISEASE. By 'STONEHENGE' With 78 Wood Engravings. 8vo., 7s. 6d.

Youatt (WILLIAM).
THE HORSE. Revised and enlarged. By W. WATSON, M.R.C.V.S. With 52 Wood Engravings. 8vo., 7s. 6d.

THE DOG. Revised and enlarged. With 33 Wood Engravings. 8vo., 6s.

Mental, Moral, and Political Philosophy.

LOGIC, RHETORIC, PSYCHOLOGY, &c.

Abbott.—THE ELEMENTS OF LOGIC. By T. K. ABBOTT, B.D.   12mo., 3s.

Aristotle.

THE ETHICS: Greek Text, Illustrated with Essay and Notes. By Sir ALEXANDER GRANT, Bart. 2 vols. 8vo., 32s.

AN INTRODUCTION TO ARISTOTLE'S ETHICS. Books I.-IV. (Book X. c. vi.-ix. in an Appendix.) With a continuous Analysis and Notes. By the Rev. EDWARD MOORE, D.D. Cr. 8vo., 10s. 6d.

Bacon (FRANCIS).

COMPLETE WORKS. Edited by R. L. ELLIS, JAMES SPEDDING, and D. D. HEATH. 7 vols. 8vo., £3 13s. 6d.

LETTERS AND LIFE, including all his occasional Works. Edited by JAMES SPEDDING. 7 vols. 8vo., £4 4s.

THE ESSAYS: with Annotations. By RICHARD WHATELY, D.D.   8vo., 10s. 6d.

THE ESSAYS: Edited, with Notes. By F. STORR and C. H. GIBSON. Cr. 8vo., 3s. 6d.

THE ESSAYS. With Introduction, Notes, and Index. By E. A. ABBOTT, D.D. 2 vols. Fcp. 8vo., 6s. The Text and Index only, without Introduction and Notes, in One Volume. Fcp. 8vo., 2s. 6d.

Bain (ALEXANDER).

MENTAL SCIENCE. Crown 8vo., 6s. 6d. MORAL SCIENCE. Crown 8vo., 4s. 6d. *The two works as above can be had in one volume, price 10s. 6d.*

SENSES AND THE INTELLECT. 8vo., 15s. EMOTIONS AND THE WILL. 8vo., 15s. LOGIC, DEDUCTIVE AND INDUCTIVE. Part I., 4s.   Part II., 6s. 6d. PRACTICAL ESSAYS. Crown 8vo., 2s.

Bray.—THE PHILOSOPHY OF NECESSITY; or Law in Mind as in Matter. By CHARLES BRAY. Crown 8vo., 5s.

Crozier (JOHN BEATTIE).

HISTORY OF INTELLECTUAL DEVELOPMENT: on the Lines of Modern Evolution.
Vol. I. Greek and Hindoo Thought; Græco-Roman Paganism; Judaism; and Christianity down to the Closing of the Schools of Athens by Justinian, 529 A.D. 8vo., 14s.

Crozier (JOHN BEATTIE)—*continued.*

CIVILISATION AND PROGRESS; being the Outlines of a New System of Political, Religious and Social Philosophy. 8vo., 14s.

Davidson.—THE LOGIC OF DEFINITION, Explained and Applied. By WILLIAM L. DAVIDSON, M.A. Crown 8vo., 6s.

Green (THOMAS HILL). The Works of. Edited by R. L. NETTLESHIP.

Vols. I. and II. Philosophical Works. 8vo., 16s. each.

Vol. III. Miscellanies. With Index to the three Volumes, and Memoir. 8vo., 21s.

LECTURES ON THE PRINCIPLES OF POLITICAL OBLIGATION. 8vo., 5s.

Hodgson (SHADWORTH H.).

TIME AND SPACE: a Metaphysical Essay. 8vo., 16s.

THE THEORY OF PRACTICE: an Ethical Inquiry. 2 vols. 8vo., 24s.

THE PHILOSOPHY OF REFLECTION. 2 vols. 8vo., 21s.

THE METAPHYSIC OF EXPERIENCE. 4 vols. I. General Analysis of Experience. II. Positive Science. III. Analysis of Conscious Action. IV. The Real Universe.

Hume.—THE PHILOSOPHICAL WORKS OF DAVID HUME. Edited by T. H. GREEN and T. H. GROSE. 4 vols. 8vo., 56s. Or separately, Essays. 2 vols. 28s. Treatise of Human Nature. 2 vols. 28s.

James.—THE WILL TO BELIEVE, and other Essays in Popular Philosophy. By WILLIAM JAMES, M.D., LL.D., &c. Crown 8vo., 7s. 6d.

Justinian.—THE INSTITUTES OF JUSTINIAN: Latin Text, chiefly that of Huschke, with English Introduction, Translation, Notes, and Summary. By THOMAS C. SANDARS, M.A. 8vo., 18s.

Kant (IMMANUEL).

CRITIQUE OF PRACTICAL REASON, AND OTHER WORKS ON THE THEORY OF ETHICS. Translated by T. K. ABBOTT, B.D. With Memoir. 8vo., 12s. 6d.

FUNDAMENTAL PRINCIPLES OF THE METAPHYSIC OF ETHICS. Translated by T. K. ABBOTT, B.D. Crown 8vo., 3s.

Mental, Moral and Political Philosophy—*continued.*

Kant (IMMANUEL)—*continued.*

INTRODUCTION TO LOGIC, AND HIS ESSAY ON THE MISTAKEN SUBTILTY OF THE FOUR FIGURES. Translated by T. K. ABBOTT. 8vo., 6*s.*

Killick.—HANDBOOK TO MILL'S SYSTEM OF LOGIC. By Rev. A. H. KILLICK, M.A. Crown 8vo., 3*s.* 6*d.*

Ladd (GEORGE TRUMBULL).

PHILOSOPHY OF KNOWLEDGE: an Inquiry into the Nature, Limits and Validity of Human Cognitive Faculty. 8vo. 18*s.*

PHILOSOPHY OF MIND: an Essay on the Metaphysics of Psychology. 8vo., 16*s.*

ELEMENTS OF PHYSIOLOGICAL PSYCHOLOGY. 8vo., 21*s.*

OUTLINES OF PHYSIOLOGICAL PSYCHOLOGY. A Text-Book of Mental Science for Academies and Colleges. 8vo., 12*s.*

PSYCHOLOGY, DESCRIPTIVE AND EXPLANATORY: a Treatise of the Phenomena, Laws, and Development of Human Mental Life. 8vo., 21*s.*

PRIMER OF PSYCHOLOGY. Crown 8vo., 5*s.* 6*d.*

Lewes.—THE HISTORY OF PHILOSOPHY, from Thales to Comte. By GEORGE HENRY LEWES. 2 vols. 8vo., 32*s.*

Lutoslawski.—THE ORIGIN AND GROWTH OF PLATO'S LOGIC. By W. LUTOSLAWSKI. 8vo., 21*s.*

Max Müller (F.).

THE SCIENCE OF THOUGHT. 8vo., 21*s.*

THREE INTRODUCTORY LECTURES ON THE SCIENCE OF THOUGHT. 8vo., 2*s.* 6*d.* net.

Mill.—ANALYSIS OF THE PHENOMENA OF THE HUMAN MIND. By JAMES MILL. 2 vols. 8vo., 28*s.*

Mill (JOHN STUART).

A SYSTEM OF LOGIC. Cr. 8vo., 3*s.* 6*d.*

ON LIBERTY. Cr. 8vo., 1*s.* 4*d.*

CONSIDERATIONS ON REPRESENTATIVE GOVERNMENT. Crown 8vo., 2*s.*

UTILITARIANISM. 8vo., 2*s.* 6*d.*

Mill (JOHN STUART)—*continued.*

EXAMINATION OF SIR WILLIAM HAMILTON'S PHILOSOPHY. 8vo., 16*s.*

NATURE, THE UTILITY OF RELIGION, AND THEISM. Three Essays. 8vo., 5*s.*

Romanes.—MIND AND MOTION AND MONISM. By GEORGE JOHN ROMANES, LL.D., F.R.S. Crown 8vo., 4*s.* 6*d.*

Stock (ST. GEORGE).

DEDUCTIVE LOGIC. Fcp. 8vo., 3*s.* 6*d.*

LECTURES IN THE LYCEUM; or, Aristotle's Ethics for English Readers. Edited by ST. GEORGE STOCK. Crown 8vo., 7*s.* 6*d.*

Sully (JAMES).

THE HUMAN MIND: a Text-book of Psychology. 2 vols. 8vo., 21*s.*

OUTLINES OF PSYCHOLOGY. Crown 8vo., 9*s.*

THE TEACHER'S HANDBOOK OF PSYCHOLOGY. Crown 8vo., 6*s.* 6*d.*

STUDIES OF CHILDHOOD. 8vo. 10*s.* 6*d.*

CHILDREN'S WAYS: being Selections from the Author's 'Studies of Childhood,' with some additional Matter. With 25 Figures in the Text. Crown 8vo., 4*s.* 6*d.*

Sutherland.—THE ORIGIN AND GROWTH OF THE MORAL INSTINCT. By ALEXANDER SUTHERLAND, M.A.

Swinburne.—PICTURE LOGIC: an Attempt to Popularise the Science of Reasoning. By ALFRED JAMES SWINBURNE, M.A. With 23 Woodcuts. Crown 8vo., 5*s.*

Weber.—HISTORY OF PHILOSOPHY. By ALFRED WEBER, Professor in the University of Strasburg, Translated by FRANK THILLY, Ph.D. 8vo., 16*s.*

Whately (ARCHBISHOP).

BACON'S ESSAYS. With Annotations. 8vo., 10*s.* 6*d.*

ELEMENTS OF LOGIC. Cr. 8vo., 4*s.* 6*d.*

ELEMENTS OF RHETORIC. Cr. 8vo., 4*s.* 6*d.*

LESSONS ON REASONING. Fcp. 8vo., 1*s.* 6*d.*

Mental, Moral and Political Philosophy—*continued*.

Zeller (Dr. EDWARD, Professor in the University of Berlin).

THE STOICS, EPICUREANS, AND SCEPTICS. Translated by the Rev. O. J. REICHEL, M.A. Crown 8vo., 15*s*.

OUTLINES OF THE HISTORY OF GREEK PHILOSOPHY. Translated by SARAH F. ALLEYNE and EVELYN ABBOTT. Crown 8vo., 10*s*. 6*d*.

Zeller (Dr. EDWARD)—*continued*.

PLATO AND THE OLDER ACADEMY. Translated by SARAH F. ALLEYNE and ALFRED GOODWIN, B.A. Crown 8vo., 18*s*.

SOCRATES AND THE SOCRATIC SCHOOLS. Translated by the Rev. O. J. REICHEL, M.A. Crown 8vo., 10*s*. 6*d*.

ARISTOTLE AND THE EARLIER PERIPATETICS. Translated by B. F. C. COSTELLOE, M.A., and J. H. MUIRHEAD, M.A. 2 vols. Cr. 8vo., 24*s*.

MANUALS OF CATHOLIC PHILOSOPHY.
(Stonyhurst Series.)

A MANUAL OF POLITICAL ECONOMY. By C. S. DEVAS, M.A. Cr. 8vo., 6*s*. 6*d*.

FIRST PRINCIPLES OF KNOWLEDGE. By JOHN RICKABY, S.J. Crown 8vo., 5*s*.

GENERAL METAPHYSICS. By JOHN RICKABY, S.J. Crown 8vo., 5*s*.

LOGIC. By RICHARD F. CLARKE, S.J. Crown 8vo., 5*s*.

MORAL PHILOSOPHY (ETHICS AND NATURAL LAW). By JOSEPH RICKABY, S.J. Crown 8vo., 5*s*.

NATURAL THEOLOGY. By BERNARD BOEDDER, S.J. Crown 8vo., 6*s*. 6*d*.

PSYCHOLOGY. By MICHAEL MAHER, S.J. Crown 8vo., 6*s*. 6*d*.

History and Science of Language, &c.

Davidson.—LEADING AND IMPORTANT ENGLISH WORDS: Explained and Exemplified. By WILLIAM L. DAVIDSON, M.A. Fcp. 8vo., 3*s*. 6*d*.

Farrar.—LANGUAGE AND LANGUAGES. By F. W. FARRAR, D.D., F.R.S., Cr. 8vo., 6*s*.

Graham.—ENGLISH SYNONYMS, Classified and Explained: with Practical Exercises. By G. F. GRAHAM. Fcap. 8vo., 6*s*.

Max Müller (F.).

THE SCIENCE OF LANGUAGE, Founded on Lectures delivered at the Royal Institution in 1861 and 1863. 2 vols. Crown 8vo., 21*s*.

BIOGRAPHIES OF WORDS, AND THE HOME OF THE ARYAS. Crown 8vo., 7*s*. 6*d*.

Max Müller (F.)—*continued*.

THREE LECTURES ON THE SCIENCE OF LANGUAGE, AND ITS PLACE IN GENERAL EDUCATION, delivered at Oxford, 1889. Crown 8vo., 3*s*. net.

Roget. — THESAURUS OF ENGLISH WORDS AND PHRASES. Classified and Arranged so as to Facilitate the Expression of Ideas and assist in Literary Composition. By PETER MARK ROGET, M.D., F.R.S. Recomposed throughout, enlarged and improved, partly from the Author's Notes, and with a full Index, by the Author's Son, JOHN LEWIS ROGET. Crown 8vo., 10*s*. 6*d*.

Whately.—ENGLISH SYNONYMS. By E. JANE WHATELY. Fcap. 8vo., 3*s*.

Political Economy and Economics.

Ashley.—ENGLISH ECONOMIC HISTORY AND THEORY. By W. J. ASHLEY. Cr. 8vo., Part I., 5*s.* Part II., 10*s.* 6*d.*

Bagehot.—ECONOMIC STUDIES. By WALTER BAGEHOT. Cr. 8vo., 3*s.* 6*d.*

Barnett.—PRACTICABLE SOCIALISM : Essays on Social Reform. By the Rev. S. A. and Mrs. BARNETT. Cr. 8vo., 6*s.*

Brassey.—PAPERS AND ADDRESSES ON WORK AND WAGES. By Lord BRASSEY. Crown 8vo., 5*s.*

Channing.—THE TRUTH ABOUT AGRI-CULTURAL DEPRESSION : An Economic Study of the Evidence of the Royal Commission. By FRANCIS ALLSTON CHANNING, M.P., one of the Commis-sion. Crown 8vo., 6*s.*

Devas.—A MANUAL OF POLITICAL ECONOMY. By C. S. DEVAS, M.A. Crown 8vo., 6*s.* 6*d.*

Dowell.—A HISTORY OF TAXATION AND TAXES IN ENGLAND, from the Earliest Times to the Year 1885. By STEPHEN DOWELL (4 vols. 8vo.). Vols. I. and II. The History of Taxation, 21*s.* Vols. III. and IV. The History of Taxes, 21*s.*

Jordan.—THE STANDARD OF VALUE. By WILLIAM LEIGHTON JORDAN. Crown 8vo., 6*s.*

Macleod (HENRY DUNNING). BIMETALISM. 8vo., 5*s.* net. THE ELEMENTS OF BANKING. Crown 8vo., 3*s.* 6*d.* THE THEORY AND PRACTICE OF BANK-ING. Vol. I. 8vo., 12*s.* Vol. II. 14*s.*

Macleod (HENRY DUNNING)—*cont.* THE THEORY OF CREDIT. 8vo. Vol. I. 10*s.* net. Vol. II., Part I., 10*s.* net. Vol. II. Part II., 10*s.* net. A DIGEST OF THE LAW OF BILLS OF EXCHANGE, BANK NOTES, &c. [*In the press.*

Mill.—POLITICAL ECONOMY. By JOHN STUART MILL. *Popular Edition.* Crown 8vo., 3*s.* 6*d.* *Library Edition.* 2 vols. 8vo., 30*s.*

Mulhall.—INDUSTRIES AND WEALTH OF NATIONS. By MICHAEL G. MUL-HALL, F.S.S. With 32 Full-page Diagrams. Crown 8vo., 8*s.* 6*d.*

Soderini.—SOCIALISM AND CATHOLI-CISM. From the Italian of Count EDWARD SODERINI. By RICHARD JENERY-SHEE. With a Preface by Cardinal VAUGHAN. Crown 8vo., 6*s.*

Symes.—POLITICAL ECONOMY : a Short Text-book of Political Economy. With a Supplementary Chapter on Socialism. By J. E. SYMES, M.A. Crown 8vo., 2*s.* 6*d.*

Toynbee.—LECTURES ON THE IN-DUSTRIAL REVOLUTION OF THE 18th CENTURY IN ENGLAND. By ARNOLD TOYNBEE. With a Memoir of the Author by BENJAMIN JOWETT, D.D. 8vo., 10*s.* 6*d.*

Webb (SIDNEY and BEATRICE). THE HISTORY OF TRADE UNIONISM. With Map and full Bibliography of the Subject. 8vo., 18*s.* INDUSTRIAL DEMOCRACY : a Study in Trade Unionism. 2 vols. 8vo., 25*s.* net.

STUDIES IN ECONOMICS AND POLITICAL SCIENCE.

Issued under the auspices of the London School of Economics and Political Science.

THE HISTORY OF LOCAL RATES IN ENG-LAND: Five Lectures. By EDWIN CANNAN, M.A. Crown 8vo., 2*s.* 6*d.*

GERMAN SOCIAL DEMOCRACY. By BERTRAND RUSSELL, B.A. With an Appendix on Social Democracy and the Woman Question in Germany by ALYS RUSSELL, B.A. Cr. 8vo., 3*s.* 6*d.*

SELECT DOCUMENTS ILLUSTRATING THE HISTORY OF TRADE UNIONISM.

  1. The Tailoring Trade. Edited by W. F. GALTON. With a Preface by SIDNEY WEBB, LL.B. Crown 8vo., 5*s.*

DEPLOIGE'S REFERENDUM EN SUISSE. Translated with Introduction and Notes, by C. P. TREVELYAN, M.A. [*In preparation*

SELECT DOCUMENTS ILLUSTRATING THE STATE REGULATION OF WAGES. Edited, with Introduction and Notes, by W. A. S. HEWINS, M.A. [*In preparation.*

HUNGARIAN GILD RECORDS. Edited by Dr. JULIUS MANDELLO, of Budapest. [*In preparation.*

THE RELATIONS BETWEEN ENGLAND AND THE HANSEATIC LEAGUE. By Miss E. A. MACARTHUR. [*In preparation.*

Evolution, Anthropology, &c.

Clodd (EDWARD).

THE STORY OF CREATION : a Plain Account of Evolution. With 77 Illustrations. Crown 8vo., 3*s.* 6*d.*

A PRIMER OF EVOLUTION : being a Popular Abridged Edition of 'The Story of Creation'. With Illustrations. Fcp. 8vo., 1*s.* 6*d.*

Lang.—CUSTOM AND MYTH : Studies of Early Usage and Belief. By ANDREW LANG. With 15 Illustrations. Crown 8vo., 3*s.* 6*d.*

Lubbock.—THE ORIGIN OF CIVILISATION and the Primitive Condition of Man. By Sir J. LUBBOCK, Bart., M.P. With 5 Plates and 20 Illustrations in the Text. 8vo., 18*s.*

Romanes (GEORGE JOHN).

DARWIN, AND AFTER DARWIN : an Exposition of the Darwinian Theory, and a Discussion on Post-Darwinian Questions.

Part I. THE DARWINIAN THEORY. With Portrait of Darwin and 125 Illustrations. Crown 8vo., 10*s.* 6*d.*

Part II. POST-DARWINIAN QUESTIONS : Heredity and Utility. With Portrait of the Author and 5 Illustrations. Cr. 8vo., 10*s.* 6*d.*

Part III. POST-DARWINIAN QUESTIONS : Isolation and Physiological Selection. Crown 8vo., 5*s.*

AN EXAMINATION OF WEISMANNISM. Crown 8vo., 6*s.*

ESSAYS. Edited by C. LLOYD MORGAN, Principal of University College, Bristol. Crown 8vo., 6*s.*

Classical Literature, Translations, &c.

Abbott.—HELLENICA. A Collection of Essays on Greek Poetry, Philosophy, History, and Religion. Edited by EVELYN ABBOTT, M.A., LL.D. 8vo., 16*s.*

Æschylus.—EUMENIDES OF ÆSCHYLUS. With Metrical English Translation. By J. F. DAVIES. 8vo., 7*s.*

Aristophanes.—The ACHARNIANS OF ARISTOPHANES, translated into English Verse. By R. Y. TYRRELL. Cr. 8vo., 1*s.*

Aristotle.—YOUTH AND OLD AGE, LIFE AND DEATH, AND RESPIRATION. Translated, with Introduction and Notes, by W. OGLE, M.A., M.D., F.R.C.P., sometime Fellow of Corpus Christi College, Oxford. 8vo., 7*s.* 6*d.*

Becker (W. A.). Translated by the Rev. F. Metcalfe, B.D.

GALLUS : or, Roman Scenes in the Time of Augustus. With 26 Illustrations. Post 8vo., 3*s.* 6*d.*

CHARICLES : or, Illustrations of the Private Life of the Ancient Greeks. With 26 Illustrations. Post 8vo., 3*s.* 6*d.*

Butler. — THE AUTHORESS OF THE ODYSSEY, WHERE AND WHEN SHE WROTE, WHO SHE WAS, THE USE SHE MADE OF THE ILIAD, AND HOW THE POEM GREW UNDER HER HANDS. By SAMUEL BUTLER, Author of 'Erewhon,' &c. With 14 Illustrations and 4 Maps. 8vo., 10*s.* 6*d.*

Cicero.—CICERO'S CORRESPONDENCE. By R. Y. TYRRELL. Vols. I., II., III. 8vo., each 12*s.* Vol. IV., 15*s.* Vol. V., 14*s.*

Egbert. — INTRODUCTION TO THE STUDY OF LATIN INSCRIPTIONS. By JAMES C. EGBERT, Junr., Ph.D. With numerous Illustrations and Facsimiles. Square crown 8vo., 16*s.*

Lang.—HOMER AND THE EPIC. By ANDREW LANG. Crown 8vo., 9*s.* net.

Lucan.—THE PHARSALIA OF LUCAN. Translated into Blank Verse. By Sir EDWARD RIDLEY. 8vo., 14*s.*

Mackail.—SELECT EPIGRAMS FROM THE GREEK ANTHOLOGY. By J. W. MACKAIL. Edited with a Revised Text, Introduction, Translation, and Notes 8vo., 16*s.*

Rich.—A DICTIONARY OF ROMAN AND GREEK ANTIQUITIES. By A. RICH, B.A. With 2000 Woodcuts. Crown 8vo., 7*s.* 6*d.*

Classical Literature, Translations, &c.—*continued.*

Sophocles.—Translated into English Verse. By ROBERT WHITELAW, M.A., Assistant Master in Rugby School. Cr. 8vo., 8*s.* 6*d.*

Tacitus.—THE HISTORY OF P. COR-NELIUS TACITUS. Translated into English, with an Introduction and Notes, Critical and Explanatory, by ALBERT WILLIAM QUILL, M.A., T.C.D. 2 Vols. Vol. I., 8vo., 7*s.* 6*d.*, Vol. II., 8vo., 12*s.* 6*d.*

Tyrrell.—TRANSLATIONS INTO GREEK AND LATIN VERSE. Edited by R. Y. TYRRELL. 8vo., 6*s.*

Virgil.—THE ÆNEID OF VIRGIL. Translated into English Verse by JOHN CONINGTON. Crown 8vo., 6*s.*

THE POEMS OF VIRGIL. Translated into English Prose by JOHN CONINGTON. Crown 8vo., 6*s.*

THE ÆNEID OF VIRGIL, freely translated into English Blank Verse. By W. J. THORNHILL. Crown 8vo., 7*s.* 6*d.*

THE ÆNEID OF VIRGIL. Translated into English Verse by JAMES RHOADES.
Books I.-VI. Crown 8vo., 5*s.*
Books VII.-XII. Crown 8vo., 5*s.*

Poetry and the Drama.

Allingham (WILLIAM).

IRISH SONGS AND POEMS. With Frontispiece of the Waterfall of Asaroe. Fcp. 8vo., 6*s.*

LAURENCE BLOOMFIELD. With Portrait of the Author. Fcp. 8vo., 3*s.* 6d.

FLOWER PIECES; DAY AND NIGHT SONGS; BALLADS. With 2 Designs by D. G. ROSSETTI. Fcp. 8vo., 6*s.*; large paper edition, 12*s.*

LIFE AND PHANTASY: with Frontispiece by Sir J. E. MILLAIS, Bart., and Design by ARTHUR HUGHES. Fcp. 8vo.. 6*s.*; large paper edition, 12*s.*

THOUGHT AND WORD, AND ASHBY MANOR: a Play. Fcp. 8vo., 6*s.*; large paper edition, 12*s.*

BLACKBERRIES. Imperial 16mo., 6*s.*

Sets of the above 6 vols. may be had in uniform half-parchment binding, price 30*s.*

Armstrong (G. F. SAVAGE).

POEMS: Lyrical and Dramatic. Fcp. 8vo., 6*s.*

KING SAUL. (The Tragedy of Israel, Part I.) Fcp. 8vo. 5*s.*

KING DAVID. (The Tragedy of Israel, Part II.) Fcp. 8vo., 6*s.*

Armstrong (G. F. SAVAGE)—*continued.*

KING SOLOMON. (The Tragedy of Israel, Part III.) Fcp. 8vo., 6*s.*

UGONE: a Tragedy. Fcp. 8vo., 6*s.*

A GARLAND FROM GREECE: Poems. Fcp. 8vo., 7*s.* 6*d.*

STORIES OF WICKLOW: Poems. Fcp. 8vo., 7*s.* 6*d.*

MEPHISTOPHELES IN BROADCLOTH: a Satire. Fcp. 8vo., 4*s.*

ONE IN THE INFINITE: a Poem. Cr. 8vo., 7*s.* 6*d.*

Armstrong.—THE POETICAL WORKS OF EDMUND J. ARMSTRONG. Fcp. 8vo., 5*s.*

Arnold.—THE LIGHT OF THE WORLD: or, the Great Consummation. By Sir EDWIN ARNOLD. With 14 Illustrations after HOLMAN HUNT. Crown 8vo., 6*s.*

Beesly (A. H.).

BALLADS, AND OTHER VERSE. Fcp. 8vo., 5*s.*

DANTON, AND OTHER VERSE. Fcp. 8vo., 4*s.* 6*d.*

Poetry and the Drama—*continued.*

Bell (Mrs. HUGH).
CHAMBER COMEDIES: a Collection of Plays and Monologues for the Drawing Room. Crown 8vo., 6s.
FAIRY TALE PLAYS, AND HOW TO ACT THEM. With 91 Diagrams and 52 Illustrations. Crown 8vo., 6s.

Cochrane (ALFRED).
THE KESTREL'S NEST, and other Verses. Fcp. 8vo., 3s. 6d.
LEVIORE PLECTRO: Occasional Verses. Fcp. 8vo., 3s. 6d.

Douglas. — POEMS OF A COUNTRY GENTLEMAN. By Sir GEORGE DOUGLAS, Bart. Crown 8vo., 3s. 6d.

Goethe.
FAUST, Part I., the German Text, with Introduction and Notes. By ALBERT M. SELSS, Ph.D., M.A. Cr. 8vo., 5s.
FAUST. Translated, with Notes. By T. E. WEBB. 8vo., 12s. 6d.

Gurney (Rev. ALFRED, M.A.).
DAY-DREAMS: Poems. Cr. 8vo, 3s. 6d.
LOVE'S FRUITION, and other Poems. Fcp. 8vo.

Hampton.—FOR REMEMBRANCE. A Record of Life's Beginnings. Three Poetical Quotations for Every Day in the Year for Birth, Baptism, Death. Illustrative of our Life, Temporal, Spiritual, Eternal. Interleaved for Names. Compiled by the Lady LAURA HAMPTON. Fcp. 8vo., 3s. 6d.

Ingelow (JEAN).
POETICAL WORKS. 2 vols. Fcp. 8vo., 12s.
Complete in One Volume. Crown 8vo., 7s. 6d.
LYRICAL AND OTHER POEMS. Selected from the Writings of JEAN INGELOW. Fcp. 8vo., 2s. 6d.; cloth plain, 3s. cloth gilt.

Lang (ANDREW).
GRASS OF PARNASSUS. Fcp. 8vo., 2s. 6d. net.
THE BLUE POETRY BOOK. Edited by ANDREW LANG. With 100 Illustrations. Crown 8vo., 6s.

Layard.—SONGS IN MANY MOODS. By NINA F. LAYARD. And THE WANDERING ALBATROSS, &c. By ANNIE CORDER. In one volume. Crown 8vo., 5s.

Lecky.—POEMS. By W. E. H. LECKY. Fcp. 8vo., 5s.

Lytton (THE EARL OF) (OWEN MEREDITH).
MARAH. Fcp. 8vo., 6s. 6d.
KING POPPY: a Fantasia. With 1 Plate and Design on Title-Page by Sir EDWARD BURNE-JONES, A.R.A. Crown 8vo., 10s. 6d.
THE WANDERER. Cr. 8vo., 10s. 6d.
LUCILE. Crown 8vo., 10s. 6d.
SELECTED POEMS. Cr. 8vo., 10s. 6d.

Macaulay.—LAYS OF ANCIENT ROME, &c. By Lord MACAULAY.
Illustrated by G. SCHARF. Fcp. 4to., 10s. 6d.
———————— Bijou Edition. 18mo., 2s. 6d., gilt top.
———————— Popular Edition. Fcp. 4to., 6d. sewed, 1s. cloth.
Illustrated by J. R. WEGUELIN. Crown 8vo., 3s. 6d.
Annotated Edition. Fcp. 8vo., 1s. sewed, 1s. 6d. cloth.

Macdonald (GEORGE, LL.D.).
A BOOK OF STRIFE, IN THE FORM OF THE DIARY OF AN OLD SOUL: Poems. 18mo., 6s.
RAMPOLLI: GROWTHS FROM A LONG-PLANTED ROOT; being Translations, new and old (mainly in verse), chiefly from the German; along with 'A Year's Diary of an Old Soul'. Crown 8vo., 6s.

Moffat.—CRICKETY CRICKET: Rhymes and Parodies. By DOUGLAS MOFFAT. With Frontispiece by Sir FRANK LOCKWOOD, Q.C., M.P., and 53 Illustrations by the Author. Crown 8vo., 2s. 6d.

Morris (WILLIAM).
POETICAL WORKS—LIBRARY EDITION. Complete in Ten Volumes. Crown 8vo., price 6s. each :—
THE EARTHLY PARADISE. 4 vols. 6s. each.
THE LIFE AND DEATH OF JASON. 6s.
THE DEFENCE OF GUENEVERE, and other Poems. 6s.
THE STORY OF SIGURD THE VOLSUNG, and the Fall of the Niblungs. 6s.
LOVE IS ENOUGH; or, The Freeing of Pharamond: a Morality; and POEMS BY THE WAY. 6s.

Poetry and the Drama—*continued.*

Morris (WILLIAM)—*continued.*

THE ODYSSEY OF HOMER. Done into English Verse. 6s.

THE ÆNEIDS OF VIRGIL. Done into English Verse. 6s.

Certain of the Poetical Works may also be had in the following Editions :—

THE EARTHLY PARADISE.
Popular Edition. 5 vols. 12mo., 25s. ; or 5s. each, sold separately.
The same in Ten Parts, 25s. ; or 2s. 6d. each, sold separately.
Cheap Edition, in 1 vol. Cr. 8vo., 7s. 6d.

LOVE IS ENOUGH ; or, The Freeing of Pharamond : a Morality. Square crown 8vo., 7s. 6d.

POEMS BY THE WAY. Square crown 8vo., 6s.

⁎ For Mr. William Morris's Prose Works, see pp. 22 and 31.

Nesbit.—LAYS AND LEGENDS. By E. NESBIT (Mrs. HUBERT BLAND). First Series. Crown 8vo., 3s. 6d. Second Series, with Portrait. Crown 8vo., 5s.

Riley (JAMES WHITCOMB).

OLD FASHIONED ROSES : Poems. 12mo., 5s.

A CHILD-WORLD : POEMS. Fcp. 8vo., 5s.

Romanes.—A SELECTION FROM THE POEMS OF GEORGE JOHN ROMANES, M.A., LL.D., F.R.S. With an Introduction by T. HERBERT WARREN, President of Magdalen College, Oxford, Crown 8vo, 4s. 6d.

Shakespeare.—BOWDLER'S FAMILY SHAKESPEARE. With 36 Woodcuts. 1 vol. 8vo., 14s. Or in 6 vols. Fcp. 8vo., 21s.

THE SHAKESPEARE BIRTHDAY BOOK. By MARY F. DUNBAR. 32mo., 1s. 6d.

Tupper.—POEMS. By JOHN LUCAS TUPPER. Selected and Edited by WILLIAM MICHAEL ROSSETTI. Crown 8vo., 5s.

⁎ *The author of these Poems was a Sculptor, and afterwards Art Instructor in Rugby School. He died in 1879, having been a very close associate of the Pre-Raphaelite Brotherhood, and contributing in verse and prose to their magazine, the 'Germ,' in 1850.*

Wordsworth. — SELECTED POEMS. By ANDREW LANG. With Photogravure Frontispiece of Rydal Mount. With 16 Illustrations and numerous Initial Letters. By ALFRED PARSONS, A.R.A. Crown 8vo., gilt edges, 6s.

Wordsworth and Coleridge.—A DESCRIPTION OF THE WORDSWORTH AND COLERIDGE MANUSCRIPTS IN THE POSSESSION OF Mr. T. NORTON LONGMAN. Edited, with Notes, by W. HALE WHITE. With 3 Facsimile Reproductions. 4to., 10s. 6d.

Fiction, Humour, &c.

Allingham.—CROOKED PATHS. By FRANCIS ALLINGHAM. Cr. 8vo., 6s.

Anstey (F., Author of ' Vice Versâ ').

VOCES POPULI. Reprinted from 'Punch'. First Series. With 20 Illustrations by J. BERNARD PARTRIDGE. Cr. 8vo., 3s. 6d.

THE MAN FROM BLANKLEY'S: a Story in Scenes, and other Sketches. With 24 Illustrations by J. BERNARD PARTRIDGE. Post 4to., 6s.

Astor.—A JOURNEY IN OTHER WORLDS: a Romance of the Future. By JOHN JACOB ASTOR. With 10 Illustrations. Cr. 8vo., 6s.

Beaconsfield (THE EARL OF).

NOVELS AND TALES.
Complete in 11 vols. Cr. 8vo., 1s. 6d. each.

Vivian Grey.	Sybil.
The Young Duke, &c.	Henrietta Temple.
Alroy, Ixion, &c.	Venetia.
Contarini Fleming, &c.	Coningsby
Tancred.	Lothair.
	Endymion.

NOVELS AND TALES. The Hughenden Edition. With 2 Portraits and 11 Vignettes. 11 vols. Cr. 8vo., 42s.

Black.—THE PRINCESS DÉSIRÉE. By CLEMENTIA BLACK. With 8 Illustrations. Crown 8vo., 6s.

Crump.—WIDE ASUNDER AS THE POLES. By ARTHUR CRUMP. Cr.8vo.,6s.

Deland (MARGARET).

PHILIP AND HIS WIFE. Cr. 8vo., 2s. 6d.

THE WISDOM OF FOOLS : Stories. Cr. 8vo., 5s.

Fiction, Humour, &c.—*continued.*

Diderot.—RAMEAU'S NEPHEW: a Translation from Diderot's Autographic Text. By SYLVIA MARGARET HILL. Crown 8vo., 3*s.* 6*d.*

Dougall.—BEGGARS ALL. By L. DOUGALL. Crown 8vo., 3*s.* 6*d.*

Doyle (A. CONAN).
MICAH CLARKE: a Tale of Monmouth's Rebellion. With 10 Illustrations. Cr. 8vo., 3*s.* 6*d.*
THE CAPTAIN OF THE POLESTAR, and other Tales. Cr. 8vo., 3*s.* 6*d.*
THE REFUGEES: a Tale of the Huguenots. With 25 Illustrations. Crown 8vo., 3*s.* 6*d.*
THE STARK-MUNRO LETTERS. Cr. 8vo., 3*s.* 6*d.*

Farrar (F. W., Dean of Canterbury).
DARKNESS AND DAWN: or, Scenes in the Days of Nero. An Historic Tale. Cr. 8vo., 7*s.* 6*d.*
GATHERING CLOUDS: a Tale of the Days of St. Chrysostom. Crown 8vo., 7*s.* 6*d.*

Fowler (EDITH H.).
THE YOUNG PRETENDERS. A Story of Child Life. With 12 Illustrations by PHILIP BURNE-JONES. Cr. 8vo., 6*s.*
THE PROFESSOR'S CHILDREN. With 24 Illustrations by ETHEL KATE BURGESS. Crown 8vo., 6*s.*

Froude.—THE TWO CHIEFS OF DUNBOY: an Irish Romance of the Last Century. By JAMES A. FROUDE. Cr. 8vo., 3*s.* 6*d.*

Gilkes.—KALLISTRATUS: An Autobiography. A Story of the Hannibal and the Second Punic War. By A. H. GILKES, M.A., Master of Dulwich College. With 3 Illustrations by MAURICE GREIFFENHAGEN. Crown 8vo., 6*s.*

Graham.—THE RED SCAUR: a Story of the North Country. By P. ANDERSON GRAHAM. Crown 8vo., 6*s.*

Gurdon.—MEMORIES AND FANCIES: Suffolk Tales and other Stories; Fairy Legends; Poems; Miscellaneous Articles. By the late LADY CAMILLA GURDON, Author of 'Suffolk Folk-Lore'. Crown 8vo., 5*s.*

Haggard (H. RIDER).
HEART OF THE WORLD. With 15 Illustrations, Crown 8vo., 6*s.*
JOAN HASTE. With 20 Illustrations. Cr. 8vo., 3*s.* 6*d.*

Haggard (H. RIDER)—*continued.*
THE PEOPLE OF THE MIST. With 16 Illustrations. Crown 8vo., 3*s.* 6*d.*
MONTEZUMA'S DAUGHTER. With 24 Illustrations. Crown 8vo., 3*s.* 6*d.*
SHE. With 32 Illustrations. Cr. 8vo., 3*s.* 6*d.*
ALLAN QUATERMAIN. With 31 Illustrations. Crown 8vo., 3*s.* 6*d.*
MAIWA'S REVENGE. Crown 8vo., 1*s.* 6*d.*
COLONEL QUARITCH, V.C. Cr. 8vo., 3*s.* 6*d.*
CLEOPATRA. With 29 Illustrations. Crown 8vo., 3*s.* 6*d.*
BEATRICE. Cr. 8vo., 3*s.* 6*d.*
ERIC BRIGHTEYES. With 51 Illustrations. Cr. 8vo., 3*s.* 6*d.*
NADA THE LILY. With 23 Illustrations. Cr. 8vo., 3*s.* 6*d.*
ALLAN'S WIFE. With 34 Illustrations. Crown 8vo., 3*s.* 6*d.*
THE WITCH'S HEAD. With 16 Illustrations. Crown 8vo., 3*s.* 6*d.*
MR. MEESON'S WILL. With 16 Illustrations. Crown 8vo., 3*s.* 6*d.*
DAWN. With 16 Illustrations. Crown 8vo., 3*s.* 6*d.*

Haggard and Lang.—THE WORLD'S DESIRE. By H. RIDER HAGGARD and ANDREW LANG. With 27 Illustrations. Crown 8vo., 3*s.* 6*d.*

Harte.—IN THE CARQUINEZ WOODS, and other Stories. By BRET HARTE. Cr. 8vo., 3*s.* 6*d.*

Hope.—THE HEART OF PRINCESS OSRA. By ANTHONY HOPE. With 9 Illustrations by JOHN WILLIAMSON. Crown 8vo., 6*s.*

Hornung.—THE UNBIDDEN GUEST. By E. W. HORNUNG. Cr. 8vo., 3*s.* 6*d.*

Jerome.—SKETCHES IN LAVENDER: Blue and Green. By JEROME K. JEROME, Author of 'Three Men in a Boat,' &c. Crown 8vo., 6*s.*

Lang.—A MONK OF FIFE: a Story of the Days of Joan of Arc. By ANDREW LANG. With 13 Illustrations by SELWYN IMAGE. Crown 8vo., 6*s.*

Levett-Yeats (S.).
THE CHEVALIER D'AURIAC. Crown 8vo., 6*s.*
A GALAHAD OF THE CREEKS, and other Stories. Crown 8vo., 6*s.*

Fiction, Humour, &c.—*continued.*

Lyall (EDNA).
THE AUTOBIOGRAPHY OF A SLANDER. Fcp. 8vo., 1s. sewed.
Presentation Edition. With 20 Illustrations by LANCELOT SPEED. Cr. 8vo., 2s. 6d. net.
THE AUTOBIOGRAPHY OF A TRUTH. Fcp. 8vo., 1s. sewed ; 1s. 6d. cloth.
DOREEN : The Story of a Singer. Cr. 8vo., 6s.
WAYFARING MEN. Crown 8vo., 6s.

Melville (G. J. WHYTE).
The Gladiators.
The Interpreter.
Good for Nothing.
The Queen's Maries.
Holmby House.
Kate Coventry.
Digby Grand.
General Bounce.
Cr. 8vo., 1s. 6d. each.

Merriman.—FLOTSAM : a Story of the Indian Mutiny. By HENRY SETON MERRIMAN. With Frontispiece and Vignette by H. G. MASSEY, A.R.E. Cr. 8vo., 6s.

Morris (WILLIAM).
THE SUNDERING FLOOD. Crown 8vo.
THE WATER OF THE WONDROUS ISLES. Crown 8vo., 7s. 6d.
THE WELL AT THE WORLD'S END. 2 vols., 8vo., 28s.
THE STORY OF THE GLITTERING PLAIN, which has been also called The Land of the Living Men, or The Acre of the Undying. Square post 8vo., 5s. net.
THE ROOTS OF THE MOUNTAINS, wherein is told somewhat of the Lives of the Men of Burgdale, their Friends, their Neighbours, their Foemen, and their Fellows-in-Arms. Written in Prose and Verse. Square cr. 8vo., 8s.
A TALE OF THE HOUSE OF THE WOLFINGS, and all the Kindreds of the Mark. Written in Prose and Verse. Second Edition. Square cr. 8vo., 6s.
A DREAM OF JOHN BALL, AND A KING'S LESSON. 12mo., 1s. 6d.
NEWS FROM NOWHERE ; or, An Epoch of Rest. Being some Chapters from an Utopian Romance. Post 8vo., 1s. 6d.
* For Mr. William Morris's Poetical Works, see p. 19.

Newman (CARDINAL).
LOSS AND GAIN : The Story of a Convert. Crown 8vo. Cabinet Edition, 6s. ; Popular Edition, 3s. 6d.
CALLISTA : A Tale of the Third Century. Crown 8vo. Cabinet Edition, 6s. ; Popular Edition, 3s. 6d.

Oliphant.—OLD MR. TREDGOLD. By Mrs. OLIPHANT. Crown 8vo., 2s. 6d.

Phillipps-Wolley.—SNAP: a Legend of the Lone Mountain. By C. PHILLIPPS-WOLLEY. With 13 Illustrations. Crown 8vo., 3s. 6d.

Quintana.—THE CID CAMPEADOR: an Historical Romance. By D. ANTONIO DE TRUEBA Y LA QUINTANA. Translated from the Spanish by HENRY J. GILL, M.A., T.C.D. Crown 8vo., 6s.

Rhoscomyl (OWEN).
THE JEWEL OF YNYS GALON : being a hitherto unprinted Chapter in the History of the Sea Rovers. With 12 Illustrations by LANCELOT SPEED. Crown 8vo., 3s. 6d.
BATTLEMENT AND TOWER : a Romance. With Frontispiece by R. CATON WOODVILLE. Crown 8vo., 6s.
FOR THE WHITE ROSE OF ARNO : A Story of the Jacobite Rising of 1745. Crown 8vo., 6s.

Sewell (ELIZABETH M.).
A Glimpse of the World.
Laneton Parsonage.
Margaret Percival.
Katharine Ashton.
The Earl's Daughter.
The Experience of Life.
Amy Herbert.
Cleve Hall.
Gertrude.
Home Life.
After Life.
Ursula. Ivors.
Cr. 8vo., 1s. 6d. each, cloth plain. 2s. 6d. each, cloth extra, gilt edges.

Stevenson (ROBERT LOUIS).
THE STRANGE CASE OF DR. JEKYLL AND MR. HYDE. Fcp. 8vo., 1s. sewed, 1s. 6d. cloth.
THE STRANGE CASE OF DR. JEKYLL AND MR. HYDE ; with Other Fables. Crown 8vo., 3s. 6d.
MORE NEW ARABIAN NIGHTS—THE DYNAMITER. By ROBERT LOUIS STEVENSON and FANNY VAN DE GRIFT STEVENSON. Crown 8vo., 3s. 6d.
THE WRONG BOX. By ROBERT LOUIS STEVENSON and LLOYD OSBOURNE. Crown 8vo., 3s. 6d.

Suttner.—LAY DOWN YOUR ARMS (*Die Waffen Nieder*) : The Autobiography of Martha Tilling. By BERTHA VON SUTTNER. Translated by T. HOLMES. Crown 8vo., 1s. 6d.

Taylor.—EARLY ITALIAN LOVE-STORIES. Edited and Retold by UNA TAYLOR. With 12 Illustrations by H. J. FORD.

Fiction, Humour, &c.—continued.

Trollope (ANTHONY).

THE WARDEN. Cr. 8vo., 1s. 6d.

BARCHESTER TOWERS. Cr. 8vo., 1s. 6d.

Walford (L. B.).

IVA KILDARE: a Matrimonial Problem. Crown 8vo., 6s.

Mr. SMITH: a Part of his Life. Crown 8vo., 2s. 6d.

THE BABY'S GRANDMOTHER. Crown 8vo., 2s. 6d

COUSINS. Crown 8vo., 2s. 6d.

TROUBLESOME DAUGHTERS. Crown 8vo., 2s. 6d.

PAULINE. Crown 8vo., 2s. 6d.

DICK NETHERBY. Crown 8vo., 2s. 6d.

THE HISTORY OF A WEEK. Crown 8vo. 2s. 6d.

A STIFF-NECKED GENERATION. Crown 8vo. 2s. 6d.

NAN, and other Stories. Cr. 8vo., 2s. 6d.

THE MISCHIEF OF MONICA. Crown 8vo., 2s. 6d.

THE ONE GOOD GUEST. Cr. 8vo. 2s. 6d.

'PLOUGHED,' and other Stories. Crown 8vo., 2s. 6d.

THE MATCHMAKER. Cr. 8vo., 2s. 6d.

Watson.—RACING AND CHASING: a Volume of Sporting Stories and Sketches. By ALFRED E. T. WATSON, Editor of the 'Badminton Magazine'. With 52 Illustrations. Crown 8vo., 7s. 6d.

Weyman (STANLEY).

THE HOUSE OF THE WOLF. Cr. 8vo., 3s. 6d.

A GENTLEMAN OF FRANCE. Cr. 8vo., 6s.

THE RED COCKADE. Cr. 8vo., 6s.

SHREWSBURY. With 24 Illustrations. Crown 8vo., 6s.

Whishaw (FRED.).

A BOYAR OF THE TERRIBLE: a Romance of the Court of Ivan the Cruel, First Tzar of Russia. With 12 Illustrations by H. G. MASSEY, A.R.E. Cr. 8vo., 6s.

A TSAR'S GRATITUDE. Cr. 8vo., 6s.

Woods.—WEEPING FERRY, and other Stories. By MARGARET L. WOODS, Author of 'A Village Tragedy'. Crown 8vo., 6s.

Popular Science (Natural History, &c.).

Butler.—OUR HOUSEHOLD INSECTS. An Account of the Insect-Pests found in Dwelling-Houses. By EDWARD A. BUTLER, B.A., B.Sc. (Lond.). With 113 Illustrations. Crown 8vo., 3s. 6d.

Furneaux (W.).

THE OUTDOOR WORLD; or, The Young Collector's Handbook. With 18 Plates, 16 of which are coloured, and 549 Illustrations in the Text. Crown 8vo., 7s. 6d.

BUTTERFLIES AND MOTHS (British). With 12 coloured Plates and 241 Illustrations in the Text. Crown 8vo., 7s. 6d.

LIFE IN PONDS AND STREAMS. With 8 coloured Plates and 331 Illustrations in the Text. Cr. 8vo., 7s. 6d.

Hartwig (Dr. GEORGE).

THE SEA AND ITS LIVING WONDERS. With 12 Plates and 303 Woodcuts. 8vo., 7s. net.

THE TROPICAL WORLD. With 8 Plates and 172 Woodcuts. 8vo., 7s. net.

THE POLAR WORLD. With 3 Maps, 8 Plates and 85 Woodcuts. 8vo., 7s. net.

Hartwig (Dr. GEORGE)—continued.

THE SUBTERRANEAN WORLD. With 3 Maps and 80 Woodcuts. 8vo., 7s. net.

THE AERIAL WORLD. With Map, 8 Plates and 60 Woodcuts. 8vo., 7s. net.

HEROES OF THE POLAR WORLD. 19 Illustrations. Crown 8vo., 2s.

WONDERS OF THE TROPICAL FORESTS. 40 Illustrations. Crown 8vo., 2s.

WORKERS UNDER THE GROUND. 29 Illustrations. Crown 8vo., 2s.

MARVELS OVER OUR HEADS. 29 Illustrations. Crown 8vo., 2s.

SEA MONSTERS AND SEA BIRDS. 75 Illustrations. Crown 8vo., 2s. 6d.

DENIZENS OF THE DEEP. 117 Illustrations. Crown 8vo., 2s. 6d.

VOLCANOES AND EARTHQUAKES. 30 Illustrations. Crown 8vo., 2s. 6d.

WILD ANIMALS OF THE TROPICS. 66 Illustrations. Crown 8vo., 3s. 6d.

Helmholtz.—POPULAR LECTURES ON SCIENTIFIC SUBJECTS. By HERMANN VON HELMHOLTZ. With 68 Woodcuts. 2 vols. Crown 8vo., 3s. 6d. each.

Popular Science (Natural History, &c.).

Hudson (W. H.).

BRITISH BIRDS. With a Chapter on Structure and Classification by FRANK E. BEDDARD, F.R.S. With 16 Plates (8 of which are Coloured), and over 100 Illustrations in the Text. Crown 8vo., 7s. 6d.

BIRDS IN LONDON. With numerous Illustrations from Drawings and Photographs.

Proctor (RICHARD A.).

LIGHT SCIENCE FOR LEISURE HOURS. Familiar Essays on Scientific Subjects. 3 vols. Crown 8vo., 5s. each.

ROUGH WAYS MADE SMOOTH. Familiar Essays on Scientific Subjects. Crown 8vo., 3s. 6d.

PLEASANT WAYS IN SCIENCE. Crown 8vo., 3s. 6d.

NATURE STUDIES. By R. A. PROCTOR, GRANT ALLEN, A. WILSON, T. FOSTER and E. CLODD. Crown 8vo., 3s. 6d.

LEISURE READINGS. By R. A. PROCTOR, E. CLODD, A. WILSON, T. FOSTER, and A. C. RANYARD. Cr. 8vo., 3s. 6d.

** *For Mr. Proctor's other books see Messrs. Longmans & Co.'s Catalogue of Scientific Works.*

Stanley.—A FAMILIAR HISTORY OF BIRDS. By E. STANLEY, D.D., formerly Bishop of Norwich. With 160 Illustrations. Crown 8vo., 3s. 6d.

Wood (Rev. J. G.).

HOMES WITHOUT HANDS : a Description of the Habitation of Animals, classed according to the Principle of Construction. With 140 Illustrations. 8vo., 7s. net.

Wood (Rev. J. G.)—*continued.*

INSECTS AT HOME . a Popular Account of British Insects, their Structure, Habits and Transformations. With 700 Illustrations. 8vo., 7s. net.

INSECTS ABROAD : a Popular Account of Foreign Insects, their Structure, Habits and Transformations. With 600 Illustrations. 8vo., 7s. net.

BIBLE ANIMALS : a Description of every Living Creature mentioned in the Scriptures. With 112 Illustrations. 8vo., 7s. net.

PETLAND REVISITED. With 33 Illustrations. Cr. 8vo., 3s. 6d.

OUT OF DOORS ; a Selection of Original Articles on Practical Natural History. With 11 Illustrations. Cr. 8vo., 3s. 6d.

STRANGE DWELLINGS : a Description of the Habitations of Animals, abridged from 'Homes without Hands '. With 60 Illustrations. Cr. 8vo., 3s. 6d.

BIRD LIFE OF THE BIBLE. 32 Illustrations. Crown 8vo., 3s. 6d.

WONDERFUL NESTS. 30 Illustrations. Crown 8vo., 3s. 6d.

HOMES UNDER THE GROUND. 28 Illustrations. Crown 8vo., 3s. 6d.

WILD ANIMALS OF THE BIBLE. 29 Illustrations. Crown 8vo., 3s. 6d.

DOMESTIC ANIMALS OF THE BIBLE. 23 Illustrations. Crown 8vo., 3s. 6d.

THE BRANCH BUILDERS. 28 Illustrations. Crown 8vo., 2s. 6d.

SOCIAL HABITATIONS AND PARASITIC NESTS. 18 Illustrations. Crown 8vo., 2s.

Works of Reference.

Longmans' GAZETTEER OF THE WORLD. Edited by GEORGE G. CHISHOLM, M.A., B.Sc. Imp. 8vo., £2 2s. cloth, £2 12s. 6d. half-morocco.

Maunder (Samuel).

BIOGRAPHICAL TREASURY. With Supplement brought down to 1889. By Rev. JAMES WOOD. Fcp. 8vo., 6s.

Maunder (Samuel)—*continued.*

TREASURY OF GEOGRAPHY, Physical, Historical, Descriptive, and Political. With 7 Maps and 16 Plates. Fcp. 8vo., 6s.

THE TREASURY OF BIBLE KNOWLEDGE. By the Rev. J. AYRE, M.A. With 5 Maps, 15 Plates, and 300 Woodcuts. Fcp. 8vo., 6s.

Works of Reference—*continued.*

Maunder (Samuel)—*continued.*

TREASURY OF KNOWLEDGE AND LIBRARY OF REFERENCE. Fcp. 8vo., 6s.

HISTORICAL TREASURY: Fcp. 8vo., 6s.

SCIENTIFIC AND LITERARY TREASURY. Fcp. 8vo., 6s.

THE TREASURY OF BOTANY. Edited by J. LINDLEY, F.R.S., and T. MOORE, F.L.S. With 274 Woodcuts and 20 Steel Plates. 2 vols. Fcp. 8vo., 12s.

Roget.—THESAURUS OF ENGLISH WORDS AND PHRASES. Classified and Arranged so as to Facilitate the Expression of Ideas and assist in Literary Composition. By PETER MARK ROGET, M.D., F.R.S. Recomposed throughout, enlarged and improved, partly from the Author's Notes and with a full Index, by the Author's Son, JOHN LEWIS ROGET. Crown 8vo., 10s. 6d.

Willich.—POPULAR TABLES for giving information for ascertaining the value of Lifehold, Leasehold, and Church Property, the Public Funds, &c. By CHARLES M. WILLICH. Edited by H. BENCE JONES. Crown 8vo., 10s. 6d.

Children's Books.

Crake (Rev. A. D.).

EDWY THE FAIR; or, the First Chronicle of Æscendune. Crown 8vo., 2s. 6d.

ALFGAR THE DANE: or, the Second Chronicle of Æscendune. Cr 8vo., 2s. 6d.

THE RIVAL HEIRS: being the Third and Last Chronicle of Æscendune. Crown 8vo., 2s. 6d.

THE HOUSE OF WALDERNE. A Tale of the Cloister and the Forest in the Days of the Barons' Wars. Crown 8vo., 2s. 6d.

BRIAN FITZ-COUNT. A Story of Wallingford Castle and Dorchester Abbey. Crown 8vo., 2s. 6d

Lang (ANDREW)—EDITED BY.

THE BLUE FAIRY BOOK. With 138 Illustrations. Crown 8vo., 6s.
THE RED FAIRY BOOK. With 100 Illustrations. Crown 8vo., 6s.
THE GREEN FAIRY BOOK. With 99 Illustrations. Crown 8vo., 6s.
THE YELLOW FAIRY BOOK. With 104 Illustrations. Crown 8vo., 6s.
THE PINK FAIRY BOOK. With 67 Illustrations. Crown 8vo., 6s.
THE BLUE POETRY BOOK. With 100 Illustrations. Crown 8vo., 6s.
THE BLUE POETRY BOOK. School Edition, without Illustrations. Fcp. 8vo., 2s. 6d.
THE TRUE STORY BOOK. With 66 Illustrations. Crown 8vo., 6s.

Lang (ANDREW)—*continued.*

THE RED TRUE STORY BOOK. With 100 Illustrations. Crown 8vo., 6s.
THE ANIMAL STORY BOOK. With 67 Illustrations. Crown 8vo., 6s.

Meade (L. T.).

DADDY'S BOY. With Illustrations. Crown 8vo., 3s. 6d.

DEB AND THE DUCHESS. With Illustrations. Crown 8vo., 3s. 6d.

THE BERESFORD PRIZE. With Illustrations. Crown 8vo., 3s. 6d.

THE HOUSE OF SURPRISES. With Illustrations. Crown 8vo., 3s. 6d.

Molesworth. — SILVERTHORNS. By Mrs. MOLESWORTH. With Illustrations. Crown 8vo., 5s.

Praeger.—THE ADVENTURES OF THE THREE BOLD BABES: Hector, Honoria and Alisander. A Story in Pictures. By S. ROSAMOND PRAEGER. With 24 Coloured Plates and 24 Outline Pictures. Oblong 4to., 3s. 6d.

Stevenson.—A CHILD'S GARDEN OF VERSES. By ROBERT LOUIS STEVENSON. fcp. 8vo., 5s.

Sullivan.—HERE THEY ARE! More Stories. Written and Illustrated by JAMES F. SULLIVAN. Crown 8vo., 6s.

Children's Books—*continued.*

Upton (FLORENCE K., and BERTHA).

THE ADVENTURES OF TWO DUTCH DOLLS AND A 'GOLLIWOGG'. With 31 Coloured Plates and numerous Illustrations in the Text. Oblong 4to., 6s.

THE GOLLIWOGG'S BICYCLE CLUB. With 31 Coloured Plates and numerous Illustrations in the Text. Oblong 4to., 6s.

Upton (FLORENCE K., and BERTHA)—*continued.*

THE VEGE-MEN'S REVENGE. With 31 Coloured Plates and numerous Illustrations in the Text. Oblong 4to., 6s.

Wordsworth.—THE SNOW GARDEN, and other Fairy Tales for Children. By ELIZABETH WORDSWORTH. With 10 Illustrations by TREVOR HADDON. Crown 8vo., 3s. 6d.

Longmans' Series of Books for Girls.

Price 2s. 6d. each.

ATELIER (THE) DU LYS: or an Art Student in the Reign of Terror.

BY THE SAME AUTHOR.

| Mademoiselle Mori: a Tale of Modern Rome. In the Olden Time: a Tale of the Peasant War in Germany. | The Younger Sister. That Child. Under a Cloud. Hester's Venture. The Fiddler of Lugau. A Child of the Revolution. |

ATHERSTONE PRIORY. By L. N. COMYN.

THE STORY OF A SPRING MORNING, &c. By Mrs. MOLESWORTH. Illustrated.

THE PALACE IN THE GARDEN. By Mrs. MOLESWORTH. Illustrated.

NEIGHBOURS. By Mrs. MOLESWORTH.

THE THIRD MISS ST. QUENTIN. By Mrs. MOLESWORTH.

VERY YOUNG; and QUITE ANOTHER STORY. Two Stories. By JEAN INGELOW.

CAN THIS BE LOVE? By LOUISA PARR.

KEITH DERAMORE. By the Author of 'Miss Molly'.

SIDNEY. By MARGARET DELAND.

AN ARRANGED MARRIAGE. By DOROTHEA GERARD.

LAST WORDS TO GIRLS ON LIFE AT SCHOOL AND AFTER SCHOOL. By MARIA GREY.

STRAY THOUGHTS FOR GIRLS. By LUCY H. M. SOULSBY, Head Mistress of Oxford High School. 16mo., 1s. 6d. net.

The Silver Library.

CROWN 8vo. 3s. 6d. EACH VOLUME.

Arnold's (Sir Edwin) Seas and Lands. With 71 Illustrations. 3s. 6d.

Bagehot's (W.) Biographical Studies. 3s. 6d.

Bagehot's (W.) Economic Studies. 3s. 6d.

Bagehot's (W.) Literary Studies. With Portrait. 3 vols. 3s. 6d. each.

Baker's (Sir S. W.) Eight Years in Ceylon. With 6 Illustrations. 3s. 6d.

Baker's (Sir S. W.) Rifle and Hound in Ceylon. With 6 Illustrations. 3s. 6d.

Baring-Gould's (Rev. S.) Curious Myths of the Middle Ages. 3s. 6d.

Baring-Gould's (Rev. S.) Origin and Development of Religious Belief. 2 vols. 3s. 6d. each.

Becker's (W. A.) Gallus: or, Roman Scenes in the Time of Augustus. With 26 Illustrations. 3s. 6d.

Becker's (W. A.) Charicles: or, Illustrations of the Private Life of the Ancient Greeks. With 26 Illustrations. 3s. 6d.

Bent's (J. T.) The Ruined Cities of Mashonaland. With 117 Illustrations. 3s. 6d.

Brassey's (Lady) A Voyage in the 'Sunbeam'. With 66 Illustrations. 3s. 6d.

Butler's (Edward A.) Our Household Insects. With 7 Plates and 113 Illustrations in the Text. 3s. 6d.

Clodd's (E.) Story of Creation: a Plain Account of Evolution. With 77 Illustrations. 3s. 6d.

The Silver Library—*continued.*

Conybeare (Rev. W. J.) and Howson's (Very Rev. J. S.) Life and Epistles of St. Paul. With 46 Illustrations. 3s. 6d.

Dougall's (L.) Beggars All; a Novel. 3s. 6d.

Doyle's (A. Conan) Micah Clarke : a Tale of Monmouth's Rebellion. With 10 Illustrations. 3s. 6d.

Doyle's (A. Conan) The Captain of the Polestar, and other Tales. 3s. 6d.

Doyle's (A. Conan) The Refugees : A Tale of the Huguenots. With 25 Illustrations, 3s. 6d.

Doyle's (A. Conan) The Stark Munro Letters. 3s. 6d.

Froude's (J. A.) The History of England, from the Fall of Wolsey to the Defeat of the Spanish Armada. 12 vols. 3s. 6d. each.

Froude's (J. A.) The English in Ireland. 3 vols. 10s. 6d.

Froude's (J. A.) The Divorce of Catherine of Aragon. 3s. 6d.

Froude's (J. A.) The Spanish Story of the Armada, and other Essays. 3s. 6d.

Froude's (J. A.) Short Studies on Great Subjects. 4 vols. 3s. 6d. each.

Froude's (J. A.) The Council of Trent. 3s. 6d.

Froude's (J. A.) Thomas Carlyle: a History of his Life.
1795-1835. 2 vols. 7s.
1834-1881. 2 vols. 7s.

Froude's (J. A.) Cæsar : a Sketch. 3s. 6d.

Froude's (J. A.) The Two Chiefs of Dunboy: an Irish Romance of the Last Century. 3s. 6d.

Gleig's (Rev. G. R.) Life of the Duke of Wellington. With Portrait. 3s. 6d.

Greville's (C. C. F.) Journal of the Reigns of King George IV., King William IV., and Queen Victoria. 8 vols. 3s. 6d. each.

Haggard's (H. R.) She: A History of Adventure. 32 Illustrations. 3s. 6d.

Haggard's (H. R.) Allan Quatermain. With 20 Illustrations. 3s. 6d.

Haggard's (H. R.) Colonel Quaritch, V.C. : a Tale of Country Life. 3s. 6d.

Haggard's (H. R.) Cleopatra. With 29 Illustrations. 3s. 6d.

Haggard's (H. R.) Eric Brighteyes. With 51 Illustrations. 3s. 6d.

Haggard's (H. R.) Beatrice. 3s. 6d.

Haggard's (H. R.) Allan's Wife. With 34 Illustrations. 3s. 6d.

Haggard's (H. R.) Montezuma's Daughter. With 25 Illustrations. 3s. 6d.

Haggard's (H. R.) The Witch's Head. With 16 Illustrations. 3s. 6d.

Haggard's (H. R.) Mr. Meeson's Will. With 16 Illustrations. 3s. 6d.

Haggard's (H. R.) Nada the Lily. With 23 Illustrations. 3s. 6d.

Haggard's (H. R.) Dawn. With 16 Illustrations. 3s. 6d.

Haggard's (H. R.) The People of the Mist. With 16 Illustrations. 3s. 6d.

Haggard's (H. R.) Joan Haste. With 20 Illustrations. 3s. 6d.

Haggard (H. R.) and Lang's (A.) The World's Desire. With 27 Illus. 3s. 6d.

Harte's (Bret) In the Carquinez Woods, and other Stories. 3s. 6d.

Helmholtz's (Hermann von) Popular Lectures on Scientific Subjects. With 68 Illustrations. 2 vols. 3s. 6d. each.

Hornung's (E. W.) The Unbidden Guest. 3s. 6d.

Howitt's (W.) Visits to Remarkable Places. With 80 Illustrations. 3s. 6d.

Jefferies' (R.) The Story of My Heart : My Autobiography. With Portrait. 3s. 6d.

Jefferies' (R.) Field and Hedgerow. With Portrait. 3s. 6d.

Jefferies' (R.) Red Deer. 17 Illus. 3s. 6d.

Jefferies' (R.) Wood Magic : a Fable. 3s. 6d.

Jefferies' (R.) The Toilers of the Field. With Portrait from the Bust in Salisbury Cathedral. 3s. 6d.

Kaye (Sir J.) and Malleson's (Colonel) History of the Indian Mutiny of 1857-8. 6 vols. 3s. 6d. each.

Knight's (E. F.) The Cruise of the 'Alerte' : the Narrative of a Search for Treasure on the Desert Island of Trinidad. With 2 Maps and 23 Illustrations. 3s. 6d.

Knight's (E. F.) Where Three Empires Meet : a Narrative of Recent Travel in Kashmir, Western Tibet, Baltistan, Gilgit. With a Map and 54 Illustrations. 3s. 6d.

Knight's (E. F.) The 'Falcon' on the Baltic. With Map and 11 Illustrations. 3s. 6d.

Kœstlin's (J.) Life of Luther. With 62 Illustrations, &c. 3s. 6d.

Lang's (A.) Angling Sketches. 20 Illustrations. 3s. 6d.

Lang's (A.) The Monk of Fife. With 13 Illustrations. 3s. 6d.

The Silver Library—*continued.*

Lang's (A.) Custom and Myth : Studies of Early Usage and Belief. 3s. 6d.

Lang's (Andrew) Cock Lane and Common-Sense. With a New Preface. 3s. 6d.

Lees (J. A.) and Clutterbuck's (W.J.)B.C. 1887, A Ramble in British Columbia. With Maps and 75 Illustrations. 3s. 6d.

Macaulay's (Lord) Essays and Lays of Ancient Rome. With Portrait and Illustration. 3s. 6d.

Macleod's (H. D.) Elements of Banking. 3s. 6d.

Marbot's (Baron de) Memoirs. Translated. 2 vols. 7s.

Marshman's (J. C.) Memoirs of Sir Henry Havelock. 3s. 6d.

Max Müller's (F.) India, what can it teach us? 3s. 6d.

Max Müller's (F.) Introduction to the Science of Religion. 3s. 6d.

Merivale's (Dean) History of the Romans under the Empire. 8 vols. 3s. 6d. ea.

Mill's (J. S.) Political Economy. 3s. 6d.

Mill's (J. S.) System of Logic. 3s. 6d.

Milner's (Geo.) Country Pleasures : the Chronicle of a Year chiefly in a garden. 3s. 6d.

Nansen's (F.) The First Crossing of Greenland. With Illustrations and a Map. 3s. 6d.

Phillipps-Wolley's (C.) Snap : a Legend of the Lone Mountain. With 13 Illustrations. 3s. 6d.

Proctor's (R. A.) The Moon. 3s. 6d.

Proctor's (R. A.) The Orbs Around Us. 3s. 6d.

Proctor's (R. A.) The Expanse of Heaven. 3s. 6d.

Proctor's (R. A.) Other Worlds than Ours. 3s. 6d.

Proctor's (R. A.) Our Place among Infinities : a Series of Essays contrasting our Little Abode in Space and Time with the Infinities around us. Crown 8vo., 3s. 6d.

Proctor's (R. A.) Other Suns than Ours. 3s. 6d.

Proctor's (R. A.) Rough Ways made Smooth. 3s. 6d.

Proctor's (R. A.) Pleasant Ways in Science. 3s. 6d.

Proctor's (R. A.) Myths and Marvels of Astronomy. 3s. 6d.

Proctor's (R. A.) Nature Studies. 3s. 6d.

Proctor's (R. A.) Leisure Readings. By R. A. PROCTOR, EDWARD CLODD, ANDREW WILSON, THOMAS FOSTER, and A. C. RANYARD. With Illustrations. 3s. 6d.

Rhoscomyl's (Owen) The Jewel of Ynys Galon. With 12 Illustrations. 3s. 6d.

Rossetti's (Maria F.) A Shadow of Dante. 3s. 6d.

Smith's (R. Bosworth) Carthage and the Carthaginians. With Maps, Plans, &c. 3s. 6d.

Stanley's (Bishop) Familiar History of Birds. With 160 Illustrations. 3s. 6d.

Stevenson's (R. L.) The Strange Case of Dr. Jekyll and Mr. Hyde ; with other Fables. 3s. 6d.

Stevenson (R. L.) and Osbourne's (Ll.) The Wrong Box. 3s. 6d.

Stevenson (Robt. Louis) and Stevenson's (Fanny van de Grift) More New Arabian Nights.—The Dynamiter. 3s. 6d.

Weyman's (Stanley J.) The House of the Wolf : a Romance. 3s. 6d.

Wood's (Rev. J. G.) Petland Revisited. With 33 Illustrations. 3s. 6d.

Wood's (Rev. J. G.) Strange Dwellings. With 60 Illustrations. 3s. 6d.

Wood's (Rev. J. G.) Out of Doors. With 11 Illustrations. 3s. 6d.

Cookery, Domestic Management, &c.

Acton.—MODERN COOKERY. By ELIZA ACTON. With 150 Woodcuts. Fcp. 8vo., 4s. 6d.

Bull (THOMAS, M.D.).
HINTS TO MOTHERS ON THE MANAGEMENT OF THEIR HEALTH DURING THE PERIOD OF PREGNANCY. Fcp. 8vo., 1s. 6d.
THE MATERNAL MANAGEMENT OF CHILDREN IN HEALTH AND DISEASE. Fcp. 8vo., 1s. 6d.

De Salis (Mrs.).
CAKES AND CONFECTIONS À LA MODE. Fcp. 8vo., 1s. 6d.

DOGS : a Manual for Amateurs. Fcp. 8vo., 1s. 6d.

DRESSED GAME AND POULTRY À LA MODE. Fcp. 8vo., 1s. 6d.

DRESSED VEGETABLES À LA MODE. Fcp. 8vo., 1s. 6d.

Cookery, Domestic Management, &c.—*continued*.

De Salis (Mrs.)—*continued*.

DRINKS À LA MODE. Fcp. 8vo., 1s. 6d.

ENTRÉES À LA MODE. Fcp. 8vo., 1s. 6d.

FLORAL DECORATIONS. Fcp. 8vo., 1s. 6d.

GARDENING À LA MODE. Fcp. 8vo.
Part I. Vegetables. 1s. 6d.
Part II. Fruits. 1s. 6d.

NATIONAL VIANDS À LA MODE. Fcp. 8vo., 1s. 6d.

NEW-LAID EGGS. Fcp. 8vo., 1s. 6d.

OYSTERS À LA MODE. Fcp. 8vo., 1s. 6d.

PUDDINGS AND PASTRY À LA MODE. Fcp. 8vo., 1s. 6d.

SAVOURIES À LA MODE. Fcp. 8vo., 1s. 6d.

SOUPS AND DRESSED FISH À LA MODE. Fcp. 8vo., 1s. 6d.

SWEETS AND SUPPER DISHES À LA MODE. Fcp. 8vo., 1s. 6d.

De Salis (Mrs.)—*continued*.

TEMPTING DISHES FOR SMALL INCOMES. Fcp. 8vo., 1s. 6d.

WRINKLES AND NOTIONS FOR EVERY HOUSEHOLD. Cr. 8vo., 1s. 6d.

Lear.—MAIGRE COOKERY. By H. L. SIDNEY LEAR. 16mo., 2s.

Poole.—COOKERY FOR THE DIABETIC. By W. H. and Mrs. POOLE. With Preface by Dr. PAVY. Fcp. 8vo., 2s. 6d.

Walker (JANE H.).
A BOOK FOR EVERY WOMAN.
Part I. The Management of Children in Health and out of Health. Cr. 8vo., 2s. 6d.
Part II. Woman in Health and out of Health. Crown 8vo, 2s. 6d.
A HANDBOOK FOR MOTHERS: being Simple Hints to Women on the Management of their Health during Pregnancy and Confinement, together with Plain Directions as to the Care of Infants. Cr. 8vo., 2s. 6d.

Miscellaneous and Critical Works.

Allingham.—VARIETIES IN PROSE. By WILLIAM ALLINGHAM. 3 vols. Cr. 8vo, 18s. (Vols. 1 and 2, Rambles, by PATRICIUS WALKER. Vol. 3, Irish Sketches, etc.)

Armstrong.—ESSAYS AND SKETCHES. By EDMUND J. ARMSTRONG. Fcp. 8vo., 5s.

Bagehot.—LITERARY STUDIES. By WALTER BAGEHOT. With Portrait. 3 vols. Crown 8vo., 3s. 6d. each.

Baring-Gould.—CURIOUS MYTHS OF THE MIDDLE AGES. By Rev. S. BARING-GOULD. Crown 8vo., 3s. 6d.

Baynes.—SHAKESPEARE STUDIES, AND OTHER ESSAYS. By the late THOMAS SPENCER BAYNES, LL.B., LL.D. With a Biographical Preface by Prof. LEWIS CAMPBELL. Crown 8vo., 7s. 6d.

Boyd (A. K. H.) ('A.K.H.B.').
And see MISCELLANEOUS THEOLOGICAL WORKS, p. 32.
AUTUMN HOLIDAYS OF A COUNTRY PARSON. Crown 8vo., 3s. 6d.
COMMONPLACE PHILOSOPHER. Crown 8vo., 3s. 6d.
CRITICAL ESSAYS OF A COUNTRY PARSON. Crown 8vo., 3s. 6d.

Boyd (A. K. H.) ('A.K.H.B.')—*continued*.
EAST COAST DAYS AND MEMORIES. Crown 8vo., 3s. 6d.
LANDSCAPES, CHURCHES AND MORALITIES. Crown 8vo., 3s. 6d.
LEISURE HOURS IN TOWN. Crown 8vo., 3s. 6d.
LESSONS OF MIDDLE AGE. Cr. 8vo., 3s. 6d.
OUR LITTLE LIFE. Two Series. Cr. 8vo., 3s. 6d. each.
OUR HOMELY COMEDY: AND TRAGEDY. Crown 8vo., 3s. 6d.
RECREATIONS OF A COUNTRY PARSON. Three Series. Cr. 8vo., 3s. 6d. each.

Brookings.—BRIEFS FOR DEBATE ON CURRENT POLITICAL, ECONOMIC AND SOCIAL TOPICS. Edited by W. DU BOIS BROOKINGS, A.B. of the Harvard Law School, and RALPH CURTIS RINGWALT, A.B., Assistant in Rhetoric in Columbia University, New York. With an Introduction on 'The Art of Debate' by ALBERT BUSHNELL HART, Ph.D., of Harvard University. With full Index Crown 8vo., 6s.

Miscellaneous and Critical Works—*continued.*

Butler (SAMUEL).
EREWHON Cr. 8vo., 5*s.*
THE FAIR HAVEN. A Work in Defence of the Miraculous Element in our Lord's Ministry. Cr. 8vo., 7*s.* 6*d.*
LIFE AND HABIT. An Essay after a Completer View of Evolution. Cr. 8vo., 7*s.* 6*d.*
EVOLUTION, OLD AND NEW. Cr. 8vo., 10*s.* 6*d.*
ALPS AND SANCTUARIES OF PIEDMONT AND CANTON TICINO. Illustrated. Pott 4to., 10*s.*6*d.*
LUCK, OR CUNNING, AS THE MAIN MEANS OF ORGANIC MODIFICATION? Cr. 8vo., 7*s.* 6*d.*
EX VOTO. An Account of the Sacro Monte or New Jerusalem at Varallo-Sesia. Crown 8vo., 10*s.* 6*d.*
THE AUTHORESS OF THE ODYSSEY, WHERE AND WHEN SHE WROTE, WHO SHE WAS, THE USE SHE MADE OF THE ILIAD, AND HOW THE POEM GREW UNDER HER HANDS. With Illustrations. 8vo.

CHARITIES REGISTER, THE ANNUAL, AND DIGEST : being a Classified Register of Charities in or available in the Metropolis, together with a Digest of Information respecting the Legal, Voluntary, and other Means for the Prevention and Relief of Distress, and the Improvement of the Condition of the Poor, and an Elaborate Index. With an Introduction by C. S. LOCH, Secretary to the Council of the Charity Organisation Society, London. 8vo., 4*s.*

Dreyfus.—LECTURES ON FRENCH LITERATURE. Delivered in Melbourne by IRMA DREYFUS. With Portrait of the Author. Large crown 8vo., 12*s.* 6*d.*

Evans.—THE ANCIENT STONE IMPLEMENTS, WEAPONS, AND ORNAMENTS OF GREAT BRITAIN. By Sir JOHN EVANS, K.C.B., D.C.L., LL.D., F.R.S., etc. With 537 Illustrations. Medium 8vo., 28*s.*

Gwilt.—AN ENCYCLOPÆDIA OF ARCHITECTURE. By JOSEPH GWILT, F.S.A. Illustrated with more than 1100 Engravings on Wood. Revised (1888), with Alterations and Considerable Additions by WYATT PAPWORTH. 8vo., £2 12*s.* 6*d.*

Hamlin.—A TEXT-BOOK OF THE HISTORY OF ARCHITECTURE. By A. D. F. HAMLIN, A.M. With 229 Illustrations. Crown 8vo., 7*s.* 6*d.*

Haweis.—MUSIC AND MORALS. By the Rev. H. R. HAWEIS. With Portrait of the Author, and numerous Illustrations, Facsimiles and Diagrams. Crown 8vo., 7*s.* 6*d.*

Hime. — STRAY MILITARY PAPERS. By Lieut.-Colonel H. W. L. HIME (late Royal Artillery). 8vo., 7*s.* 6*d.*
CONTENTS.—Infantry Fire Formations—On Marking at Rifle Matches—The Progress of Field Artillery—The Reconnoitering Duties of Cavalry.

Indian Ideals (No. 1).
NÂRADA SÛTRA : an Inquiry into Love (Bhakti-Jijnâsâ). Translated from the Sanskrit, with an Independent Commentary, by E. T. STURDY. Crown 8vo., 2*s.* 6*d.* net.

Jefferies (RICHARD).
FIELD AND HEDGEROW. With Portrait. Crown 8vo., 3*s.* 6*d.*
THE STORY OF MY HEART : my Autobiography. With Portrait and New Preface by C. J. LONGMAN. Crown 8vo., 3*s.* 6*d.*
RED DEER. With 17 Illustrations by J. CHARLTON and H. TUNALY. Crown 8vo., 3*s.* 6*d.*
THE TOILERS OF THE FIELD. With Portrait from the Bust in Salisbury Cathedral. Crown 8vo., 3*s.* 6*d.*
WOOD MAGIC : a Fable. With Frontispiece and Vignette by E. V. B. Cr. 8vo., 3*s.* 6*d.*
THOUGHTS FROM THE WRITINGS OF RICHARD JEFFERIES. Selected by H. S. HOOLE WAYLEN. 16mo., 3*s.* 6*d.*

Johnson.—THE PATENTEE'S MANUAL: a Treatise on the Law and Practice of Letters Patent. By J. & J. H. JOHNSON, Patent Agents, &c. 8vo., 10*s.* 6*d.*

Lang (ANDREW).
MODERN MYTHOLOGY. 8vo. 9*s.*
LETTERS TO DEAD AUTHORS. Fcp. 8vo., 2*s.* 6*d.* net.
BOOKS AND BOOKMEN. With 2 Coloured Plates and 17 Illustrations. Fcp. 8vo., 2*s.* 6*d.* net.
OLD FRIENDS. Fcp. 8vo., 2*s.* 6*d.* net.
LETTERS ON LITERATURE. Fcp. 8vo., 2*s.* 6*d.* net.
COCK LANE AND COMMON-SENSE. Crown 8vo., 3*s.* 6*d.*
THE BOOK OF DREAMS AND GHOSTS. Crown 8vo., 6*s.*
ESSAYS IN LITTLE. With Portrait of the Author. Crown 8vo., 2*s.* 6*d.*

Miscellaneous and Critical Works—*continued.*

Macfarren. — LECTURES ON HARMONY. By Sir GEO. A. MACFARREN. 8vo., 12s.

Madden.—THE DIARY OF MASTER WILLIAM SILENCE : a Study of Shakespeare and Elizabethan Sport. By the Right Hon. D. H. MADDEN, Vice-Chancellor of the University of Dublin. 8vo., 16s.

Max Müller (F.).

INDIA: WHAT CAN IT TEACH US ? Cr. 8vo., 3s. 6d.

CHIPS FROM A GERMAN WORKSHOP. Vol. I. Recent Essays and Addresses. Cr. 8vo., 6s. 6d. net.

Vol. II. Biographical Essays. Cr. 8vo., 6s. 6d. net.

Vol. III. Essays on Language and Literature. Cr. 8vo., 6s. 6d. net.

Vol. IV. Essays on Mythology and Folk Lore. Crown 8vo., 8s. 6d. net.

CONTRIBUTIONS TO THE SCIENCE OF MYTHOLOGY. 2 vols. 8vo., 32s.

Milner. — COUNTRY PLEASURES: the Chronicle of a Year chiefly in a Garden. By GEORGE MILNER. Cr. 8vo., 3s. 6d.

Morris (WILLIAM).

SIGNS OF CHANGE. Seven Lectures delivered on various Occasions. Post 8vo., 4s. 6d.

HOPES AND FEARS FOR ART. Five Lectures delivered in Birmingham, London, &c., in 1878-1881. Crown 8vo., 4s. 6d.

Orchard. — THE ASTRONOMY OF 'MILTON'S PARADISE LOST'. By THOMAS N. ORCHARD, M.D., Member of the British Astronomical Association. With 13 Illustrations. 8vo., 15s.

Poore(GEORGE VIVIAN, M.D., F.R.C.P.).

ESSAYS ON RURAL HYGIENE. With 13 Illustrations. Crown 8vo., 6s. 6d.

THE DWELLING HOUSE. With 36 Illustrations. Crown 8vo., 3s. 6d.

Proctor. — STRENGTH : How to get Strong and keep Strong, with Chapters on Rowing and Swimming, Fat, Age, and the Waist. By R. A. PROCTOR. With 9 Illustrations. Cr. 8vo, 2s.

Rossetti.—A SHADOW OF DANTE : being an Essay towards studying Himself, his World, and his Pilgrimage. By MARIA FRANCESCA ROSSETTI. With Frontispiece by DANTE GABRIEL ROSSETTI. Crown 8vo., 3s. 6d.

Solovyoff.—A MODERN PRIESTESS OF ISIS (MADAME BLAVATSKY). Abridged and Translated on Behalf of the Society for Psychical Research from the Russian of VSEVOLOD SERGYEEVICH SOLOVYOFF. By WALTER LEAF, Litt. D. With Appendices. Crown 8vo., 6s.

Soulsby (LUCY H. M.).

STRAY THOUGHTS ON READING. Small 8vo., 2s. 6d. net.

STRAY THOUGHTS FOR GIRLS. 16mo., 1s. 6d. net.

STRAY THOUGHTS FOR MOTHERS AND TEACHERS. Fcp. 8vo., 2s. 6d. net.

STRAY THOUGHTS FOR INVALIDS. 16mo., 2s. net.

Stevens.—ON THE STOWAGE OF SHIPS AND THEIR CARGOES. With Information regarding Freights, Charter-Parties, &c. By ROBERT WHITE STEVENS, Associate Member of the Institute of Naval Architects. 8vo. 21s.

Miscellaneous Theological Works.

** *For Church of England and Roman Catholic Works see* MESSRS. LONGMANS & CO.'S *Special Catalogues.*

Balfour.—THE FOUNDATIONS OF BELIEF : being Notes Introductory to the Study of Theology. By the Right Hon. ARTHUR J. BALFOUR, M.P. 8vo., 12s. 6d.

Bird (ROBERT).

A CHILD'S RELIGION. Crown 8vo., 2s.

JOSEPH THE DREAMER. Cr. 8vo., 5s.

Bird (ROBERT)—*continued.*

JESUS, THE CARPENTER OF NAZARETH. Twelfth Edition. Crown 8vo, 5s.

To be had also in Two Parts, price 2s. 6d. each.

Part. I.—GALILEE AND THE LAKE OF GENNESARET.

Part II.—JERUSALEM AND THE PERÆA.

Miscellaneous Theological Works—*continued.*

Boyd (A. K. H.) ('A.K.H.B.').

OCCASIONAL AND IMMEMORIAL DAYS: Discourses. Crown 8vo., 7s. 6d.

COUNSEL AND COMFORT FROM A CITY PULPIT. Crown 8vo., 3s. 6d.

SUNDAY AFTERNOONS IN THE PARISH CHURCH OF A SCOTTISH UNIVERSITY CITY. Crown 8vo., 3s. 6d.

CHANGED ASPECTS OF UNCHANGED TRUTHS. Crown 8vo., 3s. 6d.

GRAVER THOUGHTS OF A COUNTRY PARSON. Three Series. Crown 8vo., 3s. 6d. each.

PRESENT DAY THOUGHTS. Crown 8vo., 3s. 6d.

SEASIDE MUSINGS. Cr. 8vo., 3s. 6d.

'TO MEET THE DAY' through the Christian Year; being a Text of Scripture, with an Original Meditation and a Short Selection in Verse for Every Day. Crown 8vo., 4s. 6d.

Gibson.—THE ABBÉ DE LAMENNAIS AND THE LIBERAL CATHOLIC MOVEMENT IN FRANCE. By the HON. W. GIBSON. With Portrait. 8vo., 12s. 6d.

Kalisch (M. M., Ph.D.).

BIBLE STUDIES. Part I. Prophecies of Balaam. 8vo., 10s. 6d. Part II. The Book of Jonah. 8vo., 10s. 6d.

COMMENTARY ON THE OLD TESTAMENT: with a new Translation. Vol. I. Genesis. 8vo., 18s. Or adapted for the General Reader. 12s. Vol. II. Exodus. 15s. Or adapted for the General Reader. 12s. Vol. III. Leviticus, Part I. 15s. Or adapted for the General Reader. 8s. Vol. IV. Leviticus, Part II. 15s. Or adapted for the General Reader. 8s.

Macdonald (GEORGE).

UNSPOKEN SERMONS. Three Series. Crown 8vo., 3s. 6d. each.

THE MIRACLES OF OUR LORD. Crown 8vo., 3s. 6d.

Martineau (JAMES).

HOURS OF THOUGHT ON SACRED THINGS: Sermons. 2 Vols. Crown 8vo. 3s. 6d. each.

Martineau (JAMES)—*continued.*

ENDEAVOURS AFTER THE CHRISTIAN LIFE. Discourses. Cr. 8vo., 7s. 6d.

THE SEAT OF AUTHORITY IN RELIGION. 8vo., 14s.

ESSAYS, REVIEWS, AND ADDRESSES. 4 Vols. Crown 8vo., 7s. 6d. each. I. Personal; Political. II. Ecclesiastical; Historical. III. Theological; Philosophical. IV. Academical; Religious.

HOME PRAYERS, with Two Services for Public Worship. Crown 8vo. 3s. 6d.

Max Müller (F.).

HIBBERT LECTURES ON THE ORIGIN AND GROWTH OF RELIGION, as illustrated by the Religions of India. Crown 8vo., 7s. 6d.

INTRODUCTION TO THE SCIENCE OF RELIGION: Four Lectures delivered at the Royal Institution. Cr. 8vo., 3s. 6d.

NATURAL RELIGION. The Gifford Lectures, delivered before the University of Glasgow in 1888. Cr. 8vo., 10s. 6d.

PHYSICAL RELIGION. The Gifford Lectures, delivered before the University of Glasgow in 1890. Cr. 8vo., 10s. 6d.

ANTHROPOLOGICAL RELIGION. The Gifford Lectures, delivered before the University of Glasgow in 1891. Cr. 8vo., 10s. 6d.

THEOSOPHY OR PSYCHOLOGICAL RELIGION. The Gifford Lectures, delivered before the University of Glasgow in 1892. Cr. 8vo., 10s. 6d.

THREE LECTURES ON THE VEDANTA PHILOSOPHY, delivered at the Royal Institution in March, 1894. 8vo., 5s.

Romanes.—THOUGHTS ON RELIGION. By GEORGE J. ROMANES, LL.D., F.R.S. Crown 8vo., 4s. 6d.

Vivekananda.—YOGA PHILOSOPHY: Lectures delivered in New York, Winter of 1895-6, by the SWAMI VIVEKANANDA, on Raja Yoga; or, Conquering the Internal Nature; also Patanjali's Yoga Aphorisms, with Commentaries. Crown 8vo., 3s. 6d.

www.ingramcontent.com/pod-product-compliance
Lightning Source LLC
Chambersburg PA
CBHW021219270326
41929CB00010B/1185